POVERTY, DEVELOPMENT AND FOOD

Poverty, Development and Food

Essays in honour of H. W. Singer on his 75th birthday

Edited by

Edward Clay

Fellow, Institute of Development Studies, University of Sussex

and

John Shaw

Senior Economist, World Food Programme

MACMILLAN PRESS

Selection and editorial matter © Edward Clay and John Shaw 1987
Chapter 1 © Barbara Huddleston 1987
Chapter 2 © Philip Payne 1987
Chapter 3 © Tim Josling 1987
Chapter 4 © Richard Jolly 1987
Chapter 5 © Reginald Herbold Green 1987
Chapter 6 © Richard Longhurst 1987
Chapter 7 © Michael Lipton 1987
Chapter 8 © Raymond F. Hopkins 1987
Chapter 9 © John W. Mellor 1987
Chapter 10 © Jens H. Schulthes 1987
Chapter 11 © Larry Minear 1987
Chapter 12 © Robert Chambers 1987

First published in 1987

Published by
THE MACMILLAN PRESS LTD
Houndmills, Basingstoke, Hampshire RG21 2XS
and London
Companies and representatives
throughout the world

Printed in Hong Kong

British Library Cataloguing in Publication Data
Poverty, development and food : essays in
honour of H. W. Singer on his 75th birthday.
1. Food supply—Developing countries
I. Clay, Edward   II. Shaw, John
III. Singer, H. W.
388.1'9'1724   HD9018.D44
ISBN 0-333-43325-4

Contents

Notes on the Contributors

Robert Chambers is a Fellow at the Institute of Development Studies, University of Sussex.

Edward Clay is a Fellow at the Institute of Development Studies, University of Sussex.

Reginald Herbold Green is a Professorial Fellow at the Institute of Development Studies, University of Sussex.

Raymond F. Hopkins is Professor at the Department of Political Science, Swarthmore College, Pennsylvania.

Barbara Huddleston is Chief of the Food Security and Information Service of the UN Food and Agriculture Organisation, Rome.

Richard Jolly is Deputy Executive Director (Programmes) at the UN Children's Emergency Fund (UNICEF), New York.

Tim Josling is Professor at the Food Research Institute, Stanford University, California.

Michael Lipton is a Professorial Fellow at the Institute of Development Studies, University of Sussex.

Richard Longhurst is a Visiting Fellow at the Institute of Development Studies, University of Sussex.

John W. Mellor is Director of the International Food Policy Research Institute, Washington DC.

Larry Minear is the Washington-based Representative for Development Policy of Church World Service and Lutheran World Relief, two US non-governmental organisations active in the fields of development, relief and resettlement.

Philip Payne is Reader in Applied Nutrition, and Head of the Department of Human Nutrition, at the London School of Hygiene and Tropical Medicine.

Jens H. Schulthes is a senior economist in the Office of Evaluation and Policy, World Food Programme, Rome.

John Shaw is a senior economist in the Office of Evaluation and Policy, World Food Programme, Rome.

Acknowledgements

Many people have contributed to making the preparation of this volume not just a celebration but a professionally stimulating event. No one worked harder than Elizabeth Everitt in editing the contributions. Reginald Green made a considerable contribution through his careful and extensive editing of his own and Richard Jolly's drafts. Thanks too to all those participants in the seminar in December 1985 for their helpful comments and suggestions which influenced redrafting of papers and the introduction: Mike Faber, Brian van Arkadie and John White. Simon Maxwell deserves special mention for his enthusiastic support for the idea of producing such a volume and suggestions on the draft outline for the book. We would also like to acknowledge our debt to Michael Simmons of *The Guardian* for his carefully researched appreciation of Hans Singer, 'Creative Force at the UN', on his birthday. Lastly, we would like to acknowledge our debt to Hans himself, who, in his characteristically modest way, commented on many of the draft chapters during and after the seminar. His combination of idealism, practicality, and powerful advocacy of constructive action are a continuing inspiration to countless friends and colleagues throughout the world.

EDWARD CLAY
JOHN SHAW

Acknowledgements

Many people have contributed to making the preparation of this volume a pleasant as enriching ... intellectually stimulating ...

... John ...

Introduction

Edward Clay and John Shaw

ECONOMICS WITH A HUMAN FACE

The pretext for this volume was to celebrate Professor Hans Singer's 75th birthday on 29 November 1985 and the contribution that he has made for more than fifty years as a practical thinker to give a human face to economics. As Hans would consider appropriate, it is an opportunity for a serious review of development issues of current concern on which he himself has worked indefatigably almost everywhere in the world. Hans was foremost among those in the 1970s who advocated priority for the provision of basic needs in managing development. Those who have argued, with him, that an effective and ultimately sustainable development strategy must not just deliver growth but must be equitable, those who have given primacy to improving the health, education and life prospects of children on ethical grounds and as human capital, the primary resource for future development, are well represented among the contributors to this volume.

Hans Singer's writings and practical involvement in economic affairs have sustained the tradition that economics must ultimately be concerned with people and not just with the production of commodities, beginning with his work on conditions in the 'depressed areas' in the 1930s when he was a young refugee from Nazi Germany (*Men Without Work* and *Unemployment and the Unemployed*).

Hans Singer himself would see his contribution as a founder of development economics as having sustained the thesis of Keynes, that economics is not a universal truth applicable to all countries and all conditions but a framework of thinking to mould to different circumstances. For him economics is a practical discipline not primarily concerned with the elaboration of theory for its own sake. Keynes underlined the need for a soft funding aid mechanism within an international framework to sustain reconstruction after the Second World War. Hans Singer himself took up these issues directly when in 1947 he joined the newly established Economics Department of the United Nations in New York. There he played a skilfull and

1

intellectually creative role in establishing the conceptual context for important parts of the United Nations system. He was involved from the start in the Special Fund which ultimately became the United Nations Development Programme (UNDP). He has had a particular interest in the contribution which food aid could make to development. His thinking was influenced by the success of the Marshall Plan and he chaired the committee which provided the framework of ideas for the World Food Programme. He was also associated in their earliest days with the African Development Bank and the Economic Commission for Africa as well as with the United Nations' Industrial Development Organisation and Institute for Social Development.

It would be almost impossible within the scope of one book to cover the whole range of Hans Singer's interests in development. We therefore invited friends and colleagues to contribute on some of the issues with which he has been particularly concerned during the last decade: Singer quotes 'basic needs', the food problem, nutrition and the special importance of children as well as their vulnerability.

For Hans, children are the embodiment of our future and it seemed appropriate to begin by inviting contributors to look at the changing dimensions of the problems of poverty, food and the wider development context in the last decade and a half of the twentieth century. Barbara Huddleston sketches out the bounds to the problem, the difficulties in providing a sharper focus. Her timely contribution, when we are still under the shadow of the recent food crisis in Africa, looks also at what is being and what could be done to provide a better informational basis for international action. Economists have always looked to other scientific disciplines to provide solid technical foundations on which to build their analyses. But as Philip Payne shows in an important reappraisal of the nutritional issues raised by the concept of children as human capital, things are rarely so simple. The debate amongst nutritionists on the nature and extent of malnutrition continues. There are two constructive conclusions: generalised interventions that improve the overall levels of food consumption have an important part to play, whilst the core problems of severe malnutrition, which justify expensive and difficult-to-manage targeted interventions, are probably much less widespread than is often believed. The conventional wisdom, at least in developed countries, is that agricultural development must have priority in the poorer countries of the Third World. But as Tim Josling reminds us, patterns of trade have changed dramatically over the decades and for much of the Third World industrial trade has come to be more important. The developmental context of the problems of poverty and malnutrition is not to be resolved for most of the Third World through autarkic agriculture-based strategies but, as Hans Singer has always told us, through international co-operation.

What should be done? Since the late 1970s the problem of development has been for many virtually supplanted by that of 'economic adjustment' – the response of economies and public policy to the most severe economic downturn since the Great Depression. This second world depression has generated similar professional and academic conflicts of diagnosis and prescription. Economics with a human face has been under heavy attack from the new realists who have acquired powerful positions of advocacy since 1979 in developed countries and some international institutions. The generation of economists weaned on a diet of growth models in the 1950s and 1960s have perhaps lost sight of a tradition which Hans still embodies, that direct action is required not merely to ameliorate the human costs of slump but to protect the future. The society is left scarred, it does not just bounce back in a mechanical way. Richard Jolly provides a powerful restatement of the problems created when basic needs are under threat and argues cogently that recovery and subsequent development will be hampered without protecting the basic needs of the poor and the young. Nowhere are the problems more severe than in sub-Saharan Africa, and Reginald Green takes the debate from a general level to the specifics of this most vulnerable region. The problems are exemplified by the case of Ghana. A narrow economistic conception by international financial agencies and donors of the adjustment process that is required is subject to critical scrutiny. Richard Longhurst adds further detail in terms of establishing the vulnerability of rural, female-headed households and children, and the need for intervention to buffer the effects of adjustment on these groups and to facilitate decentralised food security. Michael Lipton provides a further impressive survey of the health dimension of the problem, identifying a range of opportunities for constructive intervention.

What can be done? Hans Singer has been especially associated with promoting and working to increase the effectiveness of aid transfers and 'soft financing' to sustain development. His ideas, and many of those involved in the formation of international policy in the decades after the Second World War, were much influenced by the success of the Marshall Plan and also the World Bank in contributing to rapid reconstruction of war-damaged Europe and East Asia. Ray Hopkins, re-examining the role of development economics analysis and advocacy in this period, concludes that those such as Hans Singer had a significant impact on policy practice. As a practical economist, Hans Singer has been a long-standing advocate of the possibilities of supporting development by transferring food surpluses from developed countries. John Mellor, looking again at food aid, which has been a subject of so much criticism, points up the positive side of a patchy record to underscore the opportunity once again. Food aid can contribute to ameliorating the adjustment to food crisis and can contribute to rural employment led economic growth. Aware of Hans Singer's interest in these questions, a number of the other contributors comment on issues of food aid. Reginald Green points again to the important role that food aid can play in releasing critical foreign exchange constraints on other imports and in post-food crisis rehabilitation. Richard Jolly and Richard Longhurst point to the role of food aid supported interventions in protecting the nutritional status of vulnerable groups. Ray Hopkins argues, what all economists would want to accept, that advocacy has shifted the balance of motives in the management of food aid by donors towards developmental concerns.

There is wider recognition that the possibilities of response to international problems of poverty, hunger and underdevelopment do not merely involve smoothly operating mechanisms but depend on people. Two contributors, Jens Schulthes and Larry Minear, address this issue directly. The growth of the United Nations and international aid has involved the establishment of large complex bureaucratic structures. Our expectation, Schulthes cautions, must therefore be tempered by a realistic appreciation of the possibilities and limitations of bureaucratic action. He and other contributors to this volume, to judge by the means advocated, effectively see no realistic alternative to international economic co-operation. Here perhaps is part of the agenda for research and public policy analysis in the coming decades. Some would see non-governmental organisations or voluntary agencies as an alternative to the cumbersome bureaucratic process. Larry Minear in a sympathetic assessment of the strengths and limitations of the now fashionable NGOs points to the dilemma that their strength depends upon smallness of scale and significant relative autonomy from government and international agencies. The very strengths of the NGOs will be lost if they expand rapidly to become alternative conduits for large-scale aid.

Perhaps these institutional issues will be an important part of the agenda for research and public policy analysis in the immediate future.

Pioneers such as Hans Singer recognised what institutional mechanisms were once required. The effectiveness of such institutions is now at issue. In a final provocative contribution, Robert Chambers argues that part of the problem is the way administrators and the various professionals think. Our professional framework of thinking is itself a barrier to an egalitarian public policy and scientific practice. On the main issues of poverty development and food, Hans Singer himself commented when some of the contributions were originally presented in a seminar at IDS: 'presentations on an apparently diverse set of issues showed the many interrelated aspects of the current development debates and the convergence of issues raised. A consensus emerged on the fundamental equity issue and the importance of protecting children in the present crisis for the sake of safeguarding the future.'

Part I

Dimensions of the Problem

1 Approaches to Quantifying the World Food Problem

Barbara Huddleston

THE NATURE OF THE PROBLEM

Continuing discussions about the world food problem reflect a global concern that the minimum quantities of food necessary for survival should be available to all people at all times. Although the concern is worldwide, the problem itself is specific to certain groups of people in particular locations. Further, the most severely affected areas are not static but change over time.

During the past forty years, dynamic processes have virtually eliminated the threat of hunger from Europe and parts of Asia, Latin America and the Near East, while increasing the fragility of the food situation in low-income, food-deficit countries, African ones in particular. In the longer term, therefore, the problem must be understood and quantified in terms of trends in production, income growth, demand, and trade so that areas with deteriorating food prospects can be identified and appropriate policy changes introduced. In the short term, however, the problem must be assessed in terms of how many hungry people there are, where they are located, and the kinds and amounts of food they need, so that practical help can be offered. Any comprehensive approach to quantifying the world food problem must therefore take into account both its static and its dynamic aspects.

An important point which affects both short- and long-term assessments is the fact that the world food problem is not just about food. Instead, some would argue it is not really about food at all, but is rather an aspect of the more general problem of poverty and unequal distribution of purchasing power among people and nations. A more balanced view is one which acknowledges that there are specific problems related to the supply of food which will not necessarily be solved by the overall process of economic growth, yet also recognises at policies aimed at generating productive employment opportunities for the poor must be central to any long-term solution. This thought is not new. In fact, it was one of the core ideas which gave birth to the UN/FAO World Food Programme to which Hans Singer has contributed so much.

With specific reference to the quantification of the problem, it will be useful to keep this balance between food-related and poverty-related problems, between static quantification of the numbers of hungry people and assessment of dynamic trends in the world food situation, constantly in view. There is some tendency today to identify the world food problem particularly with those countries where the trends and future prospects look most discouraging. But there are hidden hungry everywhere. The response to their food problem may need to be different in countries where there is a dynamic growth process and relative economic prosperity from that in countries where growth in per caput income and food consumption is slow or even negative. Also let us remember that the absolute number of hungry people in 1985 is greater in parts of the world which are not currently in the public eye than in Africa, where a sharp deterioration in the food situation has occurred in recent years and is likely to continue unless drastic measures are taken to turn the tide.

Quantification of the world food problem provides a necessary base of information on which to ground policy action. The remainder of this paper will consider in more detail what we already know, what more we need to know, and the implications of what we do know for future policy action.

IDENTIFYING THE HUNGRY

A periodic worldwide consumption survey would be an ideal method for identifying populations and individuals with inadequate food intake. However, both the logistical problems and the cost of such an undertaking are prohibitive. Further, if adequate information is available about other indicators such as per caput income, infant mortality rates, access to medical doctors, access to sanitary facilities and safe drinking water, and overall food availability, survey data is not required to identify population groups which either chronically or intermittently lack sufficient food.

FAO's Fifth World Survey provides a useful perspective on the problem. It notes first that, whereas hunger in the strict sense refers to undernutrition, that is, inadequate intake of calories for the size and activity level of the individual concerned, individuals may also suffer from a food problem if they lack certain essential nutrients, that is, if they are malnourished. For convenience, the World Food Survey thereafter uses the terms malnourishment and malnourished broadly to cover both lack of calories and lack of nutrients and this convention will also be followed for the remainder of this paper. The hungry then are those who are malnourished in one way or another.

Malnourishment, for most nutritionists and many medical personnel, has the characteristics of a disease, and its presence can be identified by the symptoms it exhibits. Lack of calories exhibits itself in below normal weight for height and height for age in growing children and, when severe, in marasmus; when the insufficiency is prolonged, activity levels are reduced, body wastage occurs, susceptibility to infectious disease increases, and eventually death occurs. Lack of specific nutrients, on the other hand, exhibits itself in specific nutrition-deficiency diseases such as anaemia (iron deficiency), goitre (iodine deficiency), vitamin A deficiency and kwashiorkor (protein deficiency, usually associated with lack of calories).

Since these symptoms of malnutrition can all be measured by physical indicators, it is reasonable to suppose that they could be monitored by health clinics as part of a comprehensive disease-prevention programme. Indeed, this approach would also be advantageous from another standpoint, which is the effect of health status on nutritional status. While adequate food must be present for nutritional status to be satisfactory, symptoms of malnutrition may be observed even in the presence of adequate food where health conditions are poor. For children in many developing countries water-borne diseases and parasites often prevent the nutritional value of the food that is already available from being absorbed, stunting growth and otherwise giving rise to symptoms of malnutrition.

For gross estimates of the numbers of malnourished and their locations, the monitoring of physical symptoms thus offers much promise, although clinical evidence of malnutrition needs to be combined with information about actual consumption behaviour and incidence of disease in order to determine what kind of intervention is required.

FAO's Global Information and Early Warning System found during the recent crisis in Africa that reports from health clinics and medical personnel provided some of the best and earliest indicators of emerging difficulties and rapidly changing conditions. In Mozambique, for example, reports of sharp increases in death rates in hospitals in affected areas were one of the first indications of the extent of famine. In the Sahel, Médecins sans Frontières used mobile teams to track and monitor the health conditions of nomadic populations and request help where it was needed. In these instances, however, physical indicators were monitored only at a late stage in a rapidly deteriorating situation. Greater attention to physical indicators as an aspect of regular monitoring programmes thus merits more attention.

Lacking a sufficiently wide base of health-related information for quantifying the total number of malnourished people in today's world, the Fifth World Food Survey instead used estimates of per caput food availability in relation to an estimated minimum nutritional requirement as a basis for quantifying the world food problem.

The report of a joint FAO/WHO/UNU expert consultation held in 1981 on Energy and Protein Requirements emphasised that large variations in food intake can occur among individuals and over time without detriment to nutritional status. Nevertheless, the experts agreed on a minimum survival requirement at 1.2 times the basic metabolic rate (BMR). To account for genetically determined variations among individuals' minimum requirements, an amount equal to 1.4 times was thought to be adequate. After determining overall food availability for a given population from FAO's Food Balance Sheets, a theoretical distribution of dietary energy intakes was applied by the authors of the Fifth World Food Survey, based on information obtained from sample surveys for selected countries where household-level data on food consumption had been collected. Coupled with information on household size, this provided the basis for estimating the number of individuals who were consuming less than 1.4 BMR in 1979–81. The results for developing market economies are shown in Table 1.1 below.

This indicates that nearly a quarter of the population in developing market economies suffers to some degree from lack of food, even though the situation has improved compared to a decade ago when the proportion was 28 per cent.[1]

How hungry are they? A range of estimates have been calculated, by FAO, IFPRI and USDA, among others, of the total amount of food aid required. Although these estimates vary because of differing assumptions about the magnitude of total demand and the ability of countries to meet food gaps with commercial imports, the various governing bodies of FAO and the World Food Programme have agreed that an estimate of 20 million tons of cereals a year provided a

Table 1.1 The extent of malnutrition in developing market economies
(1979–81)

	Population (billion)	Number malnourished (billion)	Malnourished as per cent of total (%)
Africa	380	99	26
Latin America	350	56	16
Near East	208	25	12
Asia and the Pacific	1252	313	25
Total	2190	494	23

Source: FAO, *Fifth World Food Survey*, Rome 1985.

useful indication of requirements for cereal food aid by 1985. Taking into account actual food aid flows of about 12 million tons in that year, the unmet need amounted to at least 8 million tons, and probably more, due to the large scale of the exceptional food shortages in drought-affected countries of Africa.[2]

The gross estimates of additional food needs, expressed in terms of cereals, give some idea of the order of magnitude of hunger in the mid-1980s. They are not operationally useful, however, for specifying the size of individual rations, the desirable commodity composition of the aid and the groups specifically in need of help, either because they are chronically malnourished or because they are facing temporary hardship because of natural or man-made disasters. For these purposes, field assessments are normally undertaken when food aid projects are being designed. These assessments determine how much and what kind of food is needed by target beneficiaries, but usually do not place the results in the context of the aggregate needs of vulnerable groups in the country.

To fill this information gap, FAO is planning to prepare a set of basic food-security information maps, initially for drought-prone countries in Africa. This study will provide baseline information on a disaggregated basis for indicators such as population distribution, cropping patterns, staple foods consumed, location and numbers of female-headed households, numbers of urban poor, land distribution, livestock ownership, access to infrastructure and services, and nutrition and health status indicators. From this information will be built up a picture of the food and nutrition status of the poor in a normal year. This area is one which promises to be most useful both for designing food aid programmes for responding to chronic malnutrition and for providing relief in an emergency.

LOOKING AHEAD

While the static food problem is one of localised shortages for which micro-indicators are needed to identify those who need immediate help, the dynamic food problem can be assessed in terms of macro-indicators and aggregate trends. Trends in per caput food production are one of the most commonly used indicators for assessing world food prospects, and the picture is not encouraging. In its Fifth Progress Report on International Agricultural Adjustment (August 1985), FAO noted that while the developing countries as a whole were making progress towards the target of an average growth rate for food and agricultural production of at least 4 per cent, more and more of the most needy countries were falling behind. In 1980–4, sixty-three countries, compared with forty-seven in 1970–80, experienced a decline in food production per caput.

The report notes that 'This dramatic increase in the number of countries with declining per caput food production is only partly due to the African drought. Indeed, out of the 29 new entrants into the negative growth rate class, nine are Latin American and eight Near Eastern/North African countries, and only ten are sub-Saharan African countries.' However, amongst the thirty-four countries which have experienced declining per caput food production throughout the 1970s and early 1980s, twenty-two were in Africa. Hence it is clear that it is on that continent that the deterioration in prospects is most widespread. (The effect of these trends on per caput consumption is shown in Fig. 1.1.)

The results of trend analysis are confirmed by the findings of a recent FAO/UNFPA/IIASA study with somewhat more operational implications. The study (reported in FAO, *Land, Food and People*, Rome 1984) considered the potential population-supporting capacities of lands in the developing world, first on the basis of agro-ecological zones and then country by country. Map 1.1 shows the countries whose total land capacity at low levels of inputs was already insufficient to support the existing population in 1975. Altogether

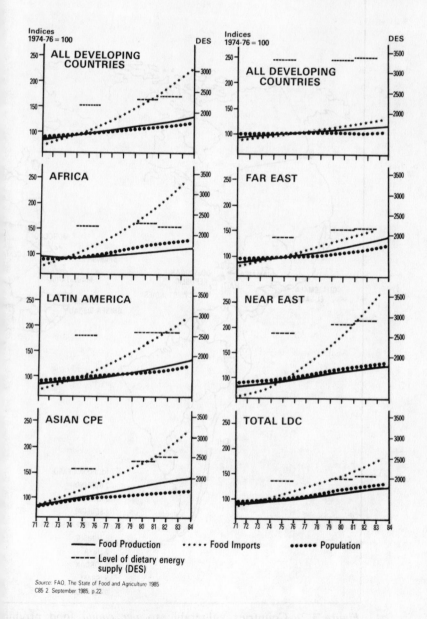

Source: FAO, The State of Food and Agriculture 1985
C85 2. September 1985, p.22.

Figure 1.1   Trends in food production, population, volumes of food
imports and levels of DES

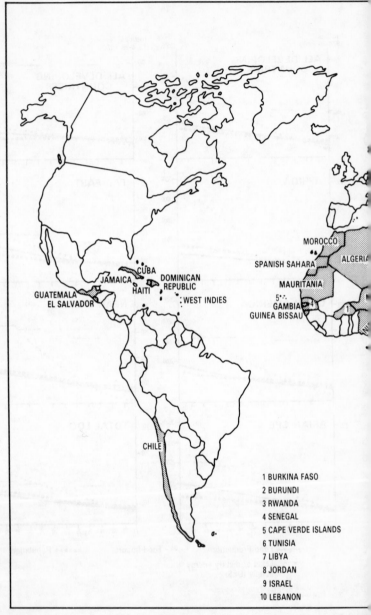

Figure 1.2 Countries vulnerable to *per capita* food produc
decline (based on population-carrying capacity of the land in 197
low levels of inputs)

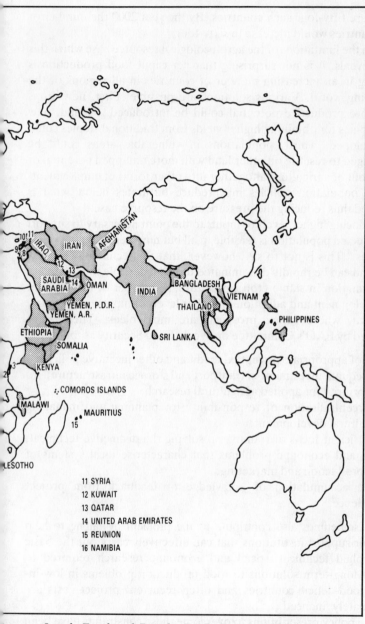

11 SYRIA
12 KUWAIT
13 QATAR
14 UNITED ARAB EMIRATES
15 REUNION
16 NAMIBIA

ource: Land, Food and People, FAO, Rome, 1984, map 3.

there were fifty-four such countries. By the year 2000 the number of such countries would increase to sixty-four.[3]

Given the limitations of the agro-ecological resource base which this study reveals, it is not surprising that per caput food production is declining in an increasing number of countries in all regions of the developing world. Various solutions are possible. First, new crops with more productive potential could be introduced. Second, new technologies for obtaining higher yields from traditional staples could be developed. Third, populations in vulnerable areas could be encouraged to resettle on other land with more untapped potential or to shift out of agriculture altogether into other forms of employment. Finally, population policies may reduce birthrates below what is projected thus reducing the pressure on the resource base.

Introducing higher levels of inputs to the point necessary to support the projected population is feasible in all but nineteen of these critical countries.[4] This is not to say, however, that the technology already exists and can be rapidly disseminated to make possible the necessary transformation in staple crop agriculture. A number of factors limit the development and adoption of higher levels of inputs, particularly in Africa, where future prospects are most bleak. These were identified by FAO's Committee on World Food Security as follows:

(a) lack of appropriate price, tax, credit and other incentive policies;
(b) inadequate investment in transport and storage infrastructure;
(c) low priority for applied agricultural research;
(d) overcentralisation of responsibility for planning and managing agricultural development;
(e) insufficient focus of training on solving the distinctive technical, social and economic problems that characterise local systems of food production and marketing;
(f) little accumulation of knowledge or feedback from project experience.

Donors sometimes also contribute to the problem by failing to help create or support institutions that can effectively carry out the basic and applied technical, social and economic research required to provide long-term solutions to food production problems in low-income, food-deficit countries and often recurrent project costs are inadequately financed.

While policy prescriptions to overcome these constraints have been numerous, they have tended to lack focus, and both the problems and the measures required to overcome them have proved difficult to quantify. Two efforts to provide tools for quantification and assessment of progress towards meeting longer term food security deserve mention. The first is contained in a document, *Proposals for Food and Agriculture Development, 1986–1990*, prepared for the Eleventh Meeting of the Conference of African Ministers in April 1985 by the Economic Commission for Africa (ECA). This document presents in simple terms the priority areas for future action and the kinds of resources required to address each of them. In brief, these were as follows:

Policy measures required	*Kinds of action required*
Increasing utility of arable land	Afforestation, soil conservation
Use of more trained manpower in agriculture	Training at all levels but especially for policy and programme managers and small farmers and rural entrepreneurs, including women
Application of improved technology	Research and development suited to local conditions
Increased use of inputs	Extension; seed, fertiliser and pesticide distribution programmes
Policies which induce investments in agriculture and production of food	Infrastructure rehabilitation, maintenance and development (roads, water supply, storage, marketing institutions); expansion of rural banking systems

Based on estimates contained in FAO's *Agriculture Toward 2000* (Rome, 1981) the Lagos Plan of Action cited a target of $4.4 billion which needed to be mobilised annually to carry out these actions. Of this, about half was to be mobilised domestically. The ECA paper considers that this is not an unrealistic goal. Taxation, mobilisation of private savings, and improved monetary policies could all be used to generate additional budgetary resources. Waste and inefficiency in state institutions could be reduced. Benefits of social expenditure could be maximised for a given cost. And the OAU Ministers, at their Summit Meeting in June 1985, pledged to make every effort to increase the share of their domestic budgets committed to agriculture.

To monitor continuously the degree to which goals established by the Lagos Plan of Action were being met, ECA proposed a simple form which could draw together statistics on resource flows and the changing food supply situation from data-gathering systems already in place in most African countries. FAO has also initiated a programme of monitoring and evaluation for socio-economic indicators which can be used to follow up implementation of the Programme of Action adopted by the World Conference on Agrarian Reform and Rural Development in 1979. These include: per caput income, nutrition, life expectancy, infant mortality, literacy, and quality of housing. These simple monitoring tools could be adapted by all developing countries to assess longer term progress in meeting food requirements.

ROLE OF THE UN SYSTEM

In all these areas the United Nations system has a double role to play. First and foremost, it must provide top quality technical assistance to developing countries who must in the end be responsible for assessing their own food situations. Second, it must carry the responsibility, on behalf of the international community, for assembling available data, carrying out analyses from a global perspective, identifying and filling in gaps, and suggesting appropriate courses of action. Because the world food situation *is* dynamic, there will always be a need for these information-related activities, even if the world food problem changes character or disappears in the form we know today. We all owe Hans Singer much for having helped set us on this track. It is, therefore, with great pleasure that I offer these few remarks on the occasion of his 75th birthday. May there be many more fruitful years ahead.

Notes

1. Based on estimates of per caput income distribution and income elasticities for food among low-income households, the World Bank has earlier estimated that some 800 million persons do not have access to enough food to maintain an active working life.

2. Although this estimate, in addition to meeting effective demand, includes a certain amount for project aid to meet the needs of the chronically malnourished, this does not fully cover the amount needed to fill the calorie gap of all those whose intake is inadequate. Various estimates put the additional amount required for this purpose at 30–40 million tons, but without more precise information on the degree of malnutrition amongst vulnerable groups, these must be considered highly provisional.

3. The consumption base used to estimate requirements was minimum per caput calorie intake recommended by FAO and WHO experts during preparation of the Fourth World Food Survey. The identification of vulnerable countries solely on the basis of natural resource limitations does not, of course, take into account economic and social factors. Some countries with insufficient land resources or poor climatic conditions may have mineral wealth or manufacturing and services industries which make it possible for them to rely on trade for their food supply. Other countries which are well endowed from the standpoint of the natural resource base may face social and institutional constraints which prevent them from fully exploiting it. In *Agriculture Toward 2000*, FAO identified fifty-two vulnerable countries in 1978–79 on the basis of economic criteria. These are also shown on Map 1.1.

4. Variable inputs are defined here as fertilisers, improved seeds, pesticides, conservation measures, and cropping patterns. Irrigation is taken as given at all input levels considered.

2 Malnutrition and Human Capital: Problems of Theory and Practice

Philip Payne

Just now there is something of a crisis of confidence in the field of applied nutrition. This may perhaps seem strange, indeed irritating to many people, in the light of so much dramatic evidence of acute starvation as well as the widespread persistence of chronic hunger. In past years, a chapter such as this might have begun with a review of the extent of different kinds of nutritional deficiency diseases and their differential causes, and would then have proceeded to describe appropriate interventions: correction of nutrient deficiencies (vitamins, minerals, and especially proteins); education programmes to correct cultural 'errors' in the use or intra-household distribution of different foods, or to correct distortions of consumer behaviour due to rapid socio-economic changes; food distribution programmes intended to bring immediate relief to those presently unable to afford an adequate diet. Now, after a very substantial investment on an international scale in basic and applied research, and in evaluation of such programmes, C. Gopalan (1980) writing about India says:

> We have therefore to conclude that during the last 30 years, in spite of all our advances in the agricultural, industrial and technological fields, and in spite of several 'applied nutrition programmes' and 'supplementary feeding programmes', we have not really made any significant dent on the problem of malnutrition in our children. We have reduced infant and child mortality to some extent and we have thus 'saved' many children whom, otherwise, the merciful hand of death would have removed. There is thus an increasing pool of survivors who have escaped death but who exist in a substandard state of health and nutrition with permanent impairment of functional competence and productivity. The result is a progressive erosion and deterioration of the 'quality' of our human resources.

Has something gone wrong? Have we simply not been trying hard enough? Is it that we do not really understand the nature and causes of the 'problem' of malnutrition? Or is it that advocacy has failed so that people and governments are still not convinced that reducing malnutrition is worthwhile or possible?

Basic research certainly seems to be directed towards revealing and quantifying more and more subtly detrimental effects of malnutrition on physical and mental function, and towards more elaborate and precise prescriptions of the amounts of nutrients needed to avoid those effects. But just as the cost of these efforts in terms of money, time and human resources increases, so their significance for application seems to become less and less clear. Thus, a major current USAID-supported research programme into the functional consequences of marginal malnutrition (Calloway *et al.*, 1980) is certain to absorb in excess of $11 million, and analysis of the data collected from three countries will probably take at least three years to complete. Evidently there are believed to be unresolved problems about the effects of malnutrition, but also it seems there are major conceptual and definitional ones. The controversy accompanying the production and interpretation of UN reports on protein and energy requirements seems to have increased with each successive one, and the most recent is still unpublished at the time of writing, five years after the preparatory meeting of experts. Are we getting to be more, or less, certain about how much food Man requires?

MEASURING MALNUTRITION: THE CONVENTIONAL VIEWPOINT

There is not only controversy about the consequences of malnutrition, but even about how to measure it. Although it is undisputed that growth and nutrient intake of children are related, it is also acknowledged that not only is the nature of that relationship complex, but that growth can be influenced by many other factors besides food. Nevertheless, it is almost universal practice to refer to anthropometry as a technique for measuring 'nutritional' status, and to equate poor growth in children with 'malnutrition'. However, although the growth of small children certainly provides a very sensitive indicator, with the passage of time it has become less clear exactly *what* it indicates. For example, Grantham-McGregor, writing in 1984, says:

Currently there is much confusion about the diagnosis and classification of malnutrition. Terms such as kwashiorkor, marasmus, 'moderate' and 'severe' malnutrition are used indiscriminately by different researchers. Some of these terms represent quite different clinical conditions which are probably associated with different social backgrounds ... A further problem is that the diagnosis of malnutrition does not reflect aetiology, and malnutrition is generally caused by a combination of inadequate food intake and infections. It is not clear exactly how important the role of infection is in the aetiology of malnutrition.

Evidently, in this last quotation, the word malnutrition is used to describe *both* the general concept and the specific measurement of growth deficits in children.

In addition to these semantic problems there is a major controversy about the significance of adaptive changes in food intake and body size. One faction asserts that the consumption patterns and growth rates achieved generally in developed countries reflect genetically determined optimum performance, and that lower intakes consumed by smaller people in poor countries must be suboptimal and therefore constitute a nutrition problem. This leads to views like that of Gopalan (1980) who says that the fact that child mortality and morbidity are strikingly lower in the state of Kerala than they are in the Punjab is evidence of great progress in 'social' development, but that the smaller size of the surviving children in Kerala means that there is more malnutrition there (twice as much in fact) than in the Punjab. Gopalan strongly rejects the view that people can adapt to different environments so as to be 'small but healthy', that it is the disease risks of the different environments which constitute the problem for policy-makers rather than the smallness *per se*. Both factions do, however, agree that there must be some degree of growth retardation which is so severe as to be beyond the limits of safe adaptation so that such individuals do suffer increased risk of early death or permanent disability.

The policy implications of this last controversy are very substantial, not only with regard to the size of the nutrition problem they identify, and hence the level of new or redistributed resources needed to deal with it, but also with respect to whether it could be argued that 'human capital' would thereby be saved, and hence to the whole question of nutrition advocacy. In Gopalan's view, only some 15 per cent of children currently born in India are destined to become 'truly healthy, physically fit, productive and intellectually capable citizens of the country', i.e. some degree of 'malnutrition' permanently affects 85 per cent of Indian children. The alternative view expressed by Sukhatme and others (1982) would put the numbers of families affected by 'serious' food intake deficits as around 15–20 per cent, and would define only the 5 per cent or so of severely growth retarded children as 'malnourished'.

It is important at this point to re-emphasise that the causes of conflict within the subject are not due to the purely technical problems of making measurements. Although there *are* methodological problems, particularly with respect to measuring food intakes, the controversies arise mainly because of different conceptual approaches to the way the measurements are interpreted. As always happens with this kind of conflict, the differences in concepts are themselves reflections of much larger divergencies between scientific paradigms, and even of different social or political ideologies (Payne and Cutler, 1984). It is tempting in fact to see the conflicts in nutrition today as very much a part of the broader conflict that overshadows the whole field of development and of economic and political change. Schaffer and Lamb (1981) have identified a number of features of neo-classical economic theory which pose critical problems regarding the improvement of equity in developing societies. Their analysis prompts a similar critique of current theory of nutrition. In attempting this I am very conscious that, unlike economists, nutritional scientists do not often make explicit the underlying structure and *a priori* assumptions of the models they use. By contrast, in nutrition the conceptual framework within which hypotheses are constructed and which serves as a source of models for analysis generally has to be inferred from accounts of research and application by a process akin to literary criticism. The main features of the conventional viewpoint are, first of all, a general assumption that the events and processes leading to changes in nutritional state operate according to a straightforward time sequence in a causal chain which is more or less invariant as between individual cases given similar environments. Accordingly, although it is accepted that interactions take place between different factors such as different nutrients, or between intake and other factors such as infections, it is believed that analytical models can be applied which treat these factors as separate explanatory variables. These are thought of as interacting with each other through continuous functional relationships (which, for the sake of simplicity, are often assumed to be linear). The outcome, the level of nutrition of the individual, is envisaged as a point lying on a graded continuum of 'states' ranging through 'mild' → 'moderate' → 'severe'. Nutritional status is thus an underlying variable, which can be represented for practical purposes by directly measured state variables such as body size or growth rate, biochemical concentrations etc.

To this is added the element of genetic determinism referred to earlier: the actual condition of an individual in respect of functional performance is seen as the extent of adjustments which have taken place, as compared to a genetically determined optimum state.

The general theory of malnutrition which emerges from these concepts has been described (Payne and Cutler, 1984) as the genetic potential model, the basic features of which are: that the body is conceived as being a system which is not only self-regulating, but self-optimising. For each individual there exists a preferred state characterised by a unique set of values of all the variables which describe the system components (weight, height, blood levels etc.). This state is an optimal one in the sense that all its functional aspects taken together are such as to maximise its fitness. If there are no constraints on diet, or continued adverse environmental influences, an individual will always tend to seek out and return to that preferred state or, in the case of children, a preferred 'road to health' or pathway of growth and development. Individuals differ from one another with respect to the values of the component variables which characterise their particular preferred state, and with respect to the levels of performance of which they are capable when at their own particular optimum states. These interindividual differences are inherent and result from differing genetic constitutions. Individuals who are prevented from returning to their preferred state, because of dietary or other constraints, are regarded as malnourished in the sense of being in a non-optimal condition. Malnourished states can be detected and graded for severity by the extent of deviation of one or more state variables from those which characterise the preferred state.

The implications of this model are:

1. Nutritional status is made consonant with the current widely held view of health as a positive condition, and not simply the absence of recognisable disease. It is important to note that the performance of a malnourished individual could be either affected currently with respect to some existing challenge, or could imply a reduced potential for dealing with some future situation such as an increased demand for work, for resisting an infection, for a psychosocial response etc. That is

to say malnutrition results in both suboptimal responses to current stresses *and* to increased risk of failure at some future time. Not only are children in Kerala pronounced to be malnourished simply because they are smaller than they could be: in terms of the 'human capital' paradigm, their present condition is also a measure of future human capital foregone.

2. If, as the model proposes, individuals with no food constraints automatically assume their preferred states of nutritional health, then studying healthy populations will provide us with normative values of variables – body dimensions, growth rates, blood levels etc. – which can be used as reference levels for indicators of nutritional status. The range of interindividual variation of these in well-fed populations can be taken as valid estimates of the extent of normal variation in genetic constitution. It is implicit in most applications that these normal values and ranges can be applied to cross-population comparisons.

3. One or more of the state variables can be used to establish nutrient requirements on an experimental basis by finding the lowest levels of intake needed by a sample of individuals to maintain those chosen indicators at the preferred (i.e. optimum) levels.

4. The procedure for quantifying malnutrition in a population is then, in theory at least, straightforward. We may either count the number of poeple who have values of status indicators which depart so much from the normal reference values as to imply that those concerned are more likely to have made some adverse adjustment to a constrained food supply than simply to have unusually low preferred values (e.g. take as being malnourished all people who have body weights less than two standard deviations below the reference mean). Alternatively, we could measure food consumption and count as either the current, or likely future, malnourished all those people whose intakes are so low as to be more likely the result of food restriction than of their having unusually low requirements for the maintenance of their preferred states.

While this seems fairly to characterise the dominant conventional view, it would not be correct to imply that these principles are universally explicit. The problem, however, is that with some notable exceptions (e.g. Frank, 1984; Margen, 1984; Seckler, 1982; and Sukhatme, 1977), they are frequently implicit, in the way data is analysed, and in the way research projects are formulated. Thus, the development of various 'classifications' or grades of malnutrition in terms of anthropometric measurements, implies not only that there is an underlying continuous gradation of effects, but that measurements of current states of individuals can provide information about differential causes. It is usual to express measurements of height, weight, etc. as percentages of international growth standards, and there are in fact perfectly sound practical reasons for this to do with grouping data from children of different ages. However, these standards are based on measurements of 'healthy' children in developed countries (usually the USA). No amount of protestation (e.g. Waterlow *et al.*, 1977) that these are to be regarded as *reference* values rather than targets can really correct the impression that any continuing deficits below the standard are evidence not only of adjustments to adverse or substandard environments, but are, as Gopalan so strongly asserts, a measure of the irretrievable loss of human capital.

In research design, the very notion of seeking for evidence to show how marginal malnutrition 'causes' functional defects in terms of morbidity, cognitive development, social competence etc., neatly expresses the main features of the theory. When interactions and multicausal sequences are acknowledged, various analytical strategies and models are adopted in order to attempt to distinguish the 'specific' effects of food intake, from other variables. This notion of the separability of effects of different explanatory variables on specific outcomes provides theoretical justification for the current emphasis on impact evaluation of nutrition interventions.

MALNUTRITION AND THE HUMAN CAPITAL THEORY

There are some fascinating parallels between the concepts underlying this conventional model of malnutrition, and those of neo-classical economic theory. For example, that individuals have sets of genetically determined preferred values for the variables and functions that characterise optimum states of nutritional health, corresponds with the view that individuals acting under scarcity will reveal consistent sets of subjective preferences as between the various commodities they choose to consume and exchange. Both imply that changes of health status in individuals (biological systems) and changes of level of consumption in population groups (market systems), can be described by deterministic models, i.e. ones in which transitions are continuous and time reversible, rather than by discontinuous transformation. Above all perhaps both the biological and the socio-economic systems are believed to be intrinsically self-optimising. Healthy individuals given free access to adequate diets will assume optimum nutritional states: populations participating in perfect markets will find 'everything for the best in the best of all possible worlds'.

Perhaps the most important link between economic and nutritional theory, however, is that the conventional model of malnutrition implies that any individual who exists below his or her optimum state of nutritional health can be regarded as having incurred a cost in terms of some loss of functional capacity. The theory therefore seems to offer the basis for quantifying the cost of malnutrition in populations in terms of the human capital foregone (either current or, in the case of children, discounted future capital).

Some of the more ardent proponents of human capital theory advocate that investment decisions, whether made by individuals or communities, should take account of human capital according to the same rules which are supposed to be applied to investment under scarcity in more tangible assets. For such purposes nutritional status measurements seem to offer a very attractive means of quantifying benefits, provided it can be shown that, for example, body size or food consumption are valid proxies for physical work capacity and efficiency, ability to learn and develop skills, competence in social relationships etc. Much research effort during the past two or three decades has consisted of attempts to demonstrate deterministic relationships between status and function, without, it has to be said, much success.

I shall refer to Schaffer and Lamb for a critique of the notion that extending neo-classical analysis to include investment in human capital could provide a basis for policy for improving equity. In particular, they emphasise that the validity of discounting future benefits as a device for making prior choices between things that in reality could only occur at different times, is crucially dependent on the assumption that all the processes and relationships are deterministic, i.e. time-reversible.[1] Obviously the suggestion that the current nutritional status of children could be used as a measure of the value of their future contribution to production is only valid to the extent that one determines the other in a consistent, quantifiable and time-reversible fashion.

In what follows we shall see that there are alternatives to this conventional model of malnutrition and that these derive from a number of different propositions about how biological systems work and from different insights into the nature of biological and social interactions. Taken together with a generally critical evaluation of the results of experimental and other interventions, these have induced many people to adopt a change of paradigm with respect to the significance of adaptive changes, and the nature of malnutrition.

ALTERNATIVE THEORIES

As has already been said, there are and have for a long time been people who have offered quite different views about the nature of malnutrition and what should be done about it. Again, it has to be said that until recently these have not been presented in any clearly integrated fashion. Thus, there is a school of thought which advocates interdisciplinary or multisectoral solutions to the problem of malnutrition rather than very specific remedies for symptoms. This has been based partly on the principle that prevention, through an attack on poverty and social discrimination, would be either a more desirable method or in the long run even a more effective one than, for example, directly targeted food interventions. But partly also on the growing evidence that interventions which are most specific in terms of concentration of resources into a single input, be it food, basic health care, education etc. and which are most highly targeted towards vulnerable groups, often seem to be least (cost) effective. Beaton and Ghassemi (1979), in a review of over 200 food supplementation projects targeted towards small children, concluded that even when as much account as possible was taken of food diverted away from target individuals, the impact of what was actually consumed in terms of measured growth improvement was very much less than would be expected on theoretical grounds, i.e. the additional food was not apparently being utilised for weight gain. Gwatkin, Wilcox and Wray (1980) reviewed basic health and nutrition interventions and, in terms of measured impacts, came to similarly gloomy conclusions about their expected outcomes.

However, these and other authors faced with similar evidence of impacts smaller than expected, have often stressed the fact that the programmes might well have been justified on other grounds. Beaton and Ghassemi speculate that the additional food may have resulted in higher levels of physical activity of the children (an effect noted in other supplementation studies), and stress also that some of the 'leakages' of food away from designated target individuals undoubtedly served instead to transfer extra income to the households, a point emphasised particularly strongly by Christiansen (1984) in his account of a family food supplementation and home stimulation programme in Bogota. Gwatkin *et al.* stress the fact that some types of healthy delivery service are effective in meeting *felt* needs of populations.

It seems that both the individual, considered as a biological system, and the household, as a social group, strongly resist attempts from outside to change one single aspect of their internal state: homeostatic mechanisms redistribute the impact of the changed input in accordance with internal priorities. Children run about more instead of growing faster; households exchange food for cash.

We certainly should not interpret the lack of specific impact of these interventions simply as evidence of the failure of programme design or management: rather, the experience should lead us to re-examine the notion of simple causality which led us to expect such specific outcomes in the first place. In doing so, it will be helpful to think of malnutrition as the outcome of the breakdown of homeostatic mechanisms rather than as a range of less desirable states of the body. We need also to consider that that end-point might be reached through any one of many different sequences of events. For example, one effect of an infectious disease may be to reduce appetite and depress intake of food. But if low intakes then act on the body so as to increase the severity of the disease, and if another effect of the infection is to increase food requirements, what we are likely to see is a self-reinforcing process which might be triggered either by an infection or by an episode of food restriction.

It seems logical to extend descriptions of processes to systems which include the interactions between the individual and those aspects of his environment which affect food entitlement. Thus whilst the first effect of a period either of illness or of food shortage might be to impair capacity of an adult for physical work, if this happens at the critical time when hard work has to be done to prepare ground for the next crop, or at the only time in the year when scarce employment becomes available, the outcome will again be the initiation of a self-reinforcing process. The capacity to produce food or cash will be progressively reduced to the point where starvation or permanent damage to health becomes likely, and where, in addition, the viability of the household or farming unit may be threatened. In neither of these cases does it make much sense to persist in asking if the *first cause* was lack of food rather than the infection or loss of employment, or vice versa.

But perhaps the most significant change in thinking results from a re-examination of the idea that the achievement of full genetic potential or maximum fitness should be the objective of good nutrition. A more logical view of fitness in evolution theory suggests that an individual's genes do not in fact uniquely determine his or her characteristics in a direct way, rather they define the range and nature of adaptive adjustments that the individual *can* make in response to the actual environment, food supply etc., to which he is exposed. A young child will respond in a relatively reversible fashion to dietary changes and may, for example, follow a period of reduced growth by a fast 'catch up'. As he ages, this potential for fully reversible responses is reduced, and growth becomes more and more 'programmed' on to a relatively less flexible course. This means that adjustments to changes can be both short term and reversible, but also long term and relatively irreversible, and that we can expect to find groups of people who have on average different patterns of physical characteristics and capacities from those of other groups living in different environments.

Looked at in this way, plasticity, i.e. the capacity to change through interacting with the environment, is itself a characteristic of fitness. It is the way the organism responds to information about the outside world, the levels of disease, food supply etc., which are current and which are likely to be encountered in the future. In addition, the concept of fitness in the evolutionary sense is seen as reflecting characteristics which maximise the changes of genotype survival rather than simply individual survival and reproduction. The fact that children under the age of 5 years from good socio-economic backgrounds all show very similar growth patterns, regardless of ethnic origin, simply means that up to this age plasticity is retained, and that the range of possible growth responses is similar.

The model for *adequate* nutrition, which results from these concepts, contrasts with the genetic potential theory of *malnutrition* in the following way.

1. The body is still viewed as a homeostatic self-regulating system whose state can be measured in terms of such variables as body size, growth rates, levels of various blood constituents etc. However, there are no preferred values for any of these variables, nor is there any internal reference which defines an optimum set of values to which the system will always tend to return.

2. The body can adapt to a range of different diets and environments, and the levels and sizes of the various components in any particular circumstances are a reflection of the adjustments that have taken place in order to achieve internal stability.

3. The state of nutrition (i.e. the sizes, levels etc. which characterise the adapted individual) and the amount of food needed to maintain that state, are thus the outcome of the relationship between the individual and his or her environment. Also, since the food available will generally depend upon the pattern and level of work done on the environment by that individual, we can say that food requirements and states of nutrition are aspects of the human energy costs of production of food and other essentials. These complementary relationships are obviously modified by the health environment. Therefore, if in addition the individual is part of a social group, these health relationships will themselves be modified by the extent of entitlement of the individual to a share of the social product of the group in the form of health provision, collaborative work, collective insurance against risks and hazards etc.

4. It is accepted that individuals are likely to vary one from another in some important respects. First, in their capacity to adapt, i.e. in the magnitudes of the adjustments they are able to make in response to environmental stresses without risk of physiological breakdown and subsequent death or disability. Secondly, in the efficiency with which they convert food to work. Thus some people may need more or less food than others in order to take up the same production possibilities: and some may be better able to exploit the potential of more extreme environments.

The contrasts between this and the more conventional viewpoint are now clear. First, the differences in body size between children (and for that matter adults) from different socio-economic environments are to be interpreted as indicators of the overall effects of those environments, since they show how much adaptive adjustment has been made by individuals living in them. To the extent that environments which result in adaptations towards small size or low food intakes frequently also carry increased chances of adverse events – infectious disease, recurrent poor harvest or other discontinuities of food supply, loss of employment, breakdown of inter-personal relationships etc. – it is to be expected that people living under such conditions will often be small in stature. However, the small size is not *in itself* a measure of the functional capacity of those people. Thus we should expect to find a larger proportion of children in socially disadvantaged households who are small for their age. In just the same way as we should expect to find that a larger proportion of such children would perform less well in tests of psychosocial capacity and responsiveness. We should not, however, infer a causal connection between the smallness and the poor performance.

The outcome of a food intervention trial in Guatemala provides an interesting illustration. Food supplements were made available to women during pregnancy and lactation, and subsequently to their offspring. This was done on a voluntary basis, subjects being given food on request at health centres. The outcomes were measured in terms of physical growth, morbidity, and a wide range of tests of cognitive development and of social interactive behaviour of the children, and on later follow-up, subsequent school performance. The results show that *on average* the growth and behavioural performance, measured in terms of spontaneous exploratory levels, competitiveness, persistance etc. of the children, were poorer for the group whose uptake of supplementary food was smaller. (In fact, these differences in behaviour were seen for the most part in boys rather than girls. *See* Barrett, Radke-Yarrow and Klein, 1982.) At the age of 6 to 8 years, these children continued to show differences in mood, levels of play activity and dependency on adults. But what are we to make of the results of a trial which shows that low *voluntary* intakes are associated with poor performance? It is said that there were no differences between the high and low uptake groups in terms of household socio-economic status. Is it therefore reasonable to say, as Barrett (1984) does, that nutrition is the *causal* agent, and that food supplementation of whole populations would greatly increase social performance and productivity? Or, would it be wiser perhaps to say that low voluntary uptake of food and smaller body size of children are telling us something about the quality of these people's physical, psychological and social environment that we are not at the moment able to measure directly?

MALNUTRITION AS FAILURE OF ADAPTATION

The newer theory does not, up to this point, say anything to us about *malnutrition*. This is to be regarded as the result of failure to maintain homeostatic control, and happens when an individual is forced beyond the limits of his adaptive range. In practice, it is accepted as corresponding to the conventional categories of severe or clinically malnourished which in children, for example, applies to some 2 to 5 per cent of under 5 year olds in poorer countries. These children are known to be likely to suffer from permanent damage, even if they survive at all. Again, however, the theory suggests that this condition is best described as the final outcome of a catastrophic process for which the triggering event may have been any one of a variety of factors, and not necessarily lack of food. Although more complex in aetiology than straightforward starvation, it not unreasonable to describe such conditions as malnutrition. They are characterised by severe loss of weight, usually by low food intakes, there is frequently some element of food deprivation, and always a need for increased food for recovery. The precipitating factors may not be simply unavailability of food, either to the individual concerned or to the household of which he is a member. Malnutrition may not, therefore, be *directly* affected by food handouts. It may, of course, be affected indirectly, through income substitution, increasing time available for child care, supporting the general socio-economic effectiveness of the household etc.

Little has been said so far about the interpretation of food intakes. Are we on any safer ground in inferring the need for programmes to increase food consumption on the basis of the existence of low intakes? There are methodological problems first of all which will probably always severely limit the utility of quantitative estimation of nutrient or energy consumption, except in highly controlled research situations. Intakes *can* be measured on individuals, but precision is bought at the expense of invasiveness as well as in money and time: it is possible to know accurately how much food a person *has eaten* over a period, but only with so much observer interference as to cast doubt on the result as an estimate of normal habitual intake. This does not of course mean that measures of household food consumption, or of changes in patterns of food availability or of critical levels of food stocks etc., are useless: simply that the widespread belief that nutritionists can 'tell what a man is by what he eats' falls sadly short of the truth. Even in many research situations, such as the Guatemalan intervention study, interpretation of effects which might be directly attributable to nutritional changes is normally limited by doubts about the validity of the intake measurements. Even if we *could* measure intakes of individuals, however, the problems of assessing the nutritional adequacy of these are essentially the same as those of interpreting differences in growth and body size. In fact it was Sukhatme's (1961) critical attack on the conventional wisdom about interpreting household intake data, and his advocacy of an approach which takes account of adaptive responses, that largely initiated the current controversy. With respect at least to energy, the problem of interpretation is made even greater because of the very wide range of adaptive responses which are made possible through altered physical activity levels.

In summary then, new perspectives of the nature of the mechanisms relating growth and body size to nutrition suggest that two distinct meanings could be attached to growth measurements. The full range of body sizes and growth rates found amongst populations of children from different backgrounds should be interpreted as a measure of the overall effects of the environment. The distribution of body sizes as between social groups, geographic locations and means of livelihood, therefore provides information about the combined effect of different factors: food security, communicable disease levels, housing standards, education, work burdens etc. Growth measurements by themselves cannot tell us much, if anything, about which of these is critical in any given situation. We should expect to find that a part of the range of body sizes reflects adaptive adjustment, and does not indicate any current or likely future costs either to the individual concerned or to society, i.e. small average sizes of children (or for that matter, of adults) in populations is not a sufficient indication of wastage of human capital.

The extent to which environment affects growth does, however, provide an indication of the level of risk that some triggering event may precipitate actual frank malnutrition by pushing individuals beyond the range of adaptive adjustment. Thus, in general we would expect to find as between population groups, correlations between the extent of overall growth reduction and the prevalence of manifest malnutrition (e.g. associated with body weights-for-age less than 60 per cent, or weights-for-height less than 80 per cent of expected values). Again, the extent and distribution of these malnourished individuals tells us little about which of the environmental risk factors is most often critical in precipitating the condition. The correlations between general growth reduction and the prevalence of malnutrition are therefore the result of a general association. As the example of Kerala as compared to the Punjab shows, interventions that change the pattern of risk factors are likely to alter the strength of this association. Secondly, the extent of severely growth retarded individuals (e.g. less than 60 per cent of expected weight-for-age, or less than 80 per cent of expected weight-for-height) gives an additional measure of that overall environmental risk, and tells us about the numbers needing immediate remedial treatment. Again, however, the prevalence of the actually malnourished does not by itself tell us much about the nature of the immediate causes.

IMPLICATIONS FOR INTERVENTION

Priorities and 'human capital'

In terms of the need to save lives and to prevent permanent loss of health, efforts should clearly be directed first of all towards reducing the extent of actual malnutrition, i.e. those severely growth retarded. If it is believed that advocacy for this will be more effective if based on the notion of saving human capital rather than on simple humanity, then resources should be preferentially directed towards these cases, either as target individuals or towards those socio-economic or other categories of households in which such children are most frequently found. The reason why this is important emerges from the arguments of Schaffer and Lamb: the appeal to human capital saving does not in itself effectively address the issue of equity unless it is accompanied by an explicit policy of redistribution. If it were really the case that 85 per cent of all Indian children could make a greater net contribution to production if they were better fed now, then presumably economic efficiency would dictate that investment be such as to increase the *total* of human capital resources, i.e. programmes should be designed to maximise the quantity (numbers × increase in productivity) and to do this at minimum cost. Other things being equal, planners should be indifferent as between a small number experiencing large improvements and a larger number experiencing small improvements, provided the total increase was the same. In practice, most experience of nutrition and health interventions suggests that problems of access, lack of control over resources, and lack of political representation mean that improving the nutrition and health of the worst off is more costly in economic and social terms. People who argue on the basis of human capital that the existence of differences in average size of children as between developing and developed countries, or between social groups, is a justification for child-oriented programmes, run the risk of obscuring the issue of redistribution. Also if they are wrong, either wholly or partly (if, for example, there *is* a deterministic relation between growth and productivity, but one which is very non-linear so that marginal gains in productivity are much smaller for small growth deficits), they bear the additional responsibility of advocating investments which may not produce the expected return. Seckler (1982) summarises the priority argument neatly:

> except where people are in clear and present danger of functional impairment due to malnutrition, interventions should be targeted to poor environments and not to poor individuals. Once the environment of small people is improved, their size will take care of itself. Until their environment is improved, their size is best left to take care of itself.

Design and evaluation

Under design, I am thinking mainly of the balance of specific project inputs and objectives. Perhaps the first question is whether the existence of smaller than expected body size could be taken as sufficient justification for programme designs which concentrate resources on food inputs, or which are designed to target those particular individuals. I think the answer must generally be no for the reasons already given: the causes are likely to be complex, and the benefits of change uncertain. However, that does not by any means imply that anthropometry has no value, or that food components of interventions are unjustified – quite the reverse. Smallness, as has been said, does tell us about the overall impact of a whole set of undesirable factors in the environment, so that a 'first round' assessment of priorities might very well be based on differences in child growth as between population groups but this would always need to be complemented by assessment of health factors, adequacy and security of food entitlement etc.

It would be a mistake to assume that, because anthropometry had a part in the selection of participants, impact on child growth should be an important component of programme evaluation. Similar arguments apply to the problem of reducing the numbers of severe cases. Here again we cannot assume that the precipitating factor is food availability, so that the real issue is the balance between prevention, which in practice means reducing the risk (i.e. improving the environment), and cure, meaning rehabilitation services for the malnourished. These latter, of course, do require food inputs in addition to health care, whether it be based on clinic or home treatment.

Experience seems also to suggest that a food (or even a nutrition education) component is not a necessary condition for programmes to have an effect on growth or malnutrition. But this need not be too disturbing for nutritionists. Some of our problems at least are due to taking too narrow a view of causality and trying to intervene, as if we were dealing with an isolated biological system rather than the hierarchy of systems – individual-family-social group-institution-state.

Advocacy

Finally there is the question of advocacy. The new theory has some very important implications for what nutritionists should be saying about their own nutrition problems whether these are in their own or other people's countries. First, while there are no short cuts or magic bullets for dealing with the problem, the extent of the kind of malnutrition that directly affects not only people's health and safety but their productive capacity is much less than has been suggested, but is likely to be much more concentrated amongst particularly deprived and high-risk households.

Secondly, those who wish to use the human capital argument as a strategy for generating concern on the part of governments would be well advised to be cautious about basing this upon the continued general smallness of children in developing countries: the large size of the problem this indicates seems as likely to deter as it is to motivate action, and in reality returns are unlikely to be realised.

Thirdly, international and social group comparisons of growth can make a useful contribution to efforts directed towards showing the existence of disparities in health, education and food security. Practical experience so far suggests that there are in any case no practical ways of reducing growth differentials by selective means – even if there were justifications for doing so. Nutrition advocacy should therefore focus attention, first, on the reduction of malnutrition, i.e. those most seriously affected, and should argue the case for a reduction of social disparities in health and food security as the primary means of improving the more general nutritional welfare of populations.

All of the above is simply a restatement of the need for a strategy for 'Putting the last first' (Chambers, 1983), or as Karl Popper (1965) puts it: 'Instead of the greatest happiness for the greatest number [we should] formulate our demands negatively, i.e. demand the elimination of suffering rather than the promotion of happiness.' Nutritional measurements can help us to identify suffering, and to characterise the condition and the constraints of those who need to be put first.

The ultimate objective of advocacy must be to establish that freedom from the risk of malnutrition and security of access to food are fundamental to the achievement of equity, and this is essentially a political issue. As Schaffer and Lamb put it: 'Equity as a concept and practice ... is an ideological construct about distribution, about the apportionment of resources in society, and therefore political in the sense of an intervention in the struggle of political ideas.'

Note

1. Prigogine and Stenger (1985) give a very precise analysis of the differences between time-reversible deterministic processes and those which are characterised by transformations initiated by random events, interspersed by phases of deterministic trends.

References

BARRETT, D. E. (1984) 'Malnutrition and child behaviour: conceptualisation of social–emotional functioning and a report on an empirical study', in *Malnutrition and Behaviour: Critical Assessment of Key Issues*, Nestle Foundation Publication Series, vol. 4 (Lausanne, Nestle Foundation) pp. 280–306.

BARRETT, D. E. *et al.* (1982) 'Chronic malnutrition and child behaviour: effects of early caloric supplementation on social and emotional functioning at school age', *Development Psychology*, vol. 18(4), pp. 541–56.

BEATON, G. H. AND H. GHASSEMI (1979) *Supplementary Feeding Programmes for Young Children in Developing Countries*, Report prepared for UNICEF and the ACC-SCN of the United Nations (Rome: FAO).

CALLOWAY, D. H. *et al.*, (1980) *Collaborative Research Support Programme on Intake and Function: Final Report to the US Agency for International Development*, Department of Nutritional Sciences (Berkeley: University of California).

CHAMBERS, R. (1983) *Rural Development: Putting the Last First* (London: Longman).

CHRISTIANSEN, N. (1984) 'Social effects of a family food supplementation and a home stimulation programme', in *Malnutrition and Behaviour: Critical Assessment of Key Issues*, Nestle Foundation Publication Series, vol. 4 (Lausanne: Nestle Foundation) pp. 520–30.

FRANK, D. A. (1984) 'Malnutrition and child behaviour: a view from the bedside', in *Malnutrition and Behaviour: Critical Assessment of Key Issues*, Nestle Foundation Publication Series, vol. 4 (Lausanne: Nestle Foundation) pp. 307–26.

GOPALAN, G. (1980) Thirteen Jawarharlal Nehru Memorial Lecture, *Jawarharlal Nehru Memorial Lectures* (New Delhi: Jawarharlal Nehru Memorial Fund, Teen Murti House) pp. 125–50.

GRANTHAM-McGREGOR, S. (1984) 'The social background of childhood malnutrition', in *Malnutrition and Behaviour: Critical Assessment of Key Issues*, Nestle Foundation Publication Series, vol. 4 (Lausanne: Nestle Foundation) pp. 358–74.

GWATKIN, D. R. *et al.*, (1980) 'Can health and nutrition interventions make a difference?', *Monograph*, no. 13 (Washington DC: Overseas Development Council).

MARGEN, S. (1984) 'Energy-protein malnutrition: a web of causes and consequences', in *Malnutrition and Behaviour: Critical Assessment of Key Issues*, Nestle Foundation Publication Series, vol. 4 (Lausanne: Nestle Foundation) pp. 20–31.

PAYNE, P. and P. CUTLER (1984) 'Measuring malnutrition: technical problems and ideological perspectives', *Economic and Political Weekly*, vol. 19(34), 25 August, pp. 1485–92.

POPPER, K. R. (1965) *The Open Society and its Enemies*, 5th ed (London: Routledge & Kegan Paul).

PRIGOGINE, I. and I. STENGER (1985) *Order out of Chaos* (London: Fontana).

SCHAFFER, B. and G. LAMB (1981) *Can Equity be Organised?* (Farnborough: Gower).

SECKLER, D. (1982) 'Small but healthy: a basic hypothesis in the theory, measurement and policy of malnutrition', in *Newer Concepts in Nutrition and their Implications for Policy* (Pune, India: Maharashtra Association for the Cultivation of Science Research Institute) pp. 127–48.

SUKHATME, P. V. (1961) 'The world's hunger and future needs in food supplies', *Journal of the Royal Statistical Society* Series A, vol. 124, pp. 463–525.

SUKHATME, P. V. (1977) 'Incidence of undernutrition', *Indian Journal of Agricultural Economics*, vol. 32(3), pp. 1–7.

SUKHATME, P. V. (1982) in *Newer Concepts in Nutrition and their Implications for Policy* (Pune, India: Maharashtra Association for the Cultivation of Science Research Institute) pp. 127–48.

WATERLOW, J. C. *et al.*, (1977) 'The presentation and use of height and weight data for comparing the nutritional status of groups of children under the age of 10 years', *WHO Bulletin*, no. 55, pp. 489–98.

3 The Changing Role of Developing Countries in International Trade[1]

Tim Josling

INTRODUCTION

It is only to be expected that the patterns of production and trade which underlie international economic relationships among countries will change over time. Sometimes this change is so slow as to allow the patterns themselves to be taken as constants; at other times the change is rapid enough to alter our conception of the world economy. Problems and issues in international trade are often identified with the problems of particular country groups. The identification of primary product export problems with developing countries is an obvious example. If, however, the world economy encounters a period of rapid change, this convenient identification of trade issues with country groups may be misleading. One such rapid change has occurred in the past decade. It is, therefore, appropriate to stop and ask whether these trade pattern changes have altered the interests of developing countries in agricultural and primary export trade.

This essay is an attempt to explore the current interests of developing countries in trade in food and agricultural products. In doing so, it is necessary to examine first the role of agriculture in the export and import pattern of developing countries and then the changes in agricultural trade that have taken place in the past decade. Whereas it is true that there is no single common 'interest' of developing countries in agricultural trade, some of the major issues of general concern can be identified.

TRADE ISSUES AND DEVELOPING COUNTRIES

A widely held preconception about developing countries is that they export agricultural products and raw materials in exchange for manufactured goods from the industrial countries. Upon such a stereotype is easily built a set of economic relationships. As both Singer and Prebisch pointed out thirty-six years ago, certain forces act in the direction of falling relative prices of primary products over time, though the effect is masked by occasional strong upward movements (Singer, 1950; Prebisch, 1950). These forces include both the intrinsic nature of supply and the use of the commodities themselves, and institutional and other characteristics of the market which influence the distribution of the gains from trade. For countries in which these commodities dominate the export pattern, the declining real price puts additional demands on the economy either to generate offsetting productivity gains in the primary product export sector or to diversify into alternative activities (export earning or import saving) to avoid the problems of falling terms of trade. These countries were also likely to lose confidence in the trading system and undertake costly import substitution policies which failed to take advantage of their comparative cost position.

The identification of commodity terms-of-trade problems with developing-country export earnings issues was broadly appropriate in the 1950s and 1960s, and became a part of the conceptual basis for the push for international commodity agreements (ICAs) in the UNCTAD. Such ICAs were proposed almost as an article of faith by the Group of 77, supported with somewhat less enthusiasm by Western Europe, and viewed with open scepticism by the United States. The resulting lack of progress became the cause of mistrust and disagreement. In the 1970s, developing countries placed the UNCTAD 'Integrated Programme for Commodities' high on their list of demands for a New International Economic Order, which promptly reduced the likelihood of its political acceptance in the West.

Singer and Ansari, writing in 1977, had already cautioned against too facile a link between commodity problems and country problems. They wrote that

the fundamental advantage of the rich countries is thus, not that they produce certain types of commodities, but rather that they are the home of modern technology and the seats of multinational corporations. It is because of this that the rich industrial countries will tend to be the direct gainers from any type of commercial relationship with the Third World – be it in the form of trade or investment.

They argued that asymetric relationships were as much to do with the indigenous institutions in developed and developing countries as with the types of goods traded. 'Hence the essential difference between the rich and poor countries is not that they produce different types of commodities, as both Prebisch and Singer initially assumed. The fact that they do, in general, produce a different "mix" of goods is merely a symptom, or indicator, of a more fundamental difference in the structure of these two types of economies' (Singer and Ansari, 1977, p. 36).

It follows that developing-country interests in international trade will change with shifts in trading patterns. To continue to identify those interests with the export of primary commodities, for instance, may be misleading. The structural differences among countries that lead to problems in international trade still exist, but they need to be seen in the context of a new pattern of commodity trade.

CHANGING TRADE PATTERNS

The change in trade patterns during the 1970s was in many respects dramatic. Table 3.1 gives an indication of the export composition for the world, developed and developing market economies, and centrally planned economies. The table indicates the magnitude of the export earnings, in current dollars. World trade expanded by 540 per cent in current dollars over the decade from 1970–2 to 1980–2. Developed market economies expanded export earnings by 473 per cent, while developing market economies increased the value of their exports by 824 per cent. This latter group increased their share of total exports from 18.0 per cent to 27.5 per cent over this period.

The major cause is not hard to find: fuel export earnings increased by 1275 per cent, jumping from $36 billion to $462 billion. Developing market economies increased their share of this market from 66 to 69 per cent. Over the same period, food and beverage export earnings rose by a more modest 418 per cent and agricultural raw materials only earned 356 per cent more. The developing market economies' share in these two markets declined from 30.0 to 28.5 per cent and from 29.7 to 26.0 per cent respectively. Manufactured products (excluding chemicals and machinery) earned 450 per cent more dollars in 1980–2 than a decade earlier, and the developing market economies raised their market share from 11.5 to 16.7 per cent. They were thus increasing their share in those export markets which were themselves expanding the fastest, and, whether by choice or happenstance, moving out of the weaker markets at a faster rate than other country groups.

To see whether this shift has been enough to bring about a change in developing country interests, it is useful to look at the trade shares by country group. This is shown in Table 3.1 (b). Reflecting the increase in the share of fuels from 10 per cent to 24 per cent of export earnings, food and beverages, agricultural raw materials and minerals and metals each declined as components in the total. For the developing market economies food and beverage exports fell from 21.8 to 10.8 per cent, while the share of agricultural raw materials declined from 11.5 to 4.4 per cent of export earnings.

The picture is even clearer when export earnings are expressed as a share of the total excluding fuel, as in Table 3.1 (c). Food and beverage exports in 1981 made up only 26.3 per cent of the developing market economies' non-fuel earnings compared with 34.6 per cent a decade earlier; agricultural raw material exports (10.9 per cent) are now less important than machinery exports (14.3 per cent) from these countries. A decade ago, primary products made up 60.8 per cent of their export earnings, compared to 36.4 per cent for manufactures: now manufactures (55 per cent) are more important than agricultural exports (37.1 per cent) and even than non-fuel primary products as a whole (42.8 per cent). At least by this measure, developing countries as a group would seem to have a greater interest in manufactured goods export markets than in those for primary products. This raises at least the possibility that the declining terms of trade for raw materials may be to the net advantage of developing countries.

It is true that such aggregates as 'developing market economies' hide vast differences among countries. This disparity may be even more true now than in the past, given the uneven distribution of oil deposits and the strong export performance of a small number of newly industrialised countries. Many countries have not begun the process of changing their export patterns. It is not surprising that it is becoming more difficult to define a 'developing-country' interest than in the past.

REGIONAL AND INTRA-DEVELOPING-COUNTRY PATTERNS

The picture of developing countries as emergent exporters of manufactured goods is, however, not uniform across regions. Table 3.2 shows

Table 3.1 Export earnings by major country groups, 1970–2 and 1980–2

US$ millions (current)	World		D'ped mkt econ		D'ping mkt econ		Central plan econ	
TOTAL	1970–2	1980–2	1970–2	1980–2	1970–2	1980–2	1970–2	1980–2
(a) Food and beverages	46 873	195 944	28 583	126 527	14 030	55 818	4 260	13 599
Agric raw materials	24 966	88 993	14 926	54 717	7 411	23 123	2 629	11 153
Minerals and metals	10 224	36 668	5 816	20 589	3 205	12 067	1 203	4 012
Fuels	36 213	461 584	8 846	92 613	23 867	318 650	3 500	50 321
Chemicals	25 088	142 284	22 204	122 361	1 073	10 139	1 811	9 784
Machinery	106 210	514 162	92 911	437 698	2 027	30 334	11 272	46 130
Manufactured products	101 703	457 872	80 194	345 440	11 648	76 377	9 861	36 055
Total exports	358 797	1 931 577	257 220	1 219 015	64 427	531 156	37 150	181 406
PER CENT OF TOTAL								
(b) Food and beverages	13.1%	10.1%	11.1%	10.4%	21.8%	10.5%	11.5%	7.5%
Agric raw materials	7.0%	4.6%	5.8%	4.5%	11.5%	4.4%	7.1%	6.1%
Minerals and metals	2.8%	1.9%	2.3%	1.7%	5.0%	2.3%	3.2%	2.2%

Fuels	10.1%	23.9%	3.4%	7.6%	37.0%	60.0%	9.4%	27.7%
Chemicals	7.0%	7.4%	8.6%	10.0%	1.7%	1.9%	4.9%	5.4%
Machinery	29.6%	26.6%	36.1%	35.9%	3.1%	5.7%	30.3%	25.4%
Manufactured products	28.3%	23.7%	31.2%	28.3%	18.1%	14.4%	26.5%	19.9%
Total exports	100.0%	100.0%	100.0%	100.0%	100.0%	100.0%	100.0%	100.0%
% OF TOTAL – LESS FUEL								
(c) Food and beverages	14.5%	13.3%	11.5%	11.2%	34.6%	26.3%	12.7%	10.4%
Agric raw materials	7.7%	6.1%	6.0%	4.9%	18.3%	10.9%	7.8%	8.5%
Minerals and metals	3.2%	2.5%	2.3%	1.8%	7.9%	5.7%	3.6%	3.1%
Chemicals	7.8%	9.7%	8.9%	10.9%	2.6%	4.8%	5.4%	7.5%
Machinery	32.9%	35.0%	37.4%	38.9%	5.0%	14.3%	33.5%	35.2%
Manufactured products	31.5%	31.1%	32.3%	30.7%	28.7%	35.9%	29.3%	27.5%
Total agriculture	22.3%	19.4%	17.5%	16.1%	52.9%	37.1%	20.5%	18.9%
Total primary products	25.4%	21.9%	19.9%	17.9%	60.8%	42.8%	24.0%	21.9%
Total manufactures	72.2%	75.8%	78.6%	80.4%	36.4%	55.0%	68.2%	70.2%

Source: FAO, *World Trade Matrices* (1985) and author's calculations.

Table 3.2 Export earnings by region, developing market economies, 1970–2 and 1980–2

US$ MILLIONS (current) TOTAL	Africa 1970–2	Africa 1980–2	Latin America 1970–2	Latin America 1980–2	Near East 1970–2	Near East 1980–2	Far East 1970–2	Far East 1980–2
(a) Food and beverages	3 040	8 374	7 350	28 489	700	3 195	2 940	15 760
Agric raw materials	1 930	3 109	1 446	5 407	684	1 046	3 351	13 561
Minerals and metals	717	2 754	1 557	5 532	106	568	825	3 213
Fuels	5 130	59 850	4 690	49 852	12 783	177 266	1 264	31 682
Chemicals	155	938	498	3 620	107	1 283	313	4 298
Machinery	76	330	512	5 524	126	2 274	1 313	22 206
Manufactured products	2 103	3 991	2 377	11 795	402	4 596	6 766	55 995
Total exports	13 223	79 812	18 500	110 916	15 003	190 358	17 701	150 070
PER CENT OF TOTAL								
(b) Food and beverages	23.0%	10.5%	39.7%	25.7%	4.7%	1.7%	16.6%	10.5%
Agric raw materials	14.6%	3.9%	7.8%	4.9%	4.6%	0.5%	18.9%	9.0%
Minerals and metals	5.4%	3.5%	8.4%	5.0%	0.7%	0.3%	4.7%	2.1%
Fuels	38.8%	75.0%	25.4%	44.9%	85.2%	93.1%	7.1%	21.1%
Chemicals	1.2%	1.2%	2.7%	3.3%	0.7%	0.7%	1.8%	2.9%
Machinery	0.6%	0.4%	2.8%	5.0%	0.8%	1.2%	7.4%	14.8%
Manufactured products	15.9%	5.0%	12.8%	10.6%	2.7%	2.4%	38.2%	37.3%
Total exports	100.0%	100.0%	100.0%	100.0%	100.0%	100.0%	100.0%	100.0%

% OF TOTAL – LESS FUEL							
(c) Food and beverages	37.6%	41.9%	53.2%	46.7%	31.5%	24.4%	17.9%	13.3%
Agric raw materials	23.8%	15.6%	10.5%	8.9%	30.8%	8.0%	20.4%	11.5%
Minerals and metals	8.9%	13.8%	11.3%	9.1%	4.8%	4.3%	5.0%	2.7%
Chemicals	1.9%	4.7%	3.6%	5.9%	4.8%	9.8%	1.9%	3.6%
Machinery	0.9%	1.7%	3.7%	9.0%	5.7%	17.4%	8.0%	18.8%
Manufactured products	26.0%	20.0%	17.2%	19.3%	18.1%	35.1%	41.2%	47.3%
Total agriculture	61.4%	57.5%	63.7%	55.5%	62.3%	32.4%	38.3%	24.8%
Total primary product	70.3%	71.3%	75.0%	64.6%	67.1%	36.7%	43.3%	27.5%
Total manufactures	28.8%	26.3%	24.5%	34.3%	28.6%	62.3%	51.1%	69.7%

Source: FAO, *World Trade Matrices* (1985) and author's calculations.

export earnings in 1970–2 reasonably evenly distributed among the four regional groups of developing market economies, from $13 billion for Africa to $18.5 billion for Latin America. A decade later export earnings from the Near East at $190 billion had outstripped Africa ($80 billion), Latin America ($111 billion) and the Far East ($150 billion), largely as a result, of course, of oil export earnings.

Once again, it is easier to see the structural changes if fuel export earnings are excluded. As can be seen from Table 3.2 (c), Africa and Latin America have retained their dependence on primary product exports, increasing the share of export earnings coming from those products from 70 to 71 per cent in the case of Africa and decreasing the share from 75 to 65 per cent for Latin America over the decade. By contrast, the Near East decreased the share of primary products in (non-fuel) export earnings from 67 to 37 per cent, and the same share in the Far East declined from 43 to 28 per cent. Manufactured exports remain relatively low in Africa (26 per cent) and Latin America (34 per cent), but have reached well over 60 per cent in the Near East and about 70 per cent in the Far East. This last group of developing countries is now as dependent upon manufactured exports as Africa is on primary products.

This regional disparity has obvious implications for the incidence of international development policy. Commodity policy becomes less applicable as a way of assisting a broad range of countries across regions. Trade negotiations aimed at improving access to manufactured markets again benefits some regions much more than others. These implications will be discussed in a later section of this paper.

Another aspect of developing-country trade patterns that has significance for international policy is the historically low level of trade among these countries themselves. In this respect there appears to have been a change in the past decade: the long-awaited increase in intra-developing-country trade flows seems finally to have arrived. Table 3.3 shows a matrix of trade by destination and origin among the developed and developing market economies and with the centrally planned economies. Trade between developing market economies increased, in total, from $13 billion to $146 billion over the period from 1971 to 1981. This represented an increase in the share of developing country exports going to other developing countries from 20 to 28 per cent. The share of imports coming from other developing countries rose from 20 to 30 per cent over this period.

In terms of manufactured trade, a remarkable 37 per cent of exports from developing market economies now go to other similarly classified

Table 3.3 Total manufactured and agricultural trade patterns among country groups – 1970–2 and 1980–2, $US millions current

	From/To	World	DME	DPME	CPE
(a) Total	World	358 797	254 934	66 177	35 610
Trade	DME	257 220	198 677	47 507	9 723
average	DPME	64 427	47 397	13 137	3 257
1970–2	CPE	37 150	8 860	5 533	22 630
Average	World	1 931 577	1 261 079	483 267	166 257
1980–2	DME	1 219 015	847 108	300 490	57 485
	DPME	531 156	357 016	145 919	22 122
	XPE	181 406	56 955	36 858	86 650
(b) Manufacture	World	233 001	162 053	45 455	24 144
Average	DME	195 309	148 395	38 263	7 554
1970–2	DPME	14 748	9 901	4 044	605
	CPE	22 944	3 757	3 148	15 985
Average	World	1 114 318	703 301	305 587	98 794
1980–2	DME	905 499	615 801	244 633	40 105
	DPME	116 850	69 070	42 687	3 924
	CPE	91 969	18 430	18 267	54 765
(c) Agriculture	World	71 839	52 447	11 860	7 118
Average	DME	43 509	34 547	6 921	1 946
1970–2	DPME	21 441	15 083	3 877	2 178
	CPE	6 889	2 817	1 062	2 994
Average	World	284 937	175 818	68 720	38 774
1980–2	DME	181 244	123 520	41 193	15 513
	DPME	78 941	43 836	21 430	13 116
	CPE	24 752	8 462	6 097	10 145

Source: FAO, *World Trade Matrices* (1985).

Key: DME (Developed market economies), DPME (Developing market economies), CPE (Centrally planned economies).

countries (up from 27 per cent a decade earlier), though this accounts for only 14 per cent of these countries' total manufactured imports. Developed market economies still provide 80 per cent of manufactured imports to, and buy 59 per cent of such exports from, the developing market economies. In agricultural products as well, trade among developing market economies has increased. Thirty-seven per cent of their exports go to, and 31 per cent of imports come from, these countries. But developed market economies still provide 60 per cent of their agricultural imports and take 56 per cent of their exports. Trade in agricultural products among the developing market economies is in fact only about one half of the value of the same trade flow in manufactured products.

In this connection, it is interesting to note the role of centrally planned countries in agricultural trade. They have turned outward over the decade, looking to the developed market economies for 40 per cent of their agricultural imports (up from 27 per cent), but still buying 34 per cent from the developing market economies. In fact they are a more important market for developing than for developed countries: centrally planned countries took 17 per cent of the agricultural exports of developing countries but only 9 per cent of the agricultural exports of developed countries in 1981. Attempts to adapt the trading institutions to better accommodate trade with centrally planned countries could benefit developing as well as developed countries.

AGRICULTURAL TRADE PATTERNS OF DEVELOPING COUNTRIES

Before attempting to draw the lessons from these changes, it is worthwhile illustrating another development in trade patterns as striking as the shift from primary products to manufactures in the export pattern of developing countries. As of 1982, developing countries became net importers of agricultural products. As can be seen from Table 3.4, developing countries exported about $15 billion (at 1981 prices) more agricultural products than they imported on average over the period 1969–71. In 1982, the excess of imports over exports was $2.2 billion. Exports rose above imports again in 1983 for developing countries as a whole, while developing market economies recorded an agricultural trade surplus of $2.7 billion (at 1981 prices).

As before, the regional pattern is instructive. Only Latin America remains a significant agricultural exporting region among the developing market economies. An increase in the real value of agricultural exports from that region, from $14 billion in 1969–71 to over $20 billion a decade later, coupled with a relatively low level of imports, generated a surplus of $12.8 billion in 1983. By contrast, developing

Table 3.4 Agricultural trade by country group and developing country region, 1969–71 to 1983

	$ billions, current				$ billions, deflated			
	1969–71	1979–81	1982	1983	1969–71	1979–81	1982	1983
AGRIC TRADE – EXPORTS								
Developed mkt econ	28.9	144.0	139.1	133.6	53.4	95.7	94.0	94.1
Developing mkt econ	17.3	65.1	59.5	61.7	32.1	43.3	40.2	43.4
Africa	3.8	9.9	8.3	8.2	7.0	6.6	5.6	5.8
Latin America	7.3	30.7	27.6	29.9	13.6	20.4	18.6	21.1
Near East	1.9	5.2	5.7	5.5	3.5	3.4	3.8	3.9
Far East	4.2	18.7	17.5	17.6	7.7	12.4	11.8	12.4
Central plan econ	5.1	14.0	13.5	12.3	9.5	9.3	9.1	8.7
Developed countries	32.7	153.7	148.2	141.8	60.5	102.2	100.2	99.9
Developing countries	18.7	69.4	63.9	65.7	34.6	46.2	43.2	46.3
WORLD	51.4	223.2	212.1	207.5	95.1	148.4	143.3	146.2
AGRIC TRADE – IMPORTS								
Developed mkt econ	40.1	150.6	139.3	137.4	74.2	100.2	94.1	96.8
Developing mtk econ	9.5	57.3	58.8	57.9	17.5	38.0	39.7	40.8
Africa	1.6	9.7	10.2	9.3	2.9	6.5	6.9	6.6
Latin America	2.3	13.1	11.5	11.8	4.3	8.7	7.8	8.3
Near East	1.7	17.9	20.3	19.4	3.2	11.9	13.7	13.7
Far East	3.6	15.8	16.1	16.7	6.7	10.5	10.9	11.7
Central plan econ	6.5	36.2	35.9	33.1	12.0	24.1	24.3	23.3
Developed countries	45.4	178.7	167.0	163.6	83.9	118.9	112.8	115.2
Developing countries	10.7	65.4	67.1	64.8	19.7	43.4	45.3	45.6
WORLD	56.0	244.0	234.1	228.4	103.6	162.3	158.2	160.8

Source: FAO Statistics Division.

market economies in Africa and the Near East have moved from export surpluses of $4.1 billion and $0.3 billion to deficits of $0.8 billion and $9.8 billion respectively by 1983. The Far East region remained a small net exporter over this period. The net deficit status of developing countries as a whole thus reflects a combination of sharply higher agricultural imports in regions with expanded incomes from oil exports (up by 13 per cent per year) and a fall in agricultural export earnings in Africa (down on average by 2 per cent per year), offset somewhat by the relatively strong performance of Latin American agricultural exports.

SIGNIFICANCE OF CHANGING COMMODITY TRADE PATTERNS

Why should the commodity composition of developing-country exports and their net balance in agricultural products be of interest and importance? On the one hand, it may influence the way in which we perceive the issues. We inevitably use 'stereotypes' in discussions of international economic policy; it is helpful if they are based on up-to-date trade patterns. To think of developing countries as being on balance more dependent upon manufactured than primary product exports, including agriculture, may cause one to specify problems and solutions differently. More fundamentally, the structural change itself has ramifications for economic interdependence and the way in which economies are linked. These changes could themselves influence policy choice at the national and international level. Countries are linked through capital and goods markets. The pattern of trade essentially determines the nature of this interaction. A country which turns from agricultural exports to manufactures undergoes a change in economic relationships somewhat in the same way as a family leaving a rural area and migrating to the city establishes a new set of linkages with economic institutions in the local economy.

The changes in the linkages with other countries as countries reduce their dependence upon agricultural exports and increase their imports of agricultural products is in turn mirrored in changes in their internal structure. Agricultural economists have documented the internal process over the years in many countries. A greater market orientation to production decisions, a declining labour force relative to other sectors, and increased productivity of labour based in part on purchases from the non-farm sector, are well-known symptoms. This process is almost a *sine qua non* for development in the rest of the economy. In some cases it has proved a spark to ignite general economic progress, in others it has followed close behind development in other areas of the economy. In either case the links between agriculture and the non-farm sector grow quickly, through participation in factor markets, competing for labour and capital, and in the goods markets, providing agricultural products in competition with overseas supplies to the extent allowed by national food and commodity policies.

The internal structural changes, of course, dictate the external linkages. A traditional agriculture, with few internal linkages to the non-farm sector other than some labour drift, will not be an integral part of the international economy, even if traditional export crops find their way to world markets through state marketing agencies. An economy with such an agriculture, and many in sub-Saharan Africa still fit that description, will face the familiar problems of declining terms of trade, widespread poverty and heavy dependence on concessional food imports. By contrast, a modern agriculture has extensive links with the non-farm sector – essentially being fully integrated into national factor markets – and a flourishing processing and marketing chain that links it with world markets. Agriculture in most developed countries has reached this point, and that in many middle income countries in approaching it rapidly.

It was once thought that this process of agricultural development led to the displacement of imports and the expansion of exports. That is, after all, a common motivation for stimulating the domestic agricultural sector. This does not appear to be the case. Agricultural development increases productivity and production per capita, but is often accompanied by falling traditional exports and an increase in other types of imports. Domestic demand for foodstuffs from the urban population takes over from cash crops for export and the stimulus for domestic expansion, but in meeting this demand the government can also call upon imports from world markets. As domestic livestock industries become established, imports of animal feed ingredients are common. In short, agricultural trade becomes somewhat more like the complex specialisation process of manufactures trade – a two-way street of components and finished products taking advantage of cost differences – than the one-way process of raw material trade, from the underdeveloped periphery to the industrial centre.

IMPLICATIONS FOR INTERNATIONAL POLICY

If the argument in this essay is correct, that the rapid shift of developing countries away from their former position as agricultural and raw material suppliers to the industrial world is due to significant internal changes in at least some of those countries, then it is useful to reflect on what this might imply for international policy. In one respect, it is a reflection of the failure of past policies. After all, if strong commodity agreements had been in effect and governments had followed the imprecations of international bodies to stimulate domestic food production, then what we should observe would be steady and remunerative traditional agricultural exports and declining imports of agricultural products.

On the other hand, it is probably just as well that this didn't happen. Manipulating commodity prices is not a very good way of helping particular countries. Many developing countries appear to have decided for themselves that whatever global commodity policy was in place their own best interests lay in trying to find a niche in the non-agricultural export market. Similarly, countries have acted as if agricultural imports, particularly the bargains to be had from the oversubsidised farm sectors in industrial countries, are worth building into the regular food and animal feed supply. Even the genuine concern about the instability of such supplies has proved no barrier to developing countries, who see the suppliers acting in fairly responsible ways (out of self-interest) when faced with shortages (Josling and Barichello, 1984).

Two complications mar this somewhat sanguine picture. First, many countries – in particular in Africa – have been left behind and are still in the traditional mould. International policy needs urgently to deal with their problems – though commodity price policy remains a weak weapon for this purpose. Second, the shift in trade patterns brings new problems. Besides greater exposure to agricultural import cost fluctuations, the general macroeconomic instability – of interest rates, exchange rates, and growth patterns – has much more direct effect on countries which have moved away from the beverages-for-machinery type of division of labour. This too presents a challenge for international policy. New ways will be needed to see that the emerging export sectors of developing countries are not the first to be hit by market shrinkage. Attempts to reduce trade barriers must be continued, and developing countries themselves may come to participate more actively in GATT affairs rather than sit on the side-lines and hope that the developed countries will remember them in their negotiations. The new GATT round may be the place to start this process.

One by-product of increased interest in manufacturing trade by developing countries, and greater emphasis on the GATT and other mechanisms for improving such trade, is that agricultural and commodity trade issues may be easier to solve. Serious problems exist with respect to market instability and high-cost production. When the level of primary product export prices is seen as an issue of 'global price support' for developing countries, solution to these problems becomes difficult. An aim of the global economy should be to reduce raw material costs in the production of usable products. Developing countries as a whole now have an economic interest in this process, which should allow them to penetrate industrial country markets. Efforts to bolster primary export earnings for particular country groups might still be desirable on distributional grounds. They should not be allowed to delay the overall process of diversification and economic maturity in developing countries which has been a hallmark of the past decade.

Note

1. The author is grateful to Richard J. Perkins and Nikos Alexandratos of FAO for several helpful discussions of this topic in the spring of 1985, while working with them on issues of agricultural trade. The trade statistics presented here are from the FAO, but the author alone is responsible for the interpretation given in this paper.

References

FAO (1985) *World Trade Matrices by Commodity Classes: 1970–72 and 1980–82 Averages*, Rome: Commodities and Trade Division, Food and Agriculture Organisation.

JOSLING, T. and R. BARICHELLO (1984) 'International trade and world food security: the role of developed countries since the World Food Conference', *Food Policy*, vol. 9(4), pp. 317–27.

PREBISCH, R. (1950) 'The economic development of Latin America', *Economic Bulletin for Latin America* (New York: United Nations Commission for Latin America).

SINGER, H. W. and J. ANSARI (1977) *Rich and Poor Countries* (London: Allen & Unwin).

SINGER, H. W. (1950) 'The distribution of gains between borrowing and investing countries', *American Economic Review*, vol. 40(2), pp. 473–85.

Part II

What Could Be Done?

4 Adjustment with a Human Face: A Broader Approach to Adjustment Policy

Richard Jolly

The 1980s will almost certainly be recorded by future development historians as a decade of rising poverty and malnutrition in many if not most countries of the world. Certainly this is true for the vast majority of countries in Africa and Latin America. It is probably true also for many of the better-off countries in the Middle East. Even in the United States, Britain and some of the other industrialised countries, poverty has been rising, and possibly malnutrition among the poorest as well. Only in the economically dynamic Asian countries can one be reasonably sure that malnutrition and poverty are declining rather than increasing, as regards both the proportion of the population affected and the depth of poverty and malnutrition they experience.

What has been happening in the majority of countries is a widespread and marked *deterioration* in the human condition.[1] The situation is one of a worsening of poverty and malnutrition, not merely its persistence. Nor, as often before, is it a matter of worsening poverty in some countries with improvements in others. The early 1980s have produced a strong, sustained and systematic set of downward international pressures on the majority of developing countries, with the consequence that living standards have deteriorated very seriously. There is still time for change, but without it the second half of the 1980s will be little better.

This paper will focus on the situation and need for offsetting action in that majority of countries whose economies are open to global influences, especially the economic repercussions of world recession. In most cases, it is extremely difficult to disentangle the effects of global and national influences and to distinguish 'causes' from the effects of policy actions they often engender. Such disentangling, however, is not essential for deciding that remedial action needs to be

61

taken. Action is the concern of this paper, just as action for development has been Hans Singer's concern in most of his life's work. This paper, therefore, concentrates on showing what a broader approach to adjustment policy would involve and how it would relate to earlier development concerns with basic needs and redistribution with growth.

THE CONTEXT – RISING MALNUTRITION AND ECONOMIC DECLINE IN THE 1980s

The increase in severe and moderate malnutrition among under-5 children in six countries of Africa is shown in Figures 4.1, 4.2 and 4.3. These diagrams are of double interest. In the first place, they show the seasonal fluctuations in levels of child malnutrition, typical in predominantly rural countries where for poor families food shortages become increasingly common in the pre-harvest period. For young children, the period of food shortages is often compounded by seasonal patterns in the incidence of diseases like measles or diarrhoea, with their own downward pressures on growth and weight gain.

In the second place, the diagrams bring out the increasing pressures on child nutrition in all parts of Africa in recent years. In Ghana, the proportion of children moderately or severely malnourished almost doubled from 1980 to 1983, the most serious of the recorded increases. Fortunately there was some improvement during 1984, though the proportion still remained well above 1980–1 levels. Botswana and Burundi also record clear increases in the proportion of children malnourished. Although changes in Lesotho, Madagascar and Rwanda are relatively small, one should note that in every case they are upward – and from unacceptably high base levels: 20 per cent or so in Lesotho, 30 per cent in Rwanda and 45 per cent in Madagascar.

A final point of these tables, to which we shall return later, is that they show that a basic indicator of the human condition can be monitored. But for the moment, let us return to the economic pressures creating or contributing to much of the human deterioration observed. With worsening terms of trade for primary commodities, sluggish world demand for manufactures, rises in interest rates and debt servicing, stagnation in private capital flows, often compounded by other influences, it is not surprising that per capita income has fallen and with it per capita consumption.

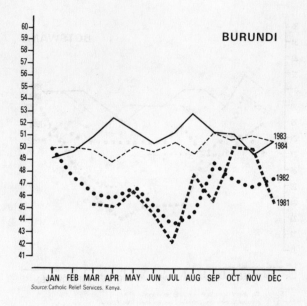

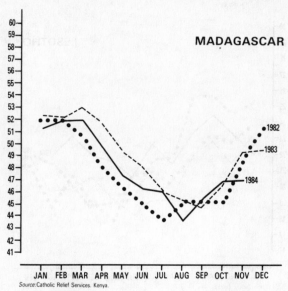

Figure 4.1   Percentage of children under five years below 80 per cent
of Harvard standard weight for age

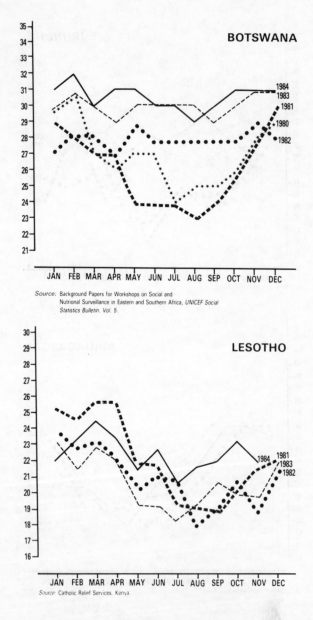

Source: Background Papers for Workshops on Social and
Nutrional Surveillance in Eastern and Southern Africa, *UNICEF Social
Statistics Bulletin. Vol. 5.*

Source: Catholic Relief Services. Kenya.

Figure 4.2   Percentage of children under five years below 80 per cent
of Harvard standard weight for age

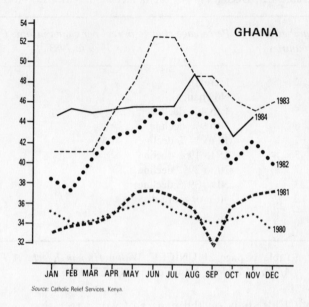

Source: Catholic Relief Services. Kenya.

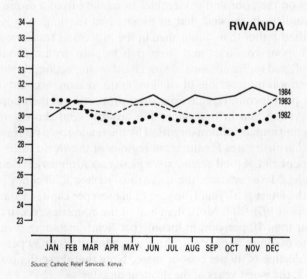

Source: Catholic Relief Services. Kenya.

Figure 4.3 Percentage of children under five years below 80 per cent
of Harvard standard weight for age

Table 4.1 Declines in per capita income in Africa 1979 to 1983

Number of countries	Percentage change in real per capita income from peak year 1979 to 1983
2	Increase
3	No change
5	1 to 4% decline
6	5 to 9% decline
7	10 to 14% decline
5	15 to 19% decline
7	20 to 29% decline
3	30 to 39% decline
2	40% or more decline
Total 40	

Source: Table 1, page 21 UNICEF, *Within Human Reach: A Future for Africa's Children*. New York: UNICEF, 1985.

UNICEF's study on the impact of world recession on children, prepared in 1983 with the assistance of Hans Singer, explored the impact on the poor and vulnerable, using data from a dozen country case-studies. It showed that in most cases the impact was usually magnified rather than diminished in the process of transmission from rich to poor countries and from rich to poor within countries. In general, and in the absence of special offsetting action, the impact on children was most serious of all. Two major reasons account for this.

The poorer countries have a greater proportion of their populations poor, young and in the vulnerable groups. And the extent of the multiplied impact is often disguised by the tendency to refer to *average annual* growth rates for the main regions of the world rather than to rates per head of total *decline since peak year* for individual countries.

Table 4.1 summarises the disastrous economic declines in Africa since the latest peak year (the year of highest per capita income during the period 1979–81). More than half of the countries record a decline greater than 10 per cent in income per head, including seven with a decline of 20 to 29 per cent; three a decline of 30 to 39 per cent and two a decline of 40 per cent or more. Note that these figures exclude 1984–5, the worst years of the drought disaster.

Within countries, this decline has a magnified impact on the poor and on children for three reasons: the tendency for cutbacks in employment and wages to hit the poor more severely than the better-off; the tendency for health education and other social sectors to be cut back more than the so-called productive sectors of government spending; the tendency for poorer families to have larger numbers of children and others who are vulnerable.

One important offsetting factor for some of the rural population is its comparative insulation from government and the urban and international economy. Just as this part of the rural population commonly received only limited benefits from the expansion of government services, so it has suffered relatively less from the cutbacks. Too much should not be made of this insulation, however, for the truly subsistence economy is a rare exception, and in terms of basic health and nutrition it has always left much to be desired, especially when land is limited and population has grown.

THE IMPACT OF ADJUSTMENT POLICY

What now of national adjustment policies, that set of domestic policy changes and international pressures and support consciously designed to curb the macro-deficits in the balance of payments and the government budget and to restore a pattern of non-inflationary economic growth over the medium term?[2]

Measures of domestic adjustment may be adopted independently or as part of some formal or informal international agreement, whereby they are part of a total package of reform and international financial support. Either way they will have further impact on the level of consumption and the living standards of the population. Usually they will involve some conscious reduction of consumption in the short run, in the hopes of restoring balance, investment and growth in the medium to longer run.

There are three possible basic effects of the adjustment process on levels of consumption, depending on whether the income distribution effects of the policies adopted are positive, neutral or negative.[3] If neutral, the consumption levels and living standards of the poorest will fall by the same proportion as those of other groups; if positive, by not so much; if negative, by more.

However, it is the argument of this paper that the *critical issue is not whether income distribution as such is worsened or unchanged, but where the consumption and living standards of the population are left in relation to their basic needs*. If the proportion of the rural or urban population with unmet basic minimum needs for nutrition, food or health is increased, and if the deficiency between their needs and their actual levels of consumption is also growing, there will be growing numbers in the country who are less and less able to support the process of economic revival and participate in its achievement. In economic parlance, there will be a disinvestment of human capital, affecting both the short and the longer run. In the short run, low levels of nutritional intake and probably increased levels of illness will have their direct effects on productivity and economic production, especially in the small-scale industrial sector and the informal urban sector. Even in the small-scale agricultural sector, where most farmers will have access to their own production, there are likely to be some repercussions as the result of cutbacks in such things as agricultural inputs, essential drugs (such as antimalarials) and other inputs for basic services.

The longer run effects may be even more serious, especially for children under 5 years old. This is the age group most vulnerable to short-term health and nutritional deficiencies and at a time of life when critical needs cannot be postponed without considerable risk. If the purpose of adjustment policy is to lay the foundations for sustained growth in the economy over the longer term, it is senseless to ignore the most basic needs of the population in the process. Yet if nutrition standards fall or basic health and education services are cut back, this is precisely what is being done.

ADJUSTMENT WITH A HUMAN FACE

This is the frame within which a broader policy of adjustment with a human face can be illustrated. It would combine the main economic elements of adjustment policy with conscious efforts to ensure that the basic nutrition and health and education needs of the entire population are satisfied. This requires special measures to raise the consumption levels of the most vulnerable to the basic needs minimum during the period of adjustment when consumption levels in general are most constrained.

As I have explained elsewhere (Jolly, 1985), this would involve three types of policy action.

First, *a clearly acknowledged concern in the goals of adjustment policy for basic human welfare and a commitment to protect the minimum nutrition levels of children and other specially vulnerable groups of a country's population.*

Second, *a broader approach to the adjustment process, which should comprise four components*:

(a) Action to maintain a floor for nutrition and other basic needs, related to what the country can in the long term sustain;
(b) Restructuring within the productive sectors – agriculture, services, industry – to rely more upon the small-scale, informal producers and to ensure their greater access to credit, internal markets and other measures which will stimulate growth in their incomes;
(c) Restructuring within health, education and other social sectors, to restore momentum and ensure maximum coverage and benefits from constrained and usually reduced resources. Already, there are important examples of what can be done to reach all of a country's population, but still at relatively low cost;
(d) More international support for these aspects of adjustment, including the provision of more, and more flexible, finance, with longer term commitments. The extremes of the present situation will often require a ceiling on outflows of interest and debt amortisation if the protection of human needs is to be feasible in the short run.

Thirdly, *a system is needed for monitoring nutrition levels and the human situation during the process of adjustment*. We should be concerned not only with inflation, balance of payments, and GNP growth – but also with nutrition, food balances and human growth. The proportion of a nation's households falling below some basic poverty line should be monitored – and treated as one of the most relevant statistics for assessing adjustment.

There is one point about adjustment with a human face which is frequently misunderstood. Because the focus is on human need, there is a common tendency, almost a reflex action of the economic mind, to think of the programme as a welfare programme. In contrast, I would stress that it is primarily one of enhancing production and investment, though in an area often overlooked and played down in spite of clear economic evidence that positive and often high returns accrue from these activities.

This is not the place for a summary of the literature but it may help to remind readers of the basic points and evidence in the key areas concerned.

Economic Efficiency of the Small-Scale Producer

Many studies have documented the relative efficiency of the small-scale producer, rural or urban. In terms of output per acre, use of inputs and returns to capital, the small farmer is usually more efficient than the large-scale one. The same is frequently true of the small-scale urban producer, in both the formal and informal sectors, though here the evidence is more limited. A strong case can be made, therefore, for expecting that a shift of emphasis to the small-scale producer will increase output and growth.

Labour intensive investment generally is both efficient and employment-creating. This was the basis of the East Asian success. It is not just a question of *adding* subscale to the existing industrial structure but of changing it radically and also shifting to rural industrialisation by:

(a) promoting agriculture;
(b) fostering strong intersectoral linkages.

Productivity

Berg (1981:14) argues that 'overcoming deficiencies in nutrition produces stronger, more energetic workers, reduces the number of work days lost because of illness, lengthens the working lifespan, and increases cognitive skills. The flow of earnings is thereby increased above what it would have been in the absence of improved nutrition and health'. He also summarises the links between improved nutrition and increases in the benefits to children and society from education, family planning programmes, anti-poverty programmes and, in general, human well-being and the capacity 'to enjoy whatever sources of human satisfaction are available'.

I would add that it is important to recognise that these nutritional benefits accrue not only by enhancing the productivity of workers in the recognised (formal) sector but also to others (especially, but not only, women) engaged in household activities, which may not be counted in national income but which greatly influence economic production and household living standards.

Investment

This long-run contribution to enhancing productivity may be even more important, especially in the case of children. For instance, the failure to provide adequate nutrition during the first five years of life may lead to life–long impairment of all the human and productive capacities mentioned above. The economic evidence of positive returns to basic levels of human investment has been frequently documented. *The World Development Report 1980* of the World Bank, for instance, gives estimates from sixty developing countries showing that the social returns from primary education and expenditure averaged 22 to 27 per cent higher than typical returns from physical investment. Moreover, they were also signficantly higher than the rates of return from investment in secondary and higher education, and showed only a mild tendency to decline over time as education expanded. In addition, investment in primary education also tends to be redistributive towards the poor, thus enhancing income distribution and poverty alleviation. These direct estimates are supported by the evidence of other long-run benefits of education, which escape quantification, focused on worker productivity: for instance, the effects of primary education on women in improving child care, reducing infant and child mortality rates and reducing fertility, and thus population growth.

Evidence of the economic return from basic health service expenditure is more limited. But there are impressive examples of the higher cost-effectiveness of preventive health services than of curative, precisely the sorts of services to which a basic needs approach would give priority.

THE IMPACT OF ADJUSTMENT WITH A HUMAN FACE ON ECONOMIC GROWTH

With these reminders of the positive contributions to productivity and investment of expenditures on basic needs, it is time to return to the effects of an adjustment strategy that protects human needs on the subsequent path of economic growth and consumption.

If the initial deficiencies in health, nutrition and incentives to the active labour force are considerable, to redress them through basic needs expenditures will have an immediate effect on production. If, at the other extreme, the immediate productivity enhancing characteristics of the basic needs expenditures are weak but the long-run investment effects are strong, the total adjustment package will still help to accelerate economic growth but only after an interval.

The timing and speed of economic recovery will also depend on the sources of support for the basic needs measures. If they are deducted from the consumption of higher income groups, or from unproductive uses of government expenditure, or from additional inflows of aid from abroad, there is every reason to expect that adjustment with a human face will do as well as growth-oriented adjustment, until at some point it accelerates and does better. If, however, the sources of support are taken from resources which would otherwise have underpinned the conventional adjustment programme, long-run growth may be accelerated (assuming the rates of return on the human investment are higher than those on the foregone physical investment) but it may take longer for the higher returns to materialise.

In the short run, there is likely to be a significant trade-off, relievable only to the extent that additional outside support is provided to ease it. In the long run, by making more rapid growth possible, the trade-off can be greatly eased if not eliminated.

This is, of course, the parallel with the arguments for redistribution with growth or for a basic needs growth strategy. Within a considerable margin of options, one can show that a country can pursue a positive-sum growth strategy, in which all groups (especially, but not only, the poor) can be better off than they would otherwise be. A number of countries have in fact achieved a combination of growth and greater basic needs satisfaction, sometimes with considerable redistribution, over the post-war period. But no one can pretend that it is the general pattern. Does this mean that the case for adjustment with a human face is fatally flawed?

Indeed, one can reasonably question the optimism when development experience evidently is so often more difficult. Two points can briefly be made in answer to this question. Other factors, including inconsistencies in national policy and inefficient execution, can warp the outcome of an adjustment strategy, as can both changes in the global economic environment and specific changes in relation to international policy towards the country concerned. But unless there is reason to believe that the inconsistencies and inefficiencies are more related to one pattern of adjustment than to another, for the reasons summarised above, the economic evidence suggests that an adjustment process giving full attention to the human dimension will be economically more efficient and effective for growth than those which do not.

Adjustment policy with a human face will remain a sham – an attempt to paint a smile on a face with tears – if it is seen only as a change in the macroeconomic policy of government. Instead it must involve a move to a more people-focused process of adjustment, a shift to greater self-reliance, decentralisation, small-scale production, community action and empowerment of people and households. These are the groups and approaches which in fact provide the goods and services and generate livelihoods for the low-income sections of most populations. They are also more often than not squeezed by conventional adjustment approaches. Yet for sheer cost effectiveness, as well as protection for the poor, they are the ones that matter.

ANTECEDENTS

Precisely because this broader approach to adjustment differs from much current theory, it may be helpful to set it within the context of earlier development thinking. The obvious links are with strategies of redistribution with growth and meeting basic needs, both part of the rethinking of development strategy in the early 1970s and both closely associated with the work of Hans Singer.

Singer himself played an important part in the evolution of redistribution from growth thinking, initially in his contributions to the ILO Kenya Mission report, *Employment, Incomes and Equality*. Later these ideas were generalised and developed more formally in the IDS/World Bank study, *Redistribution with Growth*, which explored both the economic rationale and the approaches for such strategy.

Paul Streeten (1981) has aptly summed up the emergence of basic needs thinking in the 1970s as in one sense a homecoming. 'For when the world embarked on development thirty years ago, it was primarily with the needs of the poor in mind. Third World leaders wanted economic as well as political independence, but independence was to be used for man's self-fulfilment. The process got sidetracked ...'

Streeten points out the compelling logic of basic needs. It is not only a strategy for efficiently meeting the needs of the poorest 40 per cent of the population but for increasing their productivity and thereby enabling them to contribute efficiently to their own development and the alleviation of their own poverty.

In the same book Mahbub ul-Haq sums up the core of the argument (p. viii).

It is true that the only way absolute poverty can be eliminated on a permanent and sustainable basis, is to increase the productivity of the poor. But direct methods to increase the productivity of the poor need to be supplemented with efforts to provide their unmet basic needs, for at least the following four reasons: – First, education and health are required – in addition to machines, land, and credit – to increase productivity. Sufficient empirical evidence is now available to suggest that education and health services often make a greater contribution to improving labour productivity than do most alternative investments.

– Second, many poor people have no physical assets – neither a small farm nor a small industry. They are the landless or urban poor. The only asset they possess is their own two hands and their willingness to work. In such a situation the best investment is in human resource development.

– Third, it is not enough to enable the poor to earn a reasonable income. They also need goods and services on which to spend their income. Markets do not always supply wage goods, particularly public services. Greater production of wage goods and the expansion and redistribution of public services becomes essential if basic needs of the majority of the population are to be met.

– Finally, it may take a long time to increase the productivity of the absolute poor to a level at which they can afford at least the minimum bundle of basic needs for a productive life. In the interim, some income groups – particularly the bottom 10 to 20 per cent – may need short-term subsidy programmes.

MONITORING THE HUMAN DIMENSIONS OF ADJUSTMENT

If human concerns are to be given proper attention during the adjustment process there must be a monitoring system to ensure that indicators of the extent to which human needs are met or unmet are regularly and rapidly collected, analysed and published in a form which policy-makers can take into account in devising remedial action. Experience suggests this is less momentous a task than might at first appear, even in data-weak, low-income countries. Many of the indicators required are already being collected in day-to-day operations by government departments or private organisations working at grass roots level and in touch with poor and vulnerable communities. The statistical reliability of the information may not be perfect but, almost by definition, it matches the administrative capacity and outreach of the services available to play some role in remedial action.

The challenge is, therefore, to ensure that the data is used for monitoring and policy-making at regional and national level, not only at the level at which it is collected.

The data on nutritional status given in Figures 4.1 to 4.3 provides an excellent example. In the case of Botswana it is collected as part of regular and largely routine nationwide child health activities. Each child is weighed monthly at a clinic, the weight recorded, and remedial action, including the distribution of food supplements, is taken as necessary by the clinic. In Ghana and the other four countries, the data is obtained directly from the food distribution system run by the Catholic Relief Services. In these cases only a fraction of the country's children are covered and, because child weighing is used to determine eligibility for free food, the sample of children covered by the data is undoubtedly biased. But for purposes of monitoring *changes* in the nutritional status of the poorest, including the adequacy of remedial action, the data is both relevant, and well focused. In the case of Ghana, some 250 000 children are covered by the data and tabulations are available separately for all ten provinces. Even if coverage is partial, the picture presented of the month-by-month and year-by-year change in nutritional status is indicative, and is probably much less biased statistically as an indicator of the position of the poorer sections of the population than most of the other statistical indicators available.

In addition to these data, there is a need for two other classes of information. First, the range of more conventional social indicators already widely collected, analysed and used – such as school enrolment, basic health care and consumer price and income data, production data from farms and from small-scale producers, urban and rural. Here the issue is timeliness and focus. Unlike most of the economic data used for adjustment policy, where collection, processing and often publication is expected and achieved in two or three months, the statistical lag between collection and publication for the human indicators is usually two or three years, or more. The result is that even when economic policy makers are willing to include human concerns in the adjustment deliberations, they are starved of the data which they need to do so. A priority in every country should be to develop the system for producing a core of human indicators with the same urgency and priority as is routinely accorded to some of the core economic statistics.

The second class of data required related to the functioning of the key parts of government administration which support the poor and vulnerable. Indicators are needed of the adequacy and effectiveness of these services in reaching out to the poor and in responding to their needs. Sample surveys and the routine statistical services have an important part to play.

Even with increased timeliness and a sharper focus on a critical core of indicators, there will still be a lag between data availability and the indicators needed for policy making. It is here that the world of social concerns needs to borrow from the world of economic concerns. Some short set of *leading social indicators* is needed, akin to the leading economic indicators regularly compiled and considered in many of the industrial countries. These should be available some six to nine months ahead to indicate likely trends, based on such statistics as:

– household foodstocks at end of last harvest,
– forecast rainfall,
– planned government expenditures in key areas such as primary health care,
– stocks of vaccines and essential drugs,
– maintenance of village water supplies,
– credit available for small farmer inputs and small-scale industrial producers.

The issue is not the lack of data or the intrinsic difficulty of devising appropriate weights for an effective system of leading indicators. Essentially the issue is one of perceptions and priorities. The human dimension must be recognised as central to the formulation of economic policy. Especially at times of severe economic constraint and adjustment, the condition of vulnerable groups cannot be assumed to occur as an inevitable by-product of general economic policy.

This was the Keynesian lesson of the 1930s. Out of that experience grew concern about the level of unemployment in formulating macroeconomic policy. This, in turn, begat the present system of national accounts which is a focus of much of the economic statistical work in most countries. Ironically, it was the *social* and *human* concern underlying the original GNP calculations which is now being lost in an over-preoccupation with aggregate GNP and a neglect of the people involved in its creation and use.

Notes

1. Paradoxically, the sheer size of China and India, accounting for almost 40

per cent of the world's population, makes it difficult to be sure whether (in terms of the total number of persons affected) worldwide *poverty and malnutrition* is growing, constant or declining. The economies of China and India by their size and structure are relatively insulated from world economic repercussions, their populations therefore being more affected by domestic changes of policy, the results of which in terms of poverty and malnutrition are not yet clear.
2. This is an orthodox and optimistic view of the *goals* of adjustment policy. Critics would point out that the actual measures adopted often fail to achieve them – as some of the IMF's own evaluations have made clear. There is also the matter of *international* adjustment policy: international action (or inaction) to correct major imbalances in the pattern of trade or income flows between countries, or of deficiencies in the total level of global economic activity. We return to this point later.
3. The measurement of income distribution is complex. Here I refer to the income distribution effects on consumption levels of the poor and vulnerable.

References

BERG. A. (1981) 'Malnourished people: a policy view', *Poverty and Basic Needs* series, World Bank.
JOLLY, R. (1985) *Adjustment with a Human Face* (Barbara Ward Lecture) (Rome: Society for International Development).
STREETEN, P. *et al.*, (1981) *First Things First: Meeting Basic Human Needs in the Developing Countries* (Oxford: Oxford University Press for the World Bank).

5 Sub-Saharan Africa: Poverty of Development, Development of Poverty

Reginald Herbold Green

> What do you want to be when you grow up?
> Alive.
>
> *UNICEF African poster, 1985*

INTRODUCTION

The struggle against poverty and for human conditions of life by and for poor people is not new, neither is it one limited to the poor countries of the south nor is it a static one. Participation in it – from the Temple Commission on unemployment in the UK of the 1930s, through the early days of the United Nations' economic development effort beginning at the end of the 1940s, and the International Labour Organisation's World Employment Programme in the 1970s to his present service with UNICEF – has been an abiding and integral part of Hans Singer's devotion to applied economics as a vocation – economics in its original Old Testament sense of stewardship and meeting material needs.[1] Nor is Hans a newcomer to Africa – from the founding of the Economic Commission for Africa as the 1950s turned into the 1960s, through the 1970s Kenya ILO Employment Mission to the 1984 UNICEF *State of the World's Children Report*, and study of the impact of the depression on children in Africa (Singer and Green, 1984), there is a span of twenty-five years of work.

Over that period sub-Saharan Africa has become independent; begun to grapple with both poverty and productivity; appeared to achieve (in a majority of states) a real if limited and imperfect development momentum; and, since the end of the 1970s, fallen into sustained economic unsuccess in all but a small minority of countries.[2]

That unsuccess has usually been sketched in terms of macroeconomic or political economic aggregate levels and trends (for example in World Bank, *World Development Reports* and in the bulk of the contributions to the sources cited at 2), and flashed on television screens in images of mass starvation. The first abstracts from, and anaesthetises against, the human meaning of economic disintegration – penury, hunger, illness, plague, societal distintegration (at least the outriders and forward projected shadows of the four horsemen of the apocalypse). The latter numbs by its hammer blows of horror, and creates a situation in which the struggle to meet the immediate necessity of maintaining life can push aside the need to alter the conditions which in their extreme form endanger life on a mass basis, but in their more general and more persistant form erode, degrade and shorten it in less dramatic but no less damnable ways.

The reactions to economic unsuccess in sub-Saharan Africa have been dominated by two lines:

(a) the 'new conventional wisdom'[3] centred on IMF stabilisation and World Bank structural adjustment models; and
(b) the emergency famine relief focus on keeping human beings alive.

The need to balance resources used with resources available – stabilisation – is irrefutable. No economy can avoid stabilisation indefinitely and multiterm, massive imbalance leads to conditions at least as deadly to human welfare as to GDP growth. The basic questions are ones of distribution of costs, timing and – most critical – the relevant roles of cutting resource use versus increasing domestic (produced) and external (transferred) resource supply. Similarly structural adjustment to raise production and productivity generally, and in particular to improve the balance of external resources and food availability relative to requirements, is not itself controversial. In very poor countries especially, even though growth without development is all too possible, development without growth is not. However, it is not the same thing to affirm that production is essential and to encapsulate that advice as 'Seek ye first the kingdom of production and all else shall be added unto you'. There are very real questions of distribution (dominantly turning on who is able to produce what, not on subsequent transfer payments), of basic service levels (both in respect to minimum humanly acceptable standards and to ability to produce), and of timing of gains as opposed to costs (poor people have very narrow survival margins and it is a brutal fact that the poor are dead in the short, not even in the long, run).

The emergency efforts to avoid mass death do relate to an immediate overriding necessity. For the dead there is no future. By themselves they do not answer what one is keeping people alive for, in the sense of what they will be able to make of their lives. Mass starvation in sub-Saharan Africa to date has been triggered by the interaction of drought, weak transport systems and war (and threatened, albeit to date averted, when the first two interacted particularly savagely). But it has been triggered both because the margin between 'normal' food supply and starvation is narrow, and increasingly narrowing in a majority of the region's countries, and because most poor households have neither the self-employment nor wage employment opportunity either to grow enough to eat or to be productive and well rewarded enough to buy adequate food. In normal years, inability to buy food – not its physical unavailability – is the main cause of urban malnutrition (see Reutlinger, 1985). That reality underlies the famine crises and remains even when reasonable rains return (see Please, 1985 and Green, 1985b) – as they did in many, not all, drought affected areas in the 1984–5 cropping seasons. Furthermore, peasants who have lost herds, tools, seed and other means of farming, especially if also driven from their homes into urban areas or relief camps by the search for food, cannot resume production as if nothing had happened. Flight from the land will be both difficult and slow (Burki, 1985).

Neither of these two approaches directly addresses the challenge of persistent and developing poverty. Even when many sub-Saharan Africa economies had positive per capita output growth not reversed by negative terms of trade shifts, absolute poverty at best declined slowly as a proportion of total population and even then often rose in absolute numbers of human beings affected. Similarly basic service expansion while very real is – with the partial exception of primary education – very far from achieving universal access in most states. In 1980 malnutrition in sub-Saharan Africa, defined as not enough calories for an active working life, rose to 44 per cent of the population – 150 million human beings – while 25 per cent – 90 million – were also below the calories needed to avert stunted growth and serious health risk. Both the percentages and the absolute numbers represented deterioration since 1970 (World Bank, 1986; Reutlinger, 1985). The 1970s concerns with employment (for example the World Employment Programme's country teams, such as the one to Kenya), peasant productivity, the 'informal sector', basic service access, distribution and enabling the poor to become less poor by producing more (or being more fairly paid), related to very real human and economic problems. They self-evidently remain valid in the 1980s as absolute poverty rises and basic services decay, even if the somewhat reductionist emphasis on productivity and survival has for the time being swept them to the margins of dialogue and – with exceptions – of resource allocation. The concern with persistent poverty is not a new one in economics nor one associated solely with particular ideologies. It was after all Adam Smith who made it a premise that no nation could be great and prosperous, the majority of whose people were poor and miserable.

The weakness of conventional stabilisation and structural adjustment strategies is not their focus on regaining balance between resource availability and use, still less their insistence on the need to increase and to alter the makeup of production to achieve and to sustain balance. It is the absence of two additional priorities which is open to question. These are:

(a) non-deferral of meeting basic needs – with special reference to food, water, health and education;
(b) priority to increasing productivity of and access to services by poor people and vulnerable groups.

There is no reason to assume that these goals are either economic or socio-political nonsense. The enormous cost of inadequate diet in terms of health, ability to benefit from education, capacity to work hard in lost present and future output terms is increasingly widely recognised (Reutlinger, 1985; World Bank, 1986; UNICEF, 1985b). Similarly the social disintegration and political instability caused by the immiseration of growing numbers of people who were formerly productive, non-destitute members of their societies and economies has high potential economic costs; active in the cases of disorder and insurrection, passive in those of retreat from involvement in state policy and reversion to an 'each for himself and the devil take the hindmost' variant of economic and social neo-anarchy.

The emergency relief efforts weaknesses are rather different. They do recognise that basic needs cannot be deferred and that helping human beings stay alive matters. What they have failed to do in the past is to pose two further questions:

(a) how can these people have a future – and of what kind – after their lives have been saved?

(b) how can emergency aid be designed and utilised as a first step towards self-re-establishment including increased/restored production/earned income by the recipients?

Bob Geldof's horrified comments on the need to consider what Bandaid was keeping people alive for (i.e. what human condition they faced) illustrates the growing concern with the first question. The second has been nibbled at both by analysts and practitioners but mainline action remains to treat it as unhandleable because emergencies are unpredictable, time short and relief logically separable from development.

TRANSITIONS FROM POVERTY TO POVERTY

Poverty in sub-Saharan Africa is a historic fact – as it is virtually universally. There was no golden age before the Europeans came when the land flowed with sorghum, millet and yams, with guinea fowl, cattle and fish, with palm oil, groundnuts and garden eggs, with banana beer, coconut spirits and palm wine, so that all were well fed and prosperous. But it would be equally false to treat poverty as primordial, unchanging and – implicitly – permanently immutable and inevitable.

Pre-colonial poverty turned primarily on submarginal or erratic rainfall and on technological (and therefore productivity) limitations in relation to sub-Saharan Africa's on average poor and difficult soils. The human condition was equally constrained by inadequate health knowledge, practices and services which shortened life and eroded strength. Africans, not Europeans, have always been the chief victims of African diseases and so-called adult African resistance to, for example, malaria often means no more (and no less) than that vulnerable individuals died of it as children.

None of this denies that Africans did develop technologies: some long fallow rotation system (so-called 'shifting cultivation') related admirably and sustainably to poor soils with limited, uncertain rainfall so long as populations were small and the only large demand on the land was for food; some herbal and parapsychological medical practices were far more than common sense or trial and error. Still less does it deny cultural and social achievements. The fact remains that for many Africans hunger was an annual occurrence, disease a frequent one, life short, and death an ever present danger unleashable by unpredictable and technologically unmanageable weather shifts and disease outbreaks.

Pre-colonial neo-colonialism – of slave traders and merchants manipulating African polities and agents – unleashed two additional causes of poverty and human misery. The first was the slave trade and the social and economic wastelands it created (still writ plain in the low present population of most of Nigeria's middle belt almost a century after the trade ceased). The second was the rise in the number and ferocity of wars – and the killing power available to armies – largely directly or indirectly triggered and/or made possible by European and, secondarily, Arabian interventions (see Rodney, 1972).

Colonialism in Africa rarely meant territorial economic development even in modern macroeconomic terms. Gross territorial product – as opposed to certain products of use to the colonising power and its trading partners – was rarely of central concern. James Mill's definition of a colony as a place in which the colonising power found it convenient to carry out some of its business (e.g. mining, cutting tropical timber, buying or growing tropical crops) provides much more insight into the nature of economic policy than any definition presupposing colonies were seen primarily as territorial economic units in their own right.[4]

As a direct result, poverty of Africans was not an economic concern which could appear on the colonial agenda as more than a footnote. A large export sector with a supporting food and service sector could on occasion reduce poverty – a result not unwelcome to many colonial administrators. Avoiding mass starvation (by price juggling, reserve holding, famine relief and even food for work policies which have a haunting familiarity of kind if not scale to 1970s and 1980s efforts) were sometimes priorities – for example, in the then Tanganyika Mandate – and did end mass starvation. But Adam Smith's dictum on the need for the majority to be non-poor and non-miserable as a precondition for colonial economic success would have been either incomprehensible or seen as at least as subversive as the writings of Karl Marx.[5]

Education for Africans was perceived either as a by-product of missionary endeavour (vaguely backed, tolerated or curtailed in terms of its supposed social and political impact – which was usually far more and far more deeply 'subversive' than colonial administrators, or missionaries! realised) or as an investment in clerks, semi-skilled labour and other human intermediate inputs into the colonial economy. The calculations were not in sophisticated econometric terms, but colonial education policy was early (and severely cost constrained) human resource development school in concept – even when it flowered to secondary and medical assistant levels. Health facilities for Africans (and until late in the colonial period often for Europeans[6]) were even more exiguous and dependent on missionary subsidisation of the colonial state.

However, the nature of poverty changed. Colonial rule did reduce death from war (caused by dislocation and subsequent starvation or epidemic disease more than by battle casualities); it did end the slave trade; frequently it did provide fail-safe famine relief against mass starvation. These shifts probably both increased life expectancy and (by reducing dislocation) raised rates of increase of food production. Exploitative as it was, colonial production promotion/coercion on average probably raised the command of many African households over goods and services. While there were exceptions (especially in the case of settler colonies), the territories in which most Africans were most likely to be poor and miserable were those like then Haute Volta in which, à la Joan Robinson's formulation, the colonial power and its enterprises could find no worthwhile way of exploiting them.

Poverty – or at least human deprivation – was also altered in its nature in additional ways. The first was the imposition of external rule with its impact on polity, society, self-image and self-set standards – clearly a negative shift. The second was the beginnings of education and health services which both improved the human condition of recipients and gave them – and other Africans – a fuller picture of what they were (for whatever reason) still deprived of (a much greater force in both aspects with the late colonial education and health services 'boom'). The third was an increase in population growth (presumably related to the indirect effects of law and order including famine relief and ability to produce more), which began to create pressure on land of plausible quality and security of rainfall (most severely where colonists or plantations had reduced the supply available). This trend was probably not very significant in most areas at the time but laid the foundations for much more generalised and severe problems over the last twenty years.

1960–79: DEVELOPMENT BY MODERNISATION

Development – or at least growth and expansion of both production and basic services – speeded up in the region as a whole and in most sub-Saharan economies over the two decades after independence. The dominant basic pattern was arguably a more intensive colonial *mise en valeur* emphasis on modernisation and expansion of selected output subsectors and related infrastructure, paralleled by more intensive and extensive human resource investment oriented education, and rather more attention to health and water supply. However, at least one sectoral addition – import substitution industry, one subsectoral shift – towards high capital intensity irrigated and mechanised agriculture, and one perspective shift – to see an African state as a self-contained unit for policy purposes (not an appendage of a broader unit centred abroad) were increasingly evident over time.

Output per capita and service provision coverage did rise (see World Bank, 1981). The advance was uneven – the least favoured countries in natural resource or location terms and those with chronic policy failures did not share significantly in it – slow and unstable, but real. Ironically, on average the best four years were 1976–9, the recovery following the 1973–5 shocks and preceding the 1980–5 débâcle (see sources in note 2).

Poverty, defined as low-income household inability to meet basic consumption needs, was neither rapidly nor consistently reduced. The basic cause was a failure of wages and reasonably productive self-employment to rise much – if at all – more rapidly than population plus a failure of productivity increases to become accessible to the poorest quarter to half of peasant households. Basic service accessibility did rise, albeit often so slowly that absolute numbers without access rose even though a growing share of the people was served.

While mass starvation was – with very rare exceptions – averted, it is doubtful that seasonal, cyclical and endemic hunger were reduced markedly. From about 1965 on food, and from 1970 overall, agricultural production growth lagged behind that of population – a source of subsequent immiseration on three counts: increasing inability to meet domestic food requirements from domestic production; falling per household cash income from sale of food or other crops; and falling export earnings and therefore ability to sustain overall capacity utilisation and maintenance or growth in the early and middle 1970s and more especially since 1979.

The reasons for agricultural malaise are complex, are not clearly understood (especially in terms of weight and interaction) and until the 1980s had very distinct divergences from country to country. In respect to poor farmers three stand out: concentration of resources in ways which left the small, isolated farmer with a low initial income unable to raise output; increasing population/land ratios; and static proven knowledge (and access to inputs), leading to smaller holdings, more intensive land use unsustainable under existing systems, pushing on to poorer and or higher weather-risk land. As these households usually produce primarily domestic food crops (with sales for cash a deduction from what are often at least marginally inadequate self-provisioning), and effective domestic food prices after 1960 did not in general show a cyclical fall relative to wages, there is some doubt how significant peasant/worker terms of trade shifts and state price policy (rarely effective for domestic food crops) were directly, except for the minority who produced export crops which clearly did suffer from world domestic terms of trade shifts and increases in (public and also private) marketing costs relative to export prices.

While still constituting a small proportion of total absolutely poor households, urban poverty (in low productivity, informal sector, self-or wage-employment) began to grow very rapidly. Whether the urban absolutely poor households were much less poor than the poorest half of peasant households in physical consuming power terms[7] is unclear and probably varied sharply among countries. What they did have was somewhat better access to basic services and a far higher chance – at least for some – to win their way out of absolute poverty than that of most of the poorer half of peasant households.

In the 1970s, concern about low growth of employment and of rural household incomes led to a substantial employment, technology, urban renewal and rural development studies industry and some pilot projects,[8] most to fall victim of post 1979 increases in resource stringency. Likewise concern over low food production growth led to increased real resource (including infrastructural investment and marketing working capital), institutional and policy attention to this subsector, often with renewed concentration of attention away from poor households and in most cases with no very evident net positive impact on production.[9] Finally the late 1960s/early 1970s falling off of growth and the negative 1974–5 growth during the first external shock crises led (during the 1976–9 high growth period) to a set of studies which formed the basis of the new conventional wisdom on stabilisation and structural adjustment, appearing as they did after the 1960–79 development dynamic had gone into reverse in almost all of sub-Saharan Africa.

1979–??: THE RESURGENCE OF POVERTY

Since 1979 the general performance of the region's economies has been disastrous. The combination of negative per capita physical output growth, falling external terms of trade and declining net external resource inflows (absolutely as well as per capita) have reduced real per capita command over resources to below 1970 levels for sub-Saharan Africa as a whole.[10] The World Bank's optimistic projections suggest no regional real output per capita recovery over 1985–95 and possibly some further deterioration on net per capita inflows and terms of trade (World Bank, 1984).

On what has caused this massive shift of direction there is substantial agreement that external shocks (including weather), narrow margins for riding them out and the cumulative impact of over a decade and a half of agricultural non-success were major factors. There is also agreement that government policies were not optimal (not that they had been over 1960–79 either) and were adjusted to contextual disasters too slowly, and that for some polities civil war/state disintegration and/or external aggression, which, for instance, cost the nine SADCC states about $10 000 million over 1980–4 or well over total external resource inflows for the period (SADCC, 1985), were also decisive causes. The specific weights of particular causes (and especially their interaction and their applicability to specific countries) are not agreed (see Allison and Green, 1985 and sources at note 2) nor are the directions in which policies erred (as opposed to fairly pervasive overambition in scope and underperformance in practice).

In 1984, UNICEF's *Impact of World Recession on Children* was able to produce a broad array of suggestive and scattered empirical data but no statistics comparable to those in the World Bank's annual *World Development Reports*. This was especially true for sub-Saharan Africa (see Singer and Green, 1984). The annual *Statistics on Children in UNICEF Assisted Countries* (UNICEF, 1985) illustrates the fragmentary nature of relevant data (and the three-year time lag for attaining even moderately incomplete global coverage).

Yet a number of topographical elements of the development of poverty can be drawn. Food production per capita is still declining secularly – and in the early 1980s was severely cyclically affected by a drought belt extending from the Cape Verdes through the Sahel to the Sudan and down through the Horn and East Africa to the Cape and back to the Atlantic coasts of Namibia and Angola. The officially estimated ratio of average calorie availability relative to basic requirements fell to 80 per cent in many cases and under 70 per cent in some – a chilling figure when one realises that it means that at least half the human beings in these countries have still less food than that.[11] What micro data exist suggest that the farmers hardest hit fall into several subgroups:

(a) victims of sustained drought and/or ecological degradation whose previous sources of income (including herds, seed stock, land improvements) have been wiped out;
(b) the – usually poor, often female headed – households pushed by land hunger on to more marginal (in terms of soil, weather, ecological fragility) land – i.e. the pioneers of the 'rural sponge' effect which has to date limited the rise of open unemployment;
(c) households in isolated or peripheral (to main urban centres) areas who tend to be physically and institutionally (including for private enterprise) at the end of the line for all goods and services and to suffer first and most severely from decreased flow levels;
(d) small producers – usually primarily engaged in self-provisioning but also selling food, even if in nutritional terms they have a deficit,[12] because it is their basic source of cash income – who are unable to increase or even sustain output in the face of static applicable knowledge and declining access to inputs.

Effective food prices have risen relative to wages and usually to prices but for the groups cited this does little or no good because of stagnant or falling output. Non-food crop prices have tended to fall in real terms – often dramatically – partly relating to terms of trade internationally, partly to currency overvaluation and partly to rising marketing costs. This has probably affected poor peasants less severely for two reasons: many non-food crop producers are not among the poorest peasant households; and switches from non-food to food crops by poor peasant households have been particularly marked (at least in some areas). However, there are poor peasant households presently or formerly primarily dependent on non-food crops for cash income who have been severely affected including (e.g. in northern and upper Ghana) by having to sell more of their already inadequate food production.

Formal recorded wage employment in the region as a whole has been nearly static since 1979. Meanwhile, real wages have fallen sharply – often to the point at which second and third incomes are essential to household survival. As open unemployment is not common – only those who are not absolutely poor or can depend on relatives can afford to be unemployed – this implies a rapid growth in informal sector self and non-recorded wage employment. Here too there was clearly a 'sponge effect' in the 1970s, but one which appears to be running into productivity and market limits in the 1980s, at least for most young, uneducated and female informal sector members.

Public service provision has fallen. The basic reasons are budgetary stringency (with falls in real expenditure levels on health, education and water common and draconic ones not uncommon) and foreign exchange shortages (leading to missing drugs, pump spares, textbooks, transport, etc). In some cases quantity of services has fallen markedly – for example, rural health in Zambia and Ghana. In more, quality has declined, for instance, generalised shortages of school and medical service materials and maintenance. Supply and/or usability of nominally available services is severely constrained (e.g. on average 25 per cent of rural water supply units in Tanzania are out of service at any one time because of missing spares or fuel).

The decline in services has pressed particularly hard on end of the line areas – isolated rural districts and urban slums – and on those with rapidly growing populations, again especially urban slums but also some resettlement schemes. Or, more accurately, it has pressed particularly heavily on the poor people living in them. The rise of private primary schools and clinics in poor urban areas does indeed indicate that poor Africans value these services, but also that the state supplied ones are less and less available and/or more and more unsatisfactory.

Raising or reintroducing fees for basic services has had a negative effect on access of the poor to health and education, but how much is unclear. This is true because there is no uniform pattern of fee levels (in some cases they are probably progressive relative to income but not in others), waiver possibilities and collection levels and because their supposed use to restore or sustain service levels is not to date very evident.

The most recent life expectancy and mortality data suggest that the health service cuts may – in several cases – have halted or reversed the slow improvement of life expectancy and decline of infant mortality trends which characterised sub-Saharan Africa over 1960–79. More dramatically diseases nearly eradicated in the late 1950s and 1960s (e.g. yaws and yellow fever in Ghana) have erupted at epidemic levels and remained endemic because funds and transport limited counter–campaign duration and coverage. Moderate and severe child malnutrition has reached levels of 30 per cent or above in most countries for which data exist, and is approaching 50 per cent in some even excluding famine crisis years (UNICEF, 1985 and selected UNICEF country situation reports).

Meanwhile, traditional security systems have been eroded –
probably a trend well established in the 1960–79 period but much more
nakedly evident since. Kinship and locality or origin groups are less
able to support poor members/relatives – especially in urban and
natural (or other) disaster-stricken rural areas. This is not simply a
result of shifts towards less extended families and urban residence,
relevant as these are. With economic contraction fewer and fewer
group members have resources (especially of cash or food) to spare –
all boats are sinking lower. Similarly higher cost, less available
transport reduces urban/rural kin and migrant contacts. Reciprocal
exchange – food for manufactures – has probably risen, but this is not
an avenue accessible to the very poor. To exchange one must have
something above day to day subsistence (including the cost of a trip) to
start.

The pattern and balance of absolute poverty have continued to shift.
The worst declines – excluding drought/war related famines – appear
to have been among urban poor (including for the first time a high
proportion of recorded wage employees). In consuming power terms
they are now clearly worse off than the majority of peasants and their
former advantages in respect to access to basic services and to chances
of advancing to higher real incomes are increasingly exiguous. Rural
absolute poverty has grown unevenly with the general rule of thumb
being that households in peripheral areas – geographically, politically,
in absolute agricultural potential or in perceived[13] commercialised
production – have fared worse on production and service access quite
apart from being particularly prone to drought and civil government
collapse/war debacles.

It is still true that the majority of sub-Saharan Africa's poorest of the
poor are in refugee camps and peripheral rural areas, but there is now
a rapidly growing urban household category which is almost equally
immiserised. In most of the region's economies the net resource flow –
at existing prices – is urban to rural, as much in states with an urban as
in the minority with a rural policy bias. Oddly the clearest exceptions
are two stabilisation/structural adjustment cases, Ghana and
Uganda, which are almost alone in having very high export crop
taxes. In respect of non-food crops it can be claimed that price
distortions hide a true rural to urban flow, but with both the trend and

the post 1979 realignment of food crop prices in favour of producers over wage earners it is hard to argue the same for that subsector. This does not, however, mean equal access to basic services for rural areas because state revenues from rural households and producers are much lower than from mineral and urban, so that expenditure proportional to revenue results in substantially higher per capita spending and service provision in urban areas (and for both rural and urban élites).

Table 5.1 sets out the present levels of several human condition or quality of life indicators for low-income sub-Saharan Africa as of 1982 and their evolution in Ghana over 1960–84. The absolute levels are appalling enough but their Ghanaian evolution is even more dispiriting. Moderately rapid real gains in the 1960s slowed down in the 1970s and have now gone into reverse. Two immediate basic causal inadequacies stand out – food production and the budgetary base for health and education. While Ghana's period of economic unsuccess dates to the early 1960s, not 1979, the record of change on the human condition front does not appear atypical. What was hard won over two decades has been undermined, eroded and threatened with being totally swept away in seven years. The stifling scent of despair is there – not universally, not unconditionally but widely and increasingly.

TOWARDS BROADENING THE FORMULATION OF STRUCTURAL ADJUSTMENT?

Structural adjustment – resting on its present tripod of production, state borrowing reduction and selective liberalisation (or redirection of intervention) could have positive implications for poor sub-Saharan Africans. The first (production) leg is a necessary condition for such gains. However, it would appear equally true that most present programmes have unnecessary built in biases against the poor. Since these costs come early in the adjustment process and the gains from enhanced production later, the temporal pattern is to require the poor to accept high, certain initial costs for lagged, uncertain gains – a pattern more than somewhat inconsistent with their margins above survival or their life expectancy.[14]

Table 5.1 Selected quality of life indicators: 1960–mid-1980s

	Ghana				Low-income sub-Saharan Africa (1982)
	1960	1970	Late 1970s	1980s	
1. Average life expectancy at birth	45	49	55	53	48
2. Infant mortality rate	132	107	86	107–20	118
3. Child death rate	27	21	15	25–30	24
4. Access to health facility (b)				30	45
5. Public health facility visits per person per year			0.7	0.4	2(f)
6. Health budget as % of GDP		1.2		0.26	0.95
7. Access to pure water (c)					
Rural	14	14	14	48	14
Urban	86	86	86	75	62
Total	35	35	35	60	22
8. Access to excreta disposal (d)					
Rural	40	40	40	30	25
Urban	92	92	95	65	69
Total	55	55	56	44	32
9. Average calorie availability as a % of requirements	92	97	88	68	91

10. Child malnutrition (Moderate/Severe)		36		50–55	40
11. Primary education enrolment ratio (e)	38(46)	64(75)	69(80)	–(80)	69(–)
12. Adult literacy	27	30		35–45	44
13. Education budget as % of GDP		3.9		0.85	2.81
14. Proportion of population below absolute poverty line (f)					
Rural		60–65		67-1/2 – 72-1/2	65
Urban		30–5		45–50	35

Sources: World Bank, Comparative Analysis and Data Division, Economic Analysis and Projections Department (June 1984), *World Development Report 1985*; UNICEF, *Statistics on Children* in *UNICEF Assisted Countries* (April 1985); UNICEF, *Ghana: Situation Analysis of Women and Children* (July 1984).

Notes

(a) 1960 data refer to a year between 1959 and 1961; 1970 between 1969 and 1971; later 1970s between 1975 and 1980; 1980s to 1982, 1984 or 1985.

(b) Defined in terms of location within a 5 kilometre radius. May overstate for urban population when facilities available are small to serve the entire population nominally within reach of them.

(c) 1970 and late 1970s urban figures may be overstated by failing to relate number of water points to population.

(d) 1970 and 1978 figures for urban and possibly rural areas overstate by failing to relate number of drop-holes to supposed user population.

(e) Adjusted for length of primary cycle. ( ) are unadjusted figures. Because of the primary/middle school division Ghana has a shorter primary cycle than most sub-Saharan African countries.

(f) Estimate made by author on basis of fragmentary data.

There is another – complementary – way of approaching the
interaction between stabilisation linked to structural adjustment and
poverty. This is to query whether or not success in present structural
adjustment programmes on their own terms is likely to be a sufficient
condition for reversing the deterioration of human condition indicators – and, much more important, the human conditions ·– in
sub-Saharan Africa.

On the face of it the answer is negative unless – as is most unusual –
the structural adjustment programme both posits and achieves a
sustained output growth rate of over 6 per cent and a full recovery of
real government basic service spending (or a targeted, articulated shift
towards lower unit cost basic health, education and water and away
from higher cost, limited access services), an approach endorsed by
the World Bank (1984) but not yet actually built substantially into any
existing programme.[15]

The reasoning behind this conclusion is relatively straightforward:

(a) growth rates of 4 to 5 per cent before 1979 yielded limited
    reductions in absolute poverty and slow advances in access to basic
    services;
(b) structural adjustment requires raising savings and reducing
    external deficits implying a lower growth of domestic resource use
    and especially of consumption than of GDP;
(c) most actual structural adjustment programmes – even if not the
    logic of structural adjustment – are biased against basic services
    and production by poor people.

This case is accentuated by the fact that almost all programmes have
received less external finance than external analysts – notably the
World Bank – have thought prudent, and have also been buffeted by
unanticipated external terms of trade and weather shocks.

What is usually – and quite reasonably – viewed as the model
African structural adjustment programme, that of Ghana – adopted by
the Ghanaian government in early 1983 and articulated with substantial Bank and Fund input over the subsequent year – appears to
illustrate the point:

(a) output growth has been positive in 1983, 1984 and 1985 – the first three-year run of GDP growth in over twenty years with 1984 and 1985 growth probably in the 5 to 6.5 per cent range;

(b) very substantial liberalisation has taken place (notably in respect of exchange rates and prices);

(c) the government borrowing requirement has been reduced to one-third the average for sub-Saharan Africa relative to GDP (albeit by reducing real government spending and the ratio of revenue to GDP so that both were in 1984–5 among the lowest in the world);

(d) holding the external financing position in rough balance (and reducing arrears) despite lower than targeted foreign resource inflows and lagged export recovery partly due to weather;

(e) reducing inflation from the order of 120 per cent in 1983 to perhaps 13 per cent in 1985 (admittedly partly because good 1984 and 1985 national harvests followed 1983's very severely drought curtailed crops) and thus achieving positive real interest rates.

It is difficult to envisage a much more successful structural adjustment programme than Ghana's in terms of its own macro production and balance objectives. But the poverty trend appears to remain in the wrong direction. Real cuts in health and education have virtually halved per capita public health service provision since 1981. Minimum wage levels can purchase perhaps a seventh of a plausible household consumption basket and – after late 1985 increases – remain below 1982 real levels. Real food (but to date not real non-food) grower prices are above 1982 levels, but in the poorest regions even 1985 output remains below 1982's already depressed levels, casting grave doubts on whether most small peasant producers have benefited. The situation of the – growing – proportion of urban households in absolute poverty is better than at the peak of the drought/food crisis of 1983–4, but only because of food output recovery and food price falls which are as exogenous to the structural adjustment programme as the 1983–4 food prices and availability deterioration. Inputs and supporting services (e.g. research, extension) relevant to poor farmers' ability to increase production are not being given priority – indeed no coherent framework exists for enabling such peasants to produce more. Reversal of the fall in real health and educational service provision – and some reversal of draconic declines in public service real wages to halt the loss of key personnel and the moonlighting/unofficial use of public resources and positions pattern of civil servant survival – has now become a goal, but the initial revenue increasing proposals seem to centre on user fees which are – on the face of it – likely to limit access and unlikely to be as revenue/collection cost efficient as more general tax measures.

In short, the Ghana structural adjustment programme is a notable success in its own terms. If sustained, its reversal of the declining per capita output trend is both a major achievement and a precondition for sustainable poverty reduction/basic service provision. But partly because of the formulation of some elements in the programme and even more because of what it does not include, its effect on basic service provision has to date been negative and on absolute poverty uneven but probably negative both for peasant households, the poorest rural areas and for urban slum households. This is clearly an unsatisfactory result in human terms but also in respect to human productive capacity and socio-political sustainability of the programme's successful output recovery side. The question is what can be done – in Ghana and more generally in sub-Saharan Africa – to face poverty issues more directly and with the probability of positive short- to medium-term results within existing and probable future real resource constraints?

It should be made clear that by 1983 Ghana clearly did need to undertake drastic stabilisation and structural adjustment measures. A buildup of imbalances over 1961–5 had – despite, or because of, frequent changes of regime and of verbal policy – never been tackled seriously either in terms of stabilisation or of structural adjustment. The underlying strength, viability and growth potential of the economy had been declining for over two decades with severe social and political repercussions. Apparent partial recoveries owed more to brief cocoa booms than to underlying performance, let alone purposive policy measures. The 1983 change of course (or seeking to set one as opposed to drifting) was both necessary and courageous and did seek to tackle certain key weaknesses. What is at issue is not that but whether a more inclusive articulation of stabilisation and adjustment, with greater attention to income generation by poor people and to maintaining basic health services and nutritional levels, would have been practicable and desirable on medium-term production and productivity as well as human concern grounds.

This question is not unique to the present author. It is increasingly asked by Ghanaians and within the World Bank, not with a view to abandoning structural adjustment but to redefining it to be more inclusive and more effective. From that perspective it is not useful to argue whether human condition indicator decline over 1983–5 was caused by the structural adjustment programme as executed or not. Evidently the decline began before 1983 and would not have been halted by continuation of the 1966–81 policy of resolute irresolution. Equally evidently the budgetary measures adopted have severely damaged the health service. The basic propositions are that the present trends are humanly, politically and economically unacceptable and that halting and reversing them should be specific priorities within the structural adjustment programme.

WITHIN AFRICAN REACH?

The need for emergency action is agreed in principle and in practice as – at a more speculative and non-time-targeted level – is that for basic service restoration, making possible increased production by poor peasants and, perhaps, enhancing opportunities for informal sector employment and productivity advances. However, the longer term goals are often seen as after the crisis and after structural adjustment; the emergency actions tend to be episodic and case by case; the two phases are not articulated and programmed as a sequential whole and both sets of exercises are treated as parallel to (at worst as Christmas tree ornaments on) production and balance focused macro and sectoral structural adjustment. That is simply not good enough, intellectually or operationally.

Emergency action is essential because people are dying but also because ecological, production and basic service delivery system damage once sustained is very hard to reverse and, until reversed, will continue to cost lives. The most obvious emergency support measures are food aid and interim basic medical care against killing diseases and health conditions. The first is illustrated (as are its limitations) by the responses to the stark visions of starvation in Africa screened in 1984–5. The second is best exemplified by UNICEF's evolving 'Child

Survival Revolution' programme including immunisation, anti-diarrhoeal salts (oral rehydration), nutritional monitoring, and education evolving in certain cases into more integrated but still focused primary health care (isolated rural and/or urban slum posts and clinics) support.

These programmes are essential. UNICEF's African poster with the question and answer bracketing the face of a young girl – 'What do you want to be when you grow up?' 'Alive' – sets the initial challenge starkly but realistically.

However, emergency action in sub-Saharan Africa will both need to be continued (not necessarily in the same areas) for a decade or more and to be seen as an initial phase of a broader struggle to reduce vulnerability and poverty by creating survival security structures based in Africa, and involving poor Africans as producers and subjects not receivers and objects. This perspective has several implications for emergency programmes:

(a) the question – after survival, what next? – should be posed from the start because of its implications for emergency programming. For example food aid, so delivered as to allow peasants to remain in their homes, maintain their social units and prepare for the return of the rains, is much more conducive to making survival the first step to self-rehabilitation than food aid in mass camps of dislocated, totally dependent refugees;

(b) similarly the same question implies that – for example – rural emergency food provision needs to be linked with the inputs (seed, tools, transport home, etc.) needed for an economically wiped out household to begin to produce again;

(c) in parallel, attempts to meet emergency health needs should go beyond specific injections – e.g. immunisation/vaccination campaigns and oral rehydration – to selective support for keeping a basic health service functioning, as illustrated by the UNICEF/Danida basic rural drug provision programme in Tanzania and the UNICEF inputs into selected primary health care posts in Ghana;

(d) and utilise emergency inputs – where possible without delay or sclerotic bureaucratisation – to increase productive and basic service capacity and provide a capacity for self-respect and dignity to participants (no longer pure recipients or 'targets'), e.g. Zimbabwe's rural public works scheme including agricultural infrastructure focused food for work projects;

(e) while involving recipients as participants in programme operation and – to the extent practicable – coverage and design.

None of these steps is impossible. Emergency efforts have been needed frequently and repeatedly in sub-Saharan Africa for over a decade. They will continue to be needed. The points outlined above are fairly commonly relevant to articulating programmes. African governments, international agencies, bilateral aid bodies and voluntary organisations can and should plan ahead, both as to basic capacity to finance or collect more resources and as to basic programme designs and checklists. Combined with better early warning systems on food supply and health situation deterioration – and less unwillingness to believe and act on the data until people are visibly dying or on the verge of dying from starvation or epidemics – such an approach could both increase the human survival results of emergency programmes and make them infinitely more effective as first steps towards rehabilitation/self-rehabilitation of recipients/participants who are, virtually by definition, highly vulnerable and absolutely poor.

Such an approach to emergency (human survival) programming has definite implications for longer term strategies and possibilities for reducing absolute poverty and absolute lack of access to basic services. First, if emergency assistance is to encompass initial rehabilitation it both should and can be seen within the context of longer term employment – food production – basic service – poverty reduction strategies both as an initial stage and also as a supporting measure to prevent their crippling or destruction when these strategies already existed before the emergency. Second, such a perspective suggests that the relatively watertight compartmentalisation of emergency assistance from development assistance is counter-productive for both and requires critical reassessment and 'structural adjustment'. Third, viewed in this way even emergency, human survival programmes are (or can be) relevant to sustaining and restoring human resources and production, and therefore integral to, not an unwelcome diversion from, structural adjustment (Reutlinger, 1985).

The articulation of longer term strategies and their components is beyond the scope of this essay. However, some areas for attention can be flagposted.

First, the production/productivity focus of the present World Bank structural adjustment approach is crucial. Production is important and stripping programmes of biases against production by poor people neither should nor need mean blurring that goal.

Second, the achievement of less severe external imbalance by a combination of higher exports, genuine import substitution and more concessional resource transfers is also necessary. Structural adjustment and growth of output are, at least in sub-Saharan Africa, totally inconsistent with neo-autarchy. Import strangulation is a fact weighing heavily on poor people in at least half of the region. The true dialogue is on the nature of relationships to the world economy, balance of instruments, phasing and practicable timing.

Third, unless government fiscal and monetary imbalances – and continuous resultant pressures for cuts – can be reduced, the chances of providing basic production support (extension, research, infrastructure, credit) and basic services to small peasant and/or non-agricultural informal subsectors are negligible. Prudent fiscal and monetary management is as integral to 'economic adjustment with a human face' (UNICEF, 1985:64ff) as to any other variant.

Fourth, because government resources (financial, human, physical, foreign exchange) are limited, priorities – i.e. choices as to what not to do as well as what is to be done – are necessary. For example, if primary health care is to be expanded to universal access in sub-Saharan Africa, then its share of health resources relative to limited access, high unit cost curative treatment must be expanded which may require absolute cuts in the latter. Similarly if production enhancement by low-income peasant farmers is a priority then the research, extension, input supply and other requirements to make such an increase possible must be made available, even though this means reducing allocations to large-scale, mechanised, import intensive farming (an alteration of balance likely to have positive production and external balance as well as poverty reduction results).

Up to this point what is proposed is not simply consistent with, but based on the same priority themes as, conventional structural adjustment strategy and programming. However, as argued above, this is not enough if human beings – and especially poor human beings – are seen as the subjects and the justification of development.

Fifth, increased food availability to poor people is a central goal (World Bank, 1986). Given the external balance position, this means either enhanced production or balanced regional trade expansion in all but a handful of cases. But food availability to the majority of ill-nourished Africans who are members of poor peasant households, requires that they be enabled to produce more (Burki, 1985; World Bank, 1986). This is economically feasible – indeed much more cost efficient than most large-scale agricultural programmes – and in the present food crises context probably politically and intellectually feasible as well. The problem is partly technical – articulating contextually relevant programmes based on collecting reasonably accurate data and testing/adapting new techniques for application. It is also partly institutional and partly resource management – actually giving priority to hoes and field testing, effective extension and availability of seasonal inputs on time.[16] None of these technical and institutional problems is inherently any harder to solve than those of other agricultural production promotion strategies. Similar considerations apply to enhancing poor peasant cash income which in most cases will come primarily from achieving a genuine food surplus above household self-provisioning requirements. This is not to argue against increasing non-food crop production for industrial inputs (e.g. cotton) and for export. Sub-Saharan Africa's problem is one of low agricultural growth not substitution of non-food for food crops. With rational agricultural prices peasants can judge what balance of crops to produce for self-provisioning and for sale and whether to seek saleable surpluses of food or grow non-food crops in addition to self-provisioning food production. For example, in some drought prone areas small peasant farmers are well advised to grow both cotton and food crops, with the former an anti-famine safeguard because low rainfall affects cotton far less (indeed in some areas an optimal cotton weather year results in partial food crop failure and vice versa).

Sixth, effective food availability for poor urban (or other non-agricultural) households turns on price/income relationships. Attempts to hold food prices down by squeezing growers are counter-productive (especially if growers are actually squeezed, less so if they simply use parallel markets) because they reduce supply and either result in higher effective prices to low-income consumers or in unmanageable import and subsidy bills. Higher rural productivity and larger supplies are much more likely to reduce real urban food prices. Therefore, the concentration must be on raising incomes through more, and more productive[17] employment/self-employment. How to do so is the basic question and one needing data (on what is produced how and on what the actual income sources of low-income sub-Saharan African households are, as well as on technical and institutional production/employment/productivity possibilities), plus a coherent approach (not treating 'appropriate technology' or 'the informal sector' as isolated, homogenous artifacts which they are not) linked to a systematic attempt to treat employment/distribution and production/productivity issues as joint goals and programming exercises, not separate or alternative ones.

The World Employment Programme and subsequent African basic needs mission studies do provide a foundation for devising contextual approaches on these lines. The main obstacles – once better data bases are built – would appear to be political (the urban poor in sub-Saharan Africa are neither represented in enough governing sub-class coalitions nor enough of a threat to their survival to receive priority attention in many countries) and intellectual (the depth and extent of urban poverty is still not fully comprehended, the limits of modernisation approaches are only beginning to be perceived, the somewhat faddy, sloppy and romantic approaches of some 'intermediate technology' and 'informal sector' true believers have created a climate of scepticism). The key crisis forcing rethinking is the growing realisation that with 3 per cent to 4 per cent annual economically active population growth to the end of the century, employment growth outside peasant agriculture and the large-scale, capital intensive enterprise sector is essential. Enhanced productivity and greater production, on the one hand, give the possibility of having effective urban consumer access to food and basic consumer goods and, on the other, rural producer access to basic consumer goods and agricultural inputs. Both non-agricultural workers and peasants need to become less poor and to have incentives for raising productivity (and working longer) to raise marketed output of goods and services.

Seventh, universal access to basic services (health, education, water and production support such as research and extension related to the two preceding priorities) within a finite time period (even if that must be up to twenty or twenty-five years) needs to be seen as an anti-poverty, food production, productive employment and human condition priority. Poor people, especially women and indigenous minorities, do benefit disproportionately from broadening access because when access is constricted they are the ones excluded. Literacy, nutrition, health and reduction of time spent collecting water are critical to enhancing the ability to work harder and more productively now and over time.[18] To articulate such priorities into costed, sustainable programmatic form is not impossible if: (a) non-essentials are cut out (e.g. via basic drug lists); (b) there is a real priority in personnel and policy allocation given to doing so. The obstacles are – especially for health and water – intellectual and political. Low-cost/universal access services are only now building up a cadre of professionals, a body of literature and a degree of respectability even remotely resembling that behind 'state of the art' approaches whose costs are such as to render them largely non-functional or practical only on a limited access basis in sub-Saharan Africa. Piped water to houses and high quality curative medicine do appeal directly to political decision-takers and civil servants (who use and – reasonably enough – want to have them). The balance in the intellectual dialogue is shifting towards low-cost/universal access; the political self-interest obstacle is very real and often very intractable in most of sub-Saharan Africa.

Eighth, basic survival and support mechanisms are needed because emergencies will continue to arise. People matter and the view of Nassau Senior that the Irish famine would not kill enough people to achieve adequate structural adjustment of population to land is not an acceptable political economic position today. Again there is a perfectly respectable production case – the reduction of dislocation caused by unforeseen and unprepared for emergencies could have a high pay-off in reducing their immediate and subsequent negative impact on growth. The problem is in devising approaches which do meet survival and preservation of self-rehabilitation potential needs, while being financially and institutionally feasible in specific sub-Saharan African contexts.[19] A crucial set relate to food (see Reutlinger, 1985; World Bank, 1986). Pre-planned food for work programmes (urban as well as rural) operating at some level continuously but capable of being stepped up nationally or locally when required are an example. So, where technically and financially feasible, are food reserves linked to minimum buying price safety nets for peasant producers in bumper crop years. Such an approach would also avert the danger of food aid so depressing domestic crop prices in good years as to reverse the production revival – a danger which is exacerbated by the long lag between need and supply of food aid usually resulting in large deliveries in the six months after domestic supplies have become adequate.[20] A related approach applies to submarginal argicultural–pastoral area residents. Here production returns to combined input and emergency relief (including food for work) programmes may well be low and the potential for sustained productivity increases problematic. However, in practice there is often nowhere else the human beings in these areas can go. If any value is placed on their survival and welfare, cost efficient programmes to ensure it are needed. Economic growth alone cannot proceed fast enough to end chronic food insecurity for these people. Both because their lives do matter and because chronic food insecurity reduces their productivity yet further, specific interventions in their favour – including improving their production capacity, providing additional income generating possibilities (e.g. seasonal works programmes) and emergency food and production input distribution – are needed (Reutlinger, 1985).

Ninth, environmental and ecological protection should be rescued from its European/North American upper middle class origins and related to the struggle against poverty and for sustainable production. Need can be as damaging environmentally as greed but cannot be dealt with by the same instruments. For example, deforestation (more accurately denudation by stripping all tree and bush cover) is disastrous in its impact on productivity and in its contribution to desertification (loosely defined), erosion and dust bowls. It also increases the burdens on women and girls (and reduces their ability to grow crops, attend school, secure medical attention, improve environmental sanitation). If it is caused by land-mining farmers – e.g. western Sudanese mechanised sorghum farming – or forest ravaging loggers, then financial and criminal sanctions are relevant. But if – as in a majority of the most critical sub-Saharan African cases – it is caused by an increasing population practising shorter rotations and needing to collect (for household provisioning or sale to urban areas) fuel and building materials, such measures are both normatively inappropriate and certain to fail. Imprisoning or hanging every bush cutter from Timbuktu to Gao or Mwanza to Shinyanga is hardly a plausible answer to neo-desertification in Mali or dust bowl development in Tanzania. Tree planting (encouraged by extension services but basically carried out by rural residents and/or urban fuel oriented producer co-operatives) and alternative fuel development would appear to be the only practicable basic answers[21] even if both require time and patience to build up an adequate, self-sustaining basis.

Tenth, budgetary balance should be restored primarily by increasing revenue, not cutting services. In sub-Saharan Africa, revenue to GDP ratios vary but some are almost incredibly low even for very low-income countries. Universal access basic services cannot be provided primarily on a profit-making basis both because large portions of them can operate only at a 'loss' and because external economies are large. Within revenue augmentation, attention should be focused on selective (progressive to well above the poverty line) indirect taxes and on progressive direct taxes which are in practice at least midly redistributive on both the revenue and – more particularly – the expenditure side. Fees on limited access, high cost services (e.g.

household water connections, above average use household electricity and water bills, above average health facility space and diet provision, specialist medical treatment) are at least as justifiable on this basis as luxury consumer goods taxes and are often fairly easy and low cost to collect. Charges for basic services are more problematic. Unless a quick, effective waiver system at contact point can be devised and operated, poor people, and especially their children, will be excluded. If fees can be seen to relate to services (e.g. a biannual borehole overhaul fee raised communally and paid when – and if – the overhaul takes place; local contribution of agricultural work or food to allow a primary health care worker to do health work without destroying the family nutritional base), they can help mobilise resources, increase community support and reduce net central government cost. Otherwise, they will be very unpopular in a context of fragile and often interrupted services. Large numbers of small charges have high collection costs – not least in skilled personnel time if, for example, nurses are expected to collect hundreds of small oral rehydration salts or vaccination fees as part of their daily work.[22]

Eleventh, without participation by poor people no anti-poverty programme will be fully successful even in material terms. The case for participation in production and resource mobilisation (e.g. self-help inputs of labour, materials, even cash into basic service and infrastructure provision) is presumably self-evident. What is less accepted is that poor people need to participate in programme design, ongoing management and monitoring/evaluation. The reasons are not romantic – poor people do have knowledge about their own needs and capabilities which experts do not; participation in production and 'take-up' of services is related to whether they do correspond and are responsive to users' needs and preferences; participation can create incentives for officials to be more responsive to poor people (a not inconsiderable factor in programme success, however good or weak the initial design); self-help resource mobilisation is practicable only if those who are to mobilise the resources believe their use is appropriate, for their benefit and at least partially under their control. The political and institutional obstacles to participation (and the real, if partial and limited, successes in overcoming them) do not need rehearsing and are not limited to sub-Saharan Africa. They need to be seen as conflicts to be contained, circumvented or overcome not as given and immutable barriers to action.

Participation – and accountability – pose special problems for external bodies including multilateral, bilateral and voluntary aid or development agencies. This is true even when they are intellectually committed to participation and to accountability to intended beneficiaries. First, almost by definition their personnel are 'outsiders' usually with fairly brief country experience and broad perception gaps or distance from host government officials and intellectuals, let alone African peasants, urban slum dwellers, women and children. Second, their structures of accountability run (usually hierarchically) through their own institution to its policy-makers and those to whom it is accountable, not to host governments and through them to ordinary Africans, much less directly to the latter. In a sense these tensions are not fully soluble (barring participatory, accountable, effective world government which, however desirable, cannot reasonably be posed as a side condition for the struggle against poverty in Africa). However, posing them and facing them squarely is potentially a necessary first step towards reducing tensions to manageable levels, improving host-agency relationships and to avoiding the escalation of tensions into antagonistic contradictions and the deterioration of dialogue into accusatory rhetoric.

Twelfth, while any strategy for overcoming poverty must be based on the actions of poor people and poor countries in sub-Saharan Africa, if it is to have a real chance of sustainable success, external support is critical. The resources available domestically are too limited and the exogenous shocks too great for any strategy depending wholly on domestic resources to be more than problematic in results, or more than excruciatingly slow in paying off (especially for its intended beneficiaries and participants). The need for real resource – including knowledge – transfers (from other developing countries as well as from industrial ones) is as great in respect to the broader as to the narrower aspects of structural adjustment.

A VALEDICTORY NOTE

The struggle against poverty – and especially against despairing acceptance that the fight is inevitably and irretrievably lost – in sub-Saharan Africa today is waged in an unpropitious context. But it is not an impossible context. Even more fundamental, poor Africans and those concerned with them have only that context and its present realities, limitations and potentials from which to begin. Past experience in the struggle against poverty does not suggest that the New Jerusalem can be achieved nor that partial successes once won will be easily or permanently sustainable. But nor does it suggest either that nothing can be done or that nothing can be done until production problems are largely overcome. Strategies of structural adjustment combining production and distribution, productivity and raising poor households' incomes, food balance and external balance, fiscal balance and progress towards universal access to basic services – and their partial and gradual articulation and implementation – are within human reach generally and within African reach specifically.

Notes

1. The attempt to separate technical and normative, production and distribution issues in applied economics is a fairly recent heresy or fad following about twenty centuries during which they were viewed as integrally interrelated.
2. See, for example, Rose (ed.) 1985; Green (ed.) 1985a; Ndegwa, Mureithi and Green (eds) 1985; World Bank 1984.
3. The most complete general example is usually seen as being World Bank, 1981, of which Allison and Green published a detailed review and critique in 1983.
4. Governors sometimes did, by the nature of their posts, take a more territorially self-contained view with some impact on territorial, but much less on overall, colonial policy.
5. A reading of a random selection of colonial bluebooks, reports, minutes and semi-analytical pieces – including Fabian ones on endeavours such as the post-1945 groundnut schemes – rapidly brings home the colonial economy in the service of the metropolitan economy focus, as opposed to African welfare or even overall territorial development, of colonial conceptualisation even when dealing with topics such as wages, employment or peasant production. Again some governors – for example, Sir Gordon Guggisberg in the Gold Coast and Lord Lugard in Nigeria – were partial exceptions even if rather technocratic and paternalistic in their approach to the welfare of Africans and conceptually shaky in their delineation of how to expand territorial production.
6. In German East Africa (Tanzania) examination of German tombstones suggests that diseases killed at least one German per mile of rail built, while West Africa's European health condition was as much described as caricatured by the tag 'The Bight of Benin where many go in; but few come out again'.
7. Unpublished Tanzania data suggest a 3 to 2 ratio of minimum wage-consuming power to that of the average peasant household;

scattered West African estimates include several of the same order in the mid-1970s. Much higher estimates usually compare peasant cash incomes with all urban income earners or value peasant self-provisioning in food as farmgate prices and worker food at urban retail prices, both of which distort real consuming power differentials.

8. Centred on the ILO's World Employment Programme and 'Basic Needs' conceptualisation (ILO, 1976) and the World Bank's 'Absolute Poverty' conceptualisation and projects towards its eradication.

9. In fact, in most countries of sub-Saharan Africa, a fairly steady post-1970 increase in policies aimed at enhancing growth of food production backed by generally increased resource allocations have paralleled a worsening achieved output growth trend, despite grower price/urban wage terms of trade shifts in favour of domestic food over most of the period. There are exceptions and it is probable that the causal relationship runs from the negative output trend to the policy/resource packages and not vice versa, but even on the most favourable reading policy was not in fact effective and resource allocations were not efficient in production pay-off terms.

10. See sources cited at note 2, especially Green (ed.) 1985a (contributions by S. Please and R. H. Green) and World Bank 1984.

11. The accuracy of these data is certainly open to question. Eighty per cent averages taken literally would imply starvation was rampant among at least the bottom fifth of the food distribution, and 68 per cent would suggest half the people were in the grip of a major famine. There is some reason to believe FAO (and national) estimates in some countries understate food availability, and that up to a point low height and weight represent adaptation to conditions of low food availability which do reduce minimum nutritional levels consistent with health. However, there is no reason to doubt the pattern of declining availability shown in many cases for over a decade and for almost all since the late 1970s. Equally, adaptation cannot explain the high and rising levels of clinical malnutrition in children which are based on less globalistic criteria, nor explain away the very real micro and qualitative evidence of chronic inability to work hard, to study effectively, to benefit from health care which are reported, even under non-famine conditions, in most sub-Saharan African countries.

12. Thus northern and upper Ghana are usually perceived as food deficit areas. In nutritional terms they most certainly are. But they are substantial net food (yams, groundnuts, cattle and to a lesser extent millet and guinea corn) exporters to the rest of Ghana and to Burkina Faso, except in the most severely drought affected years because most peasant households have no alternative way of meeting basic cash purchase requirements. (The regional rice surplus is less relevant to the argument as it comes from land extensive, capital intensive, large, mechanised farms not peasant growers).

13. Perceptions may be wrong – see, e.g., note 12 – but if acted on they do have objective results and are a real cause of decisions.

14. In more technical terms poor people can be expected to have high positive time and risk avoidance preferences. The implicit internal logic of structural adjustment programmes often calls for low preferences on both counts.

15. Arguably such shifts – especially within health – are incorporated in both Zimbabwean and Tanzanian structural adjustment policies. However, in neither case is the shift the result of clear macro articulation and since neither Zimbabwe nor Tanzania has secured World Bank structural adjustment loans (nor a sustained IMF high credit tranche stabilisation agreement), there is a tendency to view their policies as not constituting structural adjustment. Both have been atypical in perceiving structural adjustment as a precondition for full stabilisation, not vice versa, even though both accept that initial imbalance reduction is necessary for structural adjustment to be effective. In Zimbabwe, 1984–5 results suggest substantial success in stabilisation and some in structural adjustment, whereas in Tanzania substantial 1981–5 progress in structural adjustment has been rendered less than fully effective by distinctly limited success in attempts to reduce external and domestic resource imbalances.

16. For a programmatic sketch see Daniel, Lipton and Green, in Green (ed.) 1985a.

17. Higher productivity is basic – in the context of most informal sectors in sub-Saharan Africa – to higher real incomes. Reduction of exploitation may often also be necessary, but until they are able to raise their productivity most informal sector employees/self-employed cannot achieve minimum adequate household incomes, no matter how fairly they are paid for what they produce.

18. Interestingly, the World Bank's variant of the 'new conventional wisdom' has never fully lost sight of this point and has recently begun to reassert it. Some of the production oriented justifications of education and health are rather distressingly formulated – they would make equal sense if the 'objects' discussed were machines or cattle – but the underlying point that the productionist case reinforces the human concern one for basic services is an important and powerful one.

19. Contexts – not the sub-Saharan African context. For example, food stamps for poor households might be a fiscally and administratively feasible food security approach in Mauritius but pretty clearly not in – say – Mauretania. Similarly, large inter-year grain storage may make little sense in Botswana which is bordered by two large grain exporters and has a relatively satisfactory foreign exchange position; in Zambia, both foreign exchange constraints and the need to restructure the economy away from mining point in the other direction.

20. This may be unfair to decision-takers. With crop yields uncertain until harvest and the procurement/shipment time required long, it is prudent not to close down food aid (or other import) pipelines prematurely. However, the same cure of minimum grower prices and reserve stocks would fit equally well to alleviate the problems resulting from such prudence.

21. The role of better stoves is controversial. Those developed are with few exceptions so unpopular as to suggest serious design or overlooked side-effect weaknesses. In any case, substituting a purchased stove for three stones to save wood produced (collected) by direct labour input is not a practical prescription for poor rural households to follow.

22.　The critique on the grounds of collection cost is far from radical – it is standard Treasury practitioner wisdom aggregated from experience. That on indirect costs to unpaid collectors is not one Treasuries are so prone to make, but is one they recognise and to a degree accept – precisely because their experience is that heavy collection burdens on non-Treasury institutions or enterprises result in protests, the need to pay collection fees and/or very poor collection rates. Many of the detailed fee schemes proposed appear to be 'academic' or 'ideological' in the perjorative sense – it is hard to suppose their authors have any knowledge of revenue management and collection realities, and on occasion charging the user seems to be the goal in and of itself whether the net revenue secured is substantial, negligible or even negative. Perhaps the author is biased because for nine years he was a practising Treasury civil servant responsible *inter alia* for devising administratively feasible and cost efficient revenue measures and structures.

References

ALLISON, C. and R. H. GREEN (eds) (1983) 'Accelerated development in Sub-Saharan Africa – what agendas for action?', *IDS Bulletin*, vol. 14(1).

ALLISON, C. and R. H. GREEN (eds) (1985) 'Sub-Saharan Africa: getting the facts straight', *IDS Bulletin*, vol. 16(3).

BURKI, S. J. (1985) 'The African food crisis: looking beyond the emergency', Conference on South–South Co-operation: Experiences and Prospects, Harare, November, to be published by Third World Foundation.

DANIEL, P., R. H. GREEN and M. LIPTON (1985) 'A strategy for the rural poor', *Journal of Development Planning*, no. 15., pp. 113–36.

GREEN, R. H. (ed.) (1985a) 'Sub-Saharan Africa: towards oblivion or reconstruction', *Journal of Development Planning*, no. 15.

GREEN, R.H. (1985b) 'Sub-Saharan Africa: overall economic malaise and food production crisis', in *Famine in Africa*, House of Commons Paper 56 London: HMSO, pp. 149–53.

GREEN, R. H. (1985c) 'From deepening economic malaise towards renewed development: an overview', *Journal of Development Planning*, no. 15, pp. 9–43.

GREEN, R. H. (1985d) 'IMF stabilisation and structural adjustment in Sub-Saharan Africa: are they technically compatible?' *IDS Bulletin*, vol. 16(3), pp. 61–8.

INTERNATIONAL LABOUR ORGANISATION (ILO) (1976) *Employment Growth and Basic Needs: A One World Problem* (Geneva).

NDEGWA, P., L. MUREITHI and R. H. GREEN (eds) (1985) *Development Options for Africa in the 1980s and Beyond* (Nairobi: Oxford University Press).

PLEASE, S. (1985) 'Summary and highlights of the World Bank joint action programme', *Journal of Development Planning*, no. 15, pp. 265–72.

REUTLINGER, S. (1985) 'Food security and poverty in LDCs', *Finance and Development*, vol. 22(4).

RODNEY, W. (1972) *How Europe Underdeveloped Africa* (London: Bogle-L'overture).

ROSE, T. (ed.) (1985) *Crisis and Recovery in Sub-Saharan Africa: Realities and Complexities* (Paris: OECD, Development Centre).

SINGER, H. W. and R. H. GREEN (1984) 'Sub-Saharan Africa in depression: the impact on the welfare of children', *World Development* (Special Issue), vol. 12(3), pp. 283–95.

SOUTHERN AFRICA DEVELOPMENT CO-ORDINATION CONFERENCE (SADCC) (1985) 'An illustrative assessment of the cost of destabilisation of the member states of the SADCC', Memorandum to OAU Assembly of Heads of State and Government (Gaborone: SADCC).

UNICEF (1984) *The State of the World's Children* (New York).

UNICEF (1985a) *Statistics on Children in UNICEF Assisted Countries* (New York).

UNICEF (1985b) *Within Human Reach* (New York).

WORLD BANK (1981) *Accelerated Development in Sub-Saharan Africa: An Agenda for Action* (Washington DC).

WORLD BANK (1984) *Toward Sustained Development in Sub-Saharan Africa: A Joint Programme of Action* (Washington DC).

WORLD BANK (1986) (Reutlinger, S. and J. van Holst Pellekaan) *Ensuring Food Security in the Developing World: Issues and Options*.

6 Rural Productivity, Malnutrition and Structural Adjustment

Richard Longhurst

INTRODUCTION

The current financial recession in developing countries is deepening the problems of the poor. In Africa, a gradual decline in agricultural productivity and the provision of services to rural areas, together with recurring droughts, have accentuated impoverishment (Ghai and Radwan, 1983) and led particularly to high levels of child malnutrition. Demands by the IMF for stabilisation and by the World Bank for structural adjustment are putting pressure on governments to re-establish the balance between resource availability and use. But the price of this is deferment of basic needs policies (which would establish access by the poorest to food, water, health and education) and lower priority for increasing the productivity of vulnerable groups (UNI-CEF, 1985). In practice there have been reductions in, and even elimination of, social services, food subsidies and other government expenditure that benefits the poor. Stabilisation and adjustment processes have therefore had a disproportionate effect on the poor. Children, who have least power and fewest resources, have suffered most (Jolly and Cornea, 1984).

There is a strong humanitarian and equity argument for designing a process of adjustment which recognises that the poor, and especially children, should not be the major sufferers. But equally economic efficiency, in both the long and the short term, can be the rationale for a child-oriented stabilisation and adjustment process.

In the long term an investment in human capital is being foregone as a result of present policies. Children are being denied an adequate diet, suitable health care facilities and environmental stimulation. Poor nutrition in childhood may leave the body stunted and weak, prevent the realisation of full intellectual potential and cause permanent effects such as blindness. A synergistic reaction with

112

infection causes nutrition-related diseases which can reduce body functions. Several studies have been carried out on the economic returns to eliminating malnutrition and, although the calculations are necessarily rather speculative in view of the long time horizons involved, the evidence is none the less strong that these returns can be high (Selowsky, 1978). A recent study of supplementary feeding programmes for malnourished children in India showed that the social rate of return, even on the most pessimistic assumptions, is 10 per cent and can be as high as 21 per cent (Knudsen, 1981). There is also a great deal of evidence to indicate that for adults the capacity for hard work is lost in both present and future output if nutrition is poor (Latham 1985).

But increased productivity can also be seen in the short term. It is emerging that a major reason for declining per capita food production in most African countries has been a neglect of small farmers. Therefore, a strategy to increase their productivity could have benefits in terms of reducing food imports and increasing food exports as well as in terms of equity. When households believe that their food supply for basic subsistence is assured they are usually more innovative and willing to take advice and adopt new techniques.

RESTRUCTURING OF AGRICULTURE

Small farmers in Africa have received little assistance for the crops they grow, the credit and marketing institutions they require and the technology they use. The lack of a suitable seed technology in particular to increase yields of sorghum, millet and cassava, has compounded the problem.

But with suitable incentives and institutional development, returns to investment among poor farmers could be very high. In two senses they are potentially more productive than larger farmers. First there is the well-known 'inverse relationship' between land area operated and annual net value added per acre which was established by the Indian Farm Management Studies of thirty years ago, carried out on the type of unimproved rainfed farms that are found in most of Africa today. This relationship although varying between land types and in different areas of commercialised agriculture, exists because small farmers make greater use of family labour; find it more advantageous to employ labour to grow higher value crops; double crop or improve land in the slack season; reduce the area and duration of fallows; and enhance yields by better cultural practices (Lipton, 1985).

Second, the manner in which small farmers in some East African countries and in Asia have adopted the new maize varieties indicates that they are as responsive to, and as able to benefit from, innovations as are richer farmers. Some writers even assert that small farmers adopt modern varieties earlier and more intensively than large farmers, and that poor consumers gain most of all (Hayami 1981; Barker and Herdt, 1984). The modern varieties have been the major new technology to have an impact on the poor, and potentially on children (Lipton with Longhurst, 1985).

Recent research in villages among the World Bank agricultural projects in northern Nigeria has shown that grain production per acre can be higher under local farming systems of organic manuring, mixed cropping and high levels of family labour input, than on modernised farms growing single crops with inorganic fertiliser and a high level of hired labour (Longhurst, 1985). This suggests that too much of the indigenous farming system has been abandoned in an effort to move to a higher productivity agriculture based on large farmers.

Reports from several development agencies, notably the World Bank in Tanzania, detect a 'retreat into subsistence' in African agriculture. Farmers facing unreliable food marketing mechanisms, low prices for their products and general government neglect, have been producing sufficient food for their families but little surplus for the market or cash crops for export. As a result, the balance of payments has suffered and food prices have risen. In the Sudan, managers of the large irrigation projects of the Gezira, and especially the Rahad, have had to allow farmers to plant increasing proportions of their irrigated farms to sorghum rather than to the export crop of cotton because of the unreliability of food marketing systems. This retreat, and desire to protect household food security, indicates that poor farmers can exert some kind of power over government policies that do not have their interests at heart. It also suggests that there may be more benefit in using local entrepreneurial talent and innovation to engender development than in imposing farming systems from outside. Agricultural policies should start by improving household food security as the first step towards achieving national objectives such as improved balance of payments.

The foregoing comments have suggested linkages between small farmer productivity, household food security and hence adequate availability of food, and balance of payments. This suggests that there might be common ground between a national adjustment policy that attempts to improve a country's financial standing and the need for adequate production and consumption of food at household level.

Restructuring within agriculture needs to give greater support to indigenous cropping systems and to reinforce the means farm families employ to obtain food either through own production or off-farm employment. In particular, families experience fluctuations in supply, either regular anticipated seasonal variations or unexpected and more severe interannual fluctuations, and have mechanisms that attempt to cope with these.

Restructuring has to concentrate on those areas where national interests and those of the vulnerable groups overlap. Although many factors are relevant one of the most important is improving the returns to women's time. Most households are not a homogeneous unit of production and consumption with unified decisions made by men and women. They have separate areas of economic activity with different amounts of control over these activities. The care of children is directly related to their mothers' welfare although the overall resource level of the household is also important. Children might be best assisted by an agricultural policy which increases women's income from their own farms or reduces the amounts of labour they have to allocate to onerous household tasks. The interaction between women's time allocation and income earning occupations is now emerging as an important determinant of child nutrition (Popkin, 1978; Tripp, 1981; Wolfe and Behrmann, 1982; Berio, 1984). There can be positive and negative effects. Women with own income sources will devote some of these to improving the welfare of their children; if they cultivate their own farm plots, some of the food will be contributed to their children; if they are processing food for sale some of these products will also be devoted to children (Simmons, 1975; Longhurst, 1982). In a survey in Ghana, the children who were better nourished were those whose mothers had their own income from trading (Tripp, 1981). On the other hand, market work can take mothers away from the families, and the reduced care shows in the poorer nutritional status of the children. Also, as shown in the Philippines, poverty can necessitate a mother engaging in market work (Popkin, 1978). In such cases, educating the mother would help if it were linked with a resource, such as food aid, which might be used to increase the returns to women's work. Finally nothing should be done which might weaken the control women already have over income, especially from crop production, as has been seen in some agricultural projects (Dey, 1982; Hanger and Moris, 1973).

With this said about the economic nature of the family and the link between agricultural policy and child nutrition via women's work, three aspects of policy are especially important. These are first, export crop development, second, the key aspect of seasonality of food supply, and third the important role of food aid.

Export crops

In the past nutritionists have condemned development of export crops because the evidence has suggested that the welfare of vulnerable groups has deteriorated in their wake (e.g. Collis, 1962). And research in Jamaica linked self-reliance in food production with improved child nutrition (Marchione, 1977). However, foreign exchange earnings are an essential element in national development and in an adjustment process. Are there complementarities between foreign exchange generation by export crop production and improving the food consumption and nutrition of vulnerable groups? First of all, export crop production by smallholders, e.g. of cotton, coffee, cocoa and tea, will probably he higher among those households who have an adequate food supply, either through own production or through an effective market system, than among those who do not. This is because households usually seek to devote labour and land to meeting most of their food needs first. Increases in food crop yields and greater security of supply should encourage farmers to plant export crops; and consequent increases in farm income can lead to improved food consumption, as long as control of the marketing and of the income derived from such crops is not left entirely in the hands of male farmers.

If export crops are encouraged in isolation from the farming system and households' consumption needs it can lead to food shortages, due to a reduced acreage planted with food crops or to an increase in food prices, and have a negative nutritional impact. Studies by the FAO in Zambia and Kenya (FAO, 1984) have shown this. At a tea project in a fertile area of Kenya, malnutrition was found to be more common among the children of the tea growers than of other groups, despite the fact that their families enjoyed higher incomes as a result of a project that had been in existence for twenty years. It was found that land previously planted to food crops was now devoted to tea. Food bought by those with higher incomes was not of adequate nutritional value. In Zambia, a similar pattern emerged because there were greater incentives to grow cotton than to grow maize. Prices for maize were low and payments were late. Loans for farm development were given only to the larger cotton growing farmers. As a result maize planting declined and more land was devoted to cotton. Local food availability was reduced. The policy need is to devote equal resources to increasing the productivity of both food and export crops. There are three reasons for this from the point of view of vulnerable groups. First, incomes are improved for some without food prices rising. Second, low levels of food consumption are strongly associated with poor worker productivity. And third, intra-household control of resources is not biased further in favour of men.

Seasonality

The seasonal aspects of agriculture, when production and consumption do not coincide, place extra stresses on women and also lead to the severest periods of child malnutrition. The traditional 'hungry season' before the harvest has long been recognised as a period of stress, most of all, of course, by poor rural people who expect periods of shortage and plan as best they can for them. Several factors interact at this time. There are peaks in food prices, work requirements (and hence energy expenditure), infection levels and loan interest rates. There are troughs in food stocks, food intake and body weights. Births appear to peak at the harvest period so that women are often in their third trimester of pregnancy just before harvest when rates of child malnutrition are at their highest (Chambers, Longhurst and Pacey, 1981; Chambers, 1982).

Seasonal food imbalances show that merely planning for generally increased agricultural production is not sufficient to meet consumption objectives and nutritional needs. Agricultural policy needs to take account of seasonal factors by encouraging farmers' efforts to produce food at critical periods. There have been times when farmers were advised to give priority to non-food crops, such as cotton, at periods when food supplies were low and food prices high (e.g. in northern Nigeria, see Norman, Heywood and Hallam, 1974). Agricultural strategies that might reflect a seasonal perspective include the use of irrigation to extend the growing season, dryland farming methods, technology to reduce labour peaks in the household for women, inter-cropping as a safeguard against climatic variability, crop varieties with short maturation periods and crop breeding for drought resistance. Government food policy might consider maintaining buffer stocks, food price regulation, and decentralisation of food stores to vulnerable areas. Greater attention might be given to crop storage, although it is being increasingly recognised that at household level farmers' food losses are quite low and their storage technologies very cost effective (Boxall *et al.*, 1978).

In the area of nutrition, seasonality provides shocks to the nutritional status of children caused by poor intake, premature weaning as mothers anticipate hard field work, reduced child care and extra risk of food contamination as foods are prepared well in advance because of work pressures. Assistance to women in the form of child care facilities may bring benefits in terms of both agricultural production and child nutrition. Rural health policy must ensure that clinics are stocked with those drugs that are seasonally appropriate: if necessary rationing scarce drugs to those times of the year when diseases are most prevalent.

The seasonal problems of food supply are a major constraint to poor people; they have to divert much of their own energy and resources to surviving this period. Food surpluses at some times of the year can be appropriated by those with power in order to exploit the poor during periods of deficit.

Food aid

Food aid has become a permanent part of the scene in Africa following recurring food emergencies. Hungry people have to be fed, especially children. But food aid can be used to advantage within the context of a sound agricultural policy to prevent recurring famines. There are a number of complementary ways to ensure that with food aid, agricultural policy is more sensitive to the needs of vulnerable groups, in addition to meeting, in the short term, the problems caused by severe adjustment policies (Singer and Longhurst, 1985). For example, food aid for women can be used to increase the returns they get from low paid work by providing food-for-work projects which are more remunerative than existing work outlets. Second, food aid, either used in food-for-work schemes or sold locally to generate funds, can be used to provide the infrastructure (health clinics, small scale irrigation works, wells) that might improve both child welfare and women's work. Third, during periods of agricultural innovation, when women's crops, work and incomes could come under threat as household farms become more commercialised, food aid can be used as a buffer to dampen the effects and thus to protect vulnerable groups. Fourth, food supplements for women themselves without any work or other obligation during periods of seasonal stress can be expected to improve their activity levels and ability to cope. Fifth, food aid projects often provide an incentive effect for popular participation and community development action. It may be the only development resource that can encourage cohesiveness in a community, keeping together the traditional food system and child care network. Also, supplementary feeding programmes can encourage mothers and children to come into clinics and feeding centres, to be responsive to nutrition and health education and to receive immunisation.

Sensitively used, food aid can have several positive benefits for women and children, compatible with increasing productivity in the agricultural sector. As described above, food-for-work and other mechanisms can develop rural infrastructure and households can be made more productive and innovative. Overall, food aid projects that provide employment for women should be compatible with child care needs by allowing flexible working hours, freedom to breast feed, and the ability to carry children to the workplace (Piwoz and Viteri, 1985).

Food aid is the major means of assisting the landless: their plight has been difficult to resolve. To some extent the rice and wheat technologies in Asia have helped the landless by requiring more labour per acre but have not necessarily led to higher wage rates. Labour-displacing technology has also been introduced in some cases. The stagnation in rural wages has helped consumers, as this means that food prices have been kept down, but has not provided extra benefits for the landless.

CONCLUSIONS

Women are the economic pivot between production and consumption in many families in developing countries; between children and the outside world. National policy that takes account of this might lead to benefits in productivity at national level, compatible with stabilisation and adjustment objectives, and improvements in consumption and nutrition at household level. The two need not be conflicting objectives. Poor people can be highly productive if projects and programmes are suitably targeted. But some agricultural projects in the past have weakened the control by poor people and women over crop income (Dey, 1982; Hanger and Moris, 1973).

This paper has suggested that there need not be conflicts over household food security and export crop production, that a reorientation in agricultural policy to reduce seasonal problems can bring benefits for vulnerable groups, and that food aid has a flexible role to play. Other macro policy changes will also be required particularly in the areas of price policy, rural infrastructure and agricultural research. However, 'getting prices right' is not all that is needed.

Nearly all countries intervene to manipulate food prices in some manner. Cheap food prices do reduce producer incentives unless these are compensated for by subsidies either on inputs, where applicable, or by buying output at an artificially high price. On the other hand, increasing prices, although providing incentives and expanding production, will have a negative impact on the poor for a number of reasons: the rural group in which poverty is greatest is often the landless – they are not producers; the benefits of higher food prices may not reach rural producers, rather this may only serve to increase margins; increased production requires effective infrastructure and marketing for the benefits to be realised. Thus changes in food prices are necessary but not sufficient to bring about improvements in the welfare of rural producers (Pinstrup-Andersen, 1984).

Nation's facing the need for stabilisation and structural adjustment, should consider how to preserve minimum levels of nutrition for children. Failure to improve food production at household level is one reason for Africa's serious food crisis. Improvements in child health, leading to reductions in mortality, can be brought about both by reducing the infective environment and by improving nutrition. The importance of immunisation in reducing infant mortality is crucial. Immunisation and UNICEF's basic GOBI-FFF (Growth Monitoring, Oral Rehydration, Breast Feeding, Immunisation, Food Supplements, Family Planning, Female Education) strategy are not high-cost approaches to improving child health.

Similarly, a restructuring of agricultural policy based on increasing household food production by the landed in a way that is complementary to cash crop production, recognising the role and technical competence of women as producers in their own right, reducing the incidence of severe fluctuations in food supply and using food aid as a complementary resource is a strategy that will contribute as much to economic growth as to equity. For the landless, food-for-work projects based on food aid can be an effective income transfer if properly administered and introduced with a set of rural reforms designed to upgrade infrastructure and institutions.

Note

1. This paper was prepared with the support of UNICEF. The views expressed, however, are those of the author.

References

BARKER, R. and R. HERDT (1984) 'Who benefits from the new technology?', in *The Rice Economy of Asia*, Resources for the Future (Washington DC).

BERIO, A. J. (1984) 'The analysis of time allocation and activity patterns in nutrition and rural development planning', *Food and Nutrition Bulletin*, vol. 6(1), pp. 53–68.

BOXALL, R., M. GREELEY, D. TYAGI and M. LIPTON (1978) 'Prevention of farm-level foodgrain storage losses in India: a social cost-benefit analysis', IDS *Research Report* (Sussex).

CHAMBERS, R., R. LONGHURST and A. PACEY (eds) (1981) *Seasonal Dimensions to Rural Poverty* (London: Frances Pinter).

CHAMBERS, R. (1982) 'Health, agriculture, and rural poverty: why seasons matter', *Journal of Development Studies* vol. 18, pp. 217–38.

COLLIS, W. (1962) 'On the ecology of child health and nutrition in Nigerian villages', *Trop. Geog. Med.* vol. 14, pp. 140–63, 201–28.

DEY, J. (1982) 'Development planning in The Gambia: the gap between planners' and farmers' perceptions, expectations and objectives', *World Development*, vol. 10, pp. 377–96.

FAO (1984) 'Integrating nutrition into agricultural and rural development: six case studies', *Nutrition in Agriculture*, no. 2, (Rome).

GHAI, D. and S. RADWAN (eds) (1983) *Agrarian Policies and Rural Poverty in Africa* (Geneva: ILO).

HANGER, J. and R. J. MORIS (1973) 'Women in the household economy', in Chambers, R. and J. Moris (eds), *Mwea: An Irrigated Rice Settlement Scheme in Kenya* (Munich: Afrika Studien).

HAYAMI, Y. (1981) 'Induced innovation, green revolution and income distribution: comment', *Economic Development and Cultural Change*, vol. 30, (1), pp. 169–76.

JOLLY, R. and G. A. CORNEA (eds) (1984) *The Impact of World Recession on Children* (Oxford: Pergamon Press).

KNUDSEN, O. K. (1981) 'Economics of supplemental feeding of mal-nourished children: leakages, costs and benefits', *World Bank Staff Working Paper*, no. 451 (Washington DC).

LATHAM, M. C. (1985) 'The relationship of nutrition to productivity and wellbeing of workers', IFPRI/UNU Workshop on the Political Economy of Nutritional Improvements (West Virginia).

LIPTON, M. (1985) 'Land assets and rural poverty', *World Bank Staff Working Paper*, no. 744 (Washington DC).

LIPTON, M., with R. LONGHURST (1985) 'Modern varieties, international agricultural research and the poor', *CGIAR Study Paper*, no. 2 (Washington DC).

LONGHURST, R. (1982) 'Resource allocation and the sexual division of labor: a case study of a Moslem Hausa village in northern Nigeria' in L. Benería (ed.), *Women and Development: the Sexual Division of Labor in Rural Societies* (New York: Praeger).

LONGHURST, R. (1985) 'Farm level decision making, social structure and an agricultural development project in a northern Nigerian village', *Samaru Miscellaneous Paper 109* (Zaria: Ahmadu Bello University).

MARCHIONE, T. (1977) 'Food and nutrition in self-reliant national development: the impact on child nutrition of Jamaican government policy', *Medical Anthropology*, vol. 1, (1) pp. 57–79.

NORMAN, D., J. HAYWOOD and H. HALLAM (1974) 'An assessment of cotton growing recommendations as grown by Nigerian farmers', *Cotton Growing Review*, vol. 51, pp. 266–80.

PINSTRUP-ANDERSEN, P. (1984) 'Food prices and the poor in developing countries', Giannini Foundation Seminar (Berkeley: University of California Press).

PIWOZ, E. G. and F. E. VITERI (1985) 'Studying health and nutrition behaviour by examining household decision-making, intra-household resource distribution and the role of women in these processes', *Food and Nutrition Bulletin*, vol. 7, (4) pp. 1–31.

POPKIN, B. (1978) 'Time allocation of the mother and child and nutrition', *Ecol. Food & Nutr.*, vol. 9, pp. 1–14.

SELOWSKY, M. (1978) 'The economic dimensions of malnutrition in young children', *World Bank Staff Working Paper*, no. 294 (Washington DC).

SIMMONS, E. B. (1975) 'The small scale rural food processing industry in northern Nigeria', *Food Research Institute Studies*, vol. 45(2) pp. 147–61.

SINGER, H. and R. LONGHURST (1985) 'The role of food aid in promoting the welfare of children in developing countries', Report to UNICEF and WFP.

TRIPP, R. (1981) 'Farmers and traders: some economic determinants of nutritional status in northern Ghana', *J. Trop. Pediat.*, vol. 27, pp. 15–21.

WOLFE, B. and J. BEHRMANN (1982) 'Determinants of child mortality, health and nutrition in a developing country', *Journal of Development Economics*, vol. 11, pp. 165–93.

UNICEF (1985) *State of the World's Children* (New York).

7 The Impact of Agriculture on Third World Health: What Goals for Health Professionals?[1]

Michael Lipton

Intellectually, politically and administratively, Hans Singer has been 'in at the birth' of several international organisations full of potential to transform poor people's lives: FAO, WHO, and perhaps most directly the World Food Programme and UNICEF. I should not like to quantify the share in the reduction of age-specific death-rates since 1945 that is indirectly due to his contribution, but it is significant. Yet those death-rates, among the poorest one-fifth of Third World populations (and especially among children under 5), remain horrifyingly high. This paper argues that one major, remediable reason is the mutual unconcern of policy-makers in the fields of health (especially nutrition) and agriculture.

THE PROCESS

Agriculture involves transforming *inputs* – soils (land), sun, rain; irrigation water, labour, draught-power, agrochemicals – via *technologies* and *structures of work and ownership*, into foods and other *outputs*. All four components affect the nutrition and health of farmers, farm labourers, and their families. Also all four – especially the amount and type of food produced – may affect the health and nutrition of non-farm populations, especially as consumers. In developing countries, these four components are the main variables affecting human health. Most working time is spent in agriculture, and most income on food. For poor and vulnerable groups, the proportions are typically over two-thirds.

123

INPUTS AND HEALTH

Labour

In poor countries, most deaths occur among persons aged under 5, and their main cause is undernutrition and/or infection. Usually the poorest 20 per cent of the population suffer infant (0–1 year) and child (1–5 years) mortality rates of 150–250 and 30–60 per 1000 respectively – usually well over double the rates suffered by the richest 20 per cent in the same countries (Mitra, 1979). This is because only poor children are normally exposed to risks of periodic severe undernutrition, and of frequently recurring and untreated infection (Lipton, 1983, pp. 17–19), because their parents lack the income to buy food, healthy environments, and health care. As land gets scarcer these 'ultra-poor' depend increasingly on their labour for income, above all rural and agricultural labour. Rural infant and child mortality far exceed urban (Ibid, pp. 41–2, 46–8), and are heavily concentrated among the working poor. Hence *higher and more stable real income for persons dependent on unskilled rural labour* – in south and east Asia, and in increasingly many parts of Africa, landless and near-landless workers, rather than small family farmers – is the most important contribution that agricultural policies and projects could make to human health in developing countries.

Yet most discussions of agricultural policies and projects completely neglect the issue of health and nutrition. One excellent analysis of the impact of agricultural research on nutrition (Pinstrup-Andersen *et al.*, (eds), 1984) concentrates almost entirely on 'resource-poor farmers' (e.g. Tripp, 1984, pp. 287, 291, 293) and on consumers, and hardly mentions the impact on farm labourers (via employment and wage/food-price ratios) of the amount and stability of access to food and health care. Too often, the most marginal of labourers and even of resource-poor farmers – e.g. rural–rural migrants, and semi-legal shifting cultivators and squatters on the fringes of irrigation schemes – are invisible except as threats to the (much better) health of settled populations (Marga Inst., 1984, p. 90; FAO, 1984, p. 71, and cf. p. 111). Health professionals might well instead apply pressure to increase such people's share in the gains from agricultural policies and projects.

But it is mainly through higher employment that labourers' health can be improved. The poorest depend increasingly on farm labour for their income. It is not error, but their need to concentrate scarce health resources (i.e. mainly income from labour) on income-earning workers, that compels them to neglect child nutrition and health care. Labour income can seldom be increased by *artificially* pushing up wages (although rising population/land ratios depress real wage-rates). Minimum wage laws in the Third World often reduce the demand for labour and push up unemployment. Similarly, *artificial* depression of food prices, while temporarily raising the value of the real wage of labourers in terms of food, soon harms them by discouraging both the production of food and the employment of labour to grow it. This leaves only two effective strategies by which – until prosperity, diversification, and industrialisation are achieved – a low-income country can solve the main (child) health–food problem of its ultra-poor:

(a) the choice of agricultural programmes, including technologies and crop-mixes, that will increase the demand by farmers for unskilled labour, especially migrant and other marginalised workers;
(b) the redistribution of claims on income from project assets, especially land and draught-power, if feasible towards the poorest, otherwise to smaller farmers who employ relatively more people per hectare.

The latter strategy is discussed below, but it is hard to envisage health professionals making a substantial impact on it. The four health problems arising in relation to the former strategy, of farm labour – costs in human energy, labour hazards, women's role, seasonality – have discouraged adoption of an employment strategy as a route to 'health for all'. They are indeed obstacles to be overcome, but they are not binding constraints.

The first one – since undernutrition is such an important cause of rural ill-health – is that farm labour has high calorie requirements. Income almost always exceeds the value of calories used in work, but additional calories must be allowed for (a) travel, (b) the rise in basal metabolic rate (Miller, 1982, p. 195) for up to fifteen hours after strenuous work, (c) 'insurance' for casual labourers against being too fatigued to find or complete available work, (d) *possible* income diversion – associated with some forms of extra or new work – towards costlier foods, alcohol, bottle-feeding of children by working mothers, etc. Such problems suggest an agenda for research into: reducing the calorie costs of work-related travel (e.g. by plot consolidation, nearer drinking-water or fuel, etc.); farm innovations that would reduce physical effort (but not working time); avoiding fruitless job search (better labour-market information for workers); and preventing *possible* waste and abuses (by different means and forms of payment). Currently advisers on agricultural projects seldom seek to adjust options to reduce energy demands per hour of work. Especially at peak seasons, those households that must sell much farm labour, and can buy little, may well be in an 'energy trap', impeding their efficient conversion of work into the food (and hence health) that their families need (Longhurst, 1984, pp. 38–9, 41, 79–80). Thus health professionals should investigate ways, through agricultural projects, of getting assets or work to the poorest, while reducing the energy intensity of each hour they work.

The second problem is farm labour hazards. Growing attention is rightly paid to risks linked to pesticides, machinery, etc. But there is little analysis of how the traditional hazards of tropical farmwork – for example, snake and scorpion bites; dehydration, or inferior water; back damage (especially in transplanting) – could be reduced. Yet such hazards account for much of the time spent out of casual labour due to illness in rural India in 1977–8 (5 per cent for men and 6 per cent for women, plus 1 per cent in chronic disability) (Lipton, 1983a, p. 11). Data from other developing regions suggest higher incidences.

The third health difficulty with farm labour is its effect on participant women and children. Is 'more work for women' good or bad for their nutrition or their children's? The subject is clouded by rival and recurring anecdotes: that extra female income is offset by reduced attention to child care; or that it is likelier than extra male income to be spent on extra food for children. There is little firm evidence for such opinions (Pines, 1983, pp. 52–4). In Calcutta, Alan Berg showed that extra income from women's work did improve child nutrition, though less than proportionately to the extra income (Reutlinger and Selowsky, 1976). In eight Bangladesh villages surveyed by Greeley and his colleagues, female labour displacement, by modern methods of rice processing, harmed nutrition more than the saved grain helped it (Lipton, 1982). In Kerala, extra female income was associated with better infant birthweights and growth – a finding reversed only if the extra income was earned outside the home (or home farm), by the poorest households, *and* in the slack season (Kumar, 1977; Lipton, 1983a, p. 37); in these extremely difficult circumstances, the mother's absence from home damaged child care more than the income she earned helped it. This important finding underlines the nutritional importance of ensuring that a mother's work is compatible with child care in hungry times. Much more widespread experimentation is needed with organised child care – by exchanges, groups, schools, factories, etc. – but paid for by taxpayers or users, not by employers, who would then reduce their employment of young women. The localised seasonal impact of women's work options on infant health needs to be analysed; anecdotes, feminist or masculist, are worse than useless.

Fourth, the seasonal pattern of extra work and income greatly affects the nutritional outcome for vulnerable groups. It is in the slack, hungry agricultural seasons, especially for households most reliant on casual female income, that demand for labour (employment) is usually below average and supply of labour (participation) also falls slightly, as workers are discouraged from job search – especially if this season coincides with the 'unhealthy' period of the late rains; and because labour demand falls faster than supply, wage rates usually also fall (Lipton, 1983a, pp. 33–7, 56–60, 84–5). Household food stores are depleted, purchased food prices are high, infections prevalent, and food wages rarer. Moreover, adult men are frequently absent due to migration. For all these reasons (many of them documented in Chambers, 1982; Chambers *et al.*, 1981; Schofield, 1974; and Longhurst and Payne, 1979), it should be assumed that extra labour income for vulnerable groups normally helps nutrition most in the slack season.

Land

Three health issues need mention. First, shifting farmers, squatters with traditional and uncodified land rights, and migrant workers are too often seen only as health 'threats', yet are often the groups at greatest health risk. Seasonally migrant farm labourers are typically least resistant to diseases local to their destination, and least organised and articulate in face of agrochemical or other danger at work. Health professionals are often the only ones who know of their problems and can speak for them.

Second, urban expansion diverts land – often outstanding farmland previously controlled by poor people – to housing use. This at once raises demand for food, reduces its supply, and worsens distribution of access to it. This threat to periurban health is often neglected even in otherwise excellent 'poverty-oriented' discussions of urban expansion and land acquisition (e.g. Yeh, 1984, pp. 41–7). Health professionals could stimulate not only agricultural, but also urban, policy professionals to seek efficient ways to *replace* the cheap food (and purchasing power) lost in the process, for example, through home gardens and appropriate individual water-taps.

Third, special health problems are regularly associated with plantation farming. This is partly because of 'colonial relics' involving continued non-food monoculture and/or dependence on disfranchised ethnic groups (Beckford, 1972); and partly because, for some crops such as tea and coffee, the hilly terrains and cooler climates of many plantation systems impose heavier caloric demands, and add the infections of cooler temperatures to those of tropical latitudes. Some land uses, like that for coconuts (Marga, 1984, p. 92), add further hazards. The health problems of plantations are tractable: UNICEF regularly shows that Sri Lanka'a tea plantation districts have higher infant mortality rates than prevail elsewhere on the island, but comparable disparities apparently do not affect tea plantation workers in Kericho, Kenya (FAO, 1984, pp. 51–6). Thus the central problem of employees' health on large commercial farms – in Zimbabwe, considerably worse than the health of small family farmers (Chikanza *et al.*, 1982) – appears to lie in social organisation, not crops or climates. Health professionals can help by providing basic data to track the comparative nutritional status of plantation and other children; this has given a valuable push towards remedial action in Kenya and Sri Lanka, but too often the information is absent.

Water

Irrigation is a life-saver in poor countries, especially as population growth increasingly requires food *and work* from double-cropping. There are three scales of irrigation: 'major' surface water systems; 'minor' surface water or groundwater schemes; and farmer-controlled 'microirrigation'. It is major permanent systems, involving stationary water, in tropical areas that have been associated with serious health hazards. Schistosomiasis has spread hugely in the wake of Aswan and Gezira, and – ominously for south Asia, with its massive schemes – is beginning to emerge in Amazonia, once believed to be protected by acidic waters (Goldsmith and Hildyard, 1984, pp. 80–5). Perennial irrigation also increases tropical malaria risks by providing year-round watering for *Anopheles* and this effect is synergistic with that of greatly increased insecticide use in irrigated areas, encouraging races of *Anopheles* robust against a wide range of insecticides.

But the health case against major irrigation is often grossly overstated. First, without perennial irrigation, probably many more people would have starved than have suffered from irrigation-induced diseases. Second, conventional *minor* irrigation – especially of paddy – creates stagnant water for mosquitoes (Panikar and Soman, 1984, p. 126), often for longer periods than more modern systems of major canal irrigation management. Third, it is not irrigation as such, but bad maintenance, that – via seepage – creates much of the environment for insect vectors (Marga, 1984:97). Fourth, well-planned irrigation can complement increased drinking-water quality *and quantity*, a major dry-season health need (FAO, 1984, pp. 40–1).

Health planning, before and during irrigation project cycles, is essential if such advantages are to be realised, and possible disastrous side-effects avoided. It is alarming that major dams continue to be built without consideration of health effects and options (Goldsmith and Hildyard, 1984, pp. 89, 91, 231–2), despite the existence of clear guidelines to improving such effects by careful choice of design (McJunkin *et al.*, 1982; Hunter, 1980; World Bank *et al.*, 1985, Annex 3). Health professionals should offer not a general environmentalist critique of irrigation, but clear analyses of cost-effective options for improving the health impact of specific irrigation-system designs, maintenance and management.

Tillage and agrochemicals

The Asian shift from animals to tractors almost always displaces labour – that is what makes it profitable – and seldom raises output (Binswanger, 1978). Therefore, negative effects on nutrition are likely where many poor people live by 'landless' farm labour. Yet that shift is commonly encouraged by subsidies. The socio-economic effects, together with the directly 'physical' health–nutrition impacts of tillage options (via accident risks, ergonomics, energy uses, etc.), appear to warrant investigation.

Agrochemicals have substantial health implications, and are of three types: naturally occurring soil chemicals; organic additives (mainly manures and composts); and inorganics (mainly NPK-based fertilisers, herbicides, insecticides, and fungicides). Apart from the impassioned controversy about insecticides, most health effects of agrochemicals are ignored: NPK made available to plants on the farms of poor and vulnerable groups, especially in Africa, is overwhelmingly from the soil, secondly from organics, and least from inorganics; and herbicide and pesticide use by such groups is minimal. Only in a few much visited places in the Third World are inorganic fertilisers and pesticides intensively used by small farmers. For most poor people, the health–nutrition threats are plant vulnerability to N and P *deficiency*, weeds, insects, viruses and fungi; and *shortfalls* of output due to inaccurate use of (mostly organic) manures and composts.

Equally neglected are the health effects of alternative methods of plant nutrient enrichment: mudball techniques, the precise, repeated placing of nutrient sources in the root zone, enable farmers to raise yields without buying more fertilisers but they involve more handling of toxic substances. Health professionals need to seek inexpensive ways to identify and reduce associated health hazards.

This is also true of the problems associated with insecticides. *In any one year*, insecticides save tens of millions of tons of staple foods, and greatly increase employment income (and hence nutrition and health). But they also cause insects to develop ever more resistant races to an ever broader spectrum of poisons, so that *over the years* increasing amounts, variety and strengths of insecticide must be used to achieve the same level of protection (Bull, 1982; 1983, pp. 160–2), especially if, as with cotton and tobacco, the insecticide also kills natural predators of the pests. This 'pesticide treadmill' steadily increases not only the costs of application, but the health hazards.

There are of four main types. *Direct poisoning* by pesticides causes perhaps 10 000 deaths per year throughout the developing world, probably 7000 due to suicide (Marga, 1984, p. 94; Bull, 1983, pp. 159–60). *Pesticide build-up*, both of long-lived (but probably not very harmful) chemicals such as DDT and of harmful organochlorides, occurs throughout the food chain. It affects humans who regularly apply pesticides and/or ingest food or water contaminated with them. *Protein loss* occurs due to fish poisoning, especially as overuse of pesticides builds up (Panikar and Soman, 1984, p. 126), though poor people at nutritional risk usually get their proteins largely from vegetable sources. As for *human disease*, the most serious danger, from the use of growing amounts of stronger and more varied agroinsecticides, is the robust races of insect vectors, above all of malaria (Goldsmith and Hildyard, 1984, p. 77, citing WHO sources). Arguably, agroinsecticides are the main cause of the recrudescence of malaria and the abandonment of the elimination strategy (Ibid., pp. 77–8; Bull, 1982). This interacts with selective insectiside damage to fish species, and to the introduction of Nile carp (*tilapia*), which preys on the small fish that lived off mosquito larvae (Goldsmith and Hildyard, 1984, p. 80).

Health professionals cannot decide the 'right' balance between more food from pesticides now (saving human life), and more deaths from treadmill effects later (wasting it). They can, however, estimate the health effects of alternative strategies to control insect pests, and help to design strategies for inexpensively reducing health damage. Among the more appealing are:

(a) To experiment with schemes to insure farmers against pest recurrence; farmers' current tendency to insure *themselves* against pests by applying pesticides too often, in too heavy doses, is a major cause of the 'treadmill' (Panikar and Soman, 1984, p. 126).

(b) To help research stations select priorities in the search either for crop varieties that are pest-resistant without agrochemicals, or for natural predators of the pests that would permit phasing-out of the most risky or 'treadmill-prone' insecticides (an example for potatoes is Valle-Riestra, 1984, p. 65).

(c) Internationally, to press all major exporters to ratify an international convention requiring all pesticide exports, and home-produced competitors, to be clearly labelled (and/or colour-coded) at the smallest unit-of-use level, with the health hazards, maximum advised dosages, and pictorially illustrated safety precautions (e.g. simple face-masks and protective clothing for sprayers; washing after use) in the language of the potential users (Bull, 1983).

HEALTH AND THE CHOICE OF AGRICULTURAL OUTPUTS

Most effects of agricultural policies and projects – on input availability, research, transport, water regimes, etc. – alter farmers' incentives, making some outputs more attractive to grow, and others less so. There are six main issues of concern to the health professional. Should the intended output-mix consist of more expensive (high quality) outputs, or a higher proportion of cheaper locally consumed crops? Of food crops, or cash crops? Within foods, aimed at calories, proteins, or micronutrients? Of outputs mainly for promising regions or poor ones? Of high-yielding or robust products? And how should the issue of dangerous products be handled?

Cheap or expensive outputs?

For farmers expensive crops are better than cheap ones, but from a health viewpoint, this may not apply to food crops. Even at farm level, a reliable supply of calories is important, and may involve some sacrifice of (a) higher, but less reliable, outputs of calories; (b) outputs of saleable non-food products, usually valuable enough to buy ample calories, but sometimes fetching very low prices; (c) food products with high value-per-acre and/or good cooking quality, taste, and protein content, but low fat or carbohydrate content and unsure prospects of market exchange for adequate calories, especially when these are in short supply at national level. Thus research into high-protein or 'aesthetic' food-crop varieties may well be misplaced (Ryan, 1984, pp. 199–204), even for farmers.

In questions of commodity choice affecting total communities of vulnerable groups (not just farmers), the issues are even starker. Health and nutrition are damaged by the neglect of poor people's staple crops in African agricultural research (to the benefit of export crops of high but uncertain value, and more recently of fashionable high-protein crops like soybeans (Lipton, 1985a)). Similar 'bias (against) commodities consumed primarily by the poor' has to be reversed 'to alleviate malnutrition in urban Latin America' (Pachico, 1984:30). Advocacy of dairy development on the grounds of 'proteins for the poor' should be questioned; the poor get their proteins (usually adequately) from affordable cereals and pulses, and lose as consumers when land and farmworkers are diverted to animal husbandry, though they may gain (Jul, 1979) as producers if they own one or two milking animals. General neglect of minor crops – especially local roots, beansprouts, and melons and plantains – slights their *seasonal* importance to caloric adequacy for very poor rural people in pre-harvest seasons (Longhurst, 1985, p. 11) and in the home gardens of very poor urban and plantation workers (FAO, 1984, p. 56).

Food or other crops?

These agruments, however, do not constitute a general health case for food crops against cash crops. Very often, the value and employment-intensity of output are such that income – and hence command over food – provided to nutritionally vulnerable groups from appropriate cash crops far exceeds what might be provided by use of the land for food crops. Generally, 'differences in nutritional status' at a given level of income-per-person have little to do with 'type of crop grown' (FAO, 1984, p. 128), though the health professional should enquire whether policies that depress cash crop prices may deprive vulnerable farming families of command over necessary calories. Often, as in Kenya and Zambia, payment is swifter – even if still set at artificially low levels – for export crops than for food crops (Ibid., pp. 8, 122); small farmers who grow and sell maize cobs, but must buy processed meal, may in the process be compelled to underfeed their children.

At both local and national level, the choice among producing food crops for home consumption, food or cash crops for exchange internally, or export crops, has complex health implications. These include seasonal considerations, dependent on storability and credit markets; and gender considerations, dependent on who in a household controls crop income and how s/he uses it. Such issues are specific to crops, regions, and forms of social organisation. They are research-able, but currently clouded by a miasma of self-serving anecdotes. Agricultural planners must be asked not for a policy for localised food self-sufficiency that would appear to prevent exchange altogether (Twose, 1984), nor for a policy for free trade and specialisation in advance of any guarantees for food security, but for research into the likely health consequences of the choices made. By co-operating with them, health professionals could help to end the disgraceful situation in which 'few project appraisal reports make mention of potential declines in the production of foods for home consumption', or of changes in the seasonal and annual riskiness of vulnerable groups' command over calories, associated with planned changes in the crop-mix (Reutlinger, 1983, p. 15, 21).

An important health consequence of strategic shifts in crop-mix, towards cash-cropping, is to shift consumption, even among vulner-able groups, from locally grown millet and sorghum, to maize meal processed in cities (Africa) and to imported wheat flour (some of Africa and much of Asia). This can greatly increase food insecurity. The impression that 'self-sufficiency' is being approached because net imports of the traditional main staple diminish – neglecting the fact that they are replaced by a new import, e.g. rice by wheat in Sri Lanka (Marga, 1984, p. 34) – dangerously reduces political awareness of the new nutritional dangers.

These are greater where tastes are developed for imported crops, such as wheat in much of tropical Africa, that for agroclimatic reasons cannot be grown locally without major diversion of inputs and research (Ryan, 1984, p. 214) from currently grown foods with more promise, calories-per-acre, and consumption by the rural poor. Even where the new crops can be grown locally, the concentration of research, credit and especially marketing upon the newly popular 'urban' crop frequently wipes out large parts of the production of much more drought-resistant local staples; the shift from sorghum to *katumani* maize in Machakos, Kenya, greatly increased nutritional vulnerability in the 1982–4 droughts (FAO, 1984, pp. 33–40). Shifts to finer grains are an irreversible, indeed desirable, part of develop- ment; nor should local crops be advocated for their own sake. However, the development of appropriate flour mixes – using sorghum, millet, and/or cassava as well as wheat or maize – could do much to soften the harsh side-effects, and to reduce the dangers of increasing reliance on vulnerable monocultures.

Calories, proteins or micronutrients?

In developing countries, the overriding fact of caloric shortfall, and the need for simply monitored data, both point to caloric adequacy as the main health goal of agriculture. Few underfed people, if they received enough calories, would be short of protein (FAO, 1983, pp. 63, 75; Pinstrup-Andersen, 1981, pp. 175–7; Muscat, 1983, p. 4; Lipton, 1983, p. 8). Iodine or Vitamin A deficiencies are usually more cost-effectively met by fortification, e.g. of salt, than by trying to alter cropping patterns.

Thus health professionals seldom need to worry about the effects of the spread of cereals upon availability of pulse proteins. High-yielding wheats and rices have indeed displaced large areas of pulses in Asia. However, first, the health gain from the extra calories-per-acre greatly outweighs the loss from any possible protein displacement. Second, for poor people, cereals are a cheaper source of protein (and even of most key amino-acids) than pulses. Third, high-yielding wheat often produces three times the food weight per hectare of the pulses it displaces and its protein content per kilogram is often 35–40 per cent as high; so the shift to grain can often increase even protein availability. However, it normally remains important to incorporate pulse or leaf protein into weaning gruels, because otherwise bulk may prevent the weanling from obtaining enough protein before s/he is full. This is even more important with root crops, where bulk can even impede adequate calorie intake by weanlings.

Poor regions or promising regions?

Health advice is rarely sought or offered, and is desperately needed, on the issue of regional balance. The comforting simplicities of advocating support for food production in poorer regions or in promising ones offset each other. Food availability is best advanced at national level by concentrating resources for food production where the returns are highest; at local level, where the need is greatest. For nutritional impact, it is the context of public policy that matters. If extra output of cheap staples will replace imports (or build stocks) rather than increase consumption per person – because poor people's average purchasing-power is not increasing, as in India – then health considerations indicate that a larger proportion of inputs and research should go towards locating extra food output in the poorest areas than would be indicated by considerations of efficiency alone. However, if a government can ensure that vulnerable groups' claims on food – their incomes per person – rise, it does best, even on health grounds, to locate resources to grow more food where the returns are highest. Thus health professionals would probably advise the government of India to shift some agricultural support from the high-yielding, progressive north-west towards the neglected poverty belts of north-east India. Conversely, the Indian state government of Kerala (where the power balance favours equitable distribution of gains, but has failed to achieve rapid growth (Panikar and Soman, 1984)) might well achieve a better health impact by concentrating resources in the most promising regions, and distributing some of the gains to the highlands, where health levels are worse than elsewhere.

Agricultural policy research (e.g. Pachico, 1984, p. 39) often assumes that poorer *regions* contain a higher proportion of poorer and hence nutritionally vulnerable *people*. This need not be so, in view of the greater internal equality within more remote, less commercialised villages and areas (Dasgupta, 1977), and the effects of migration. In poor regions, moreover, the poorest people are deficit farmers and landless labourers, who may gain if scarce resources are used to grow more food in more promising (even if 'prosperous') areas and thus to cut food prices (Mason, 1983, p. 106). However, some poor regions have been so long neglected that they may be more promising users of scarce government support than the pampered 'progressive' areas.

Otherwise, vulnerable groups in poor regions may gain more from accessible food stores, rural non-farm expansion and employment guarantee schemes (Dandekar and Sathe, 1980) than from farm outlays for their own unresponsive agroclimates.

Yield or robustness?

Breeding for robustness stabilises farm incomes, as well as food available to consumers (Pachico, 1984, p. 38). There need be no conflict between output and stability – irrigation normally improves both; and much breeding research achieves high yields largely by, not at the expense of, selecting for resistance to pests and drought (cf. ICRISAT's expenditure pattern (Jodha, 1984, p. 110)). However, *maximum* average yield and *maximum* stability will normally require quite different policies. In surplus areas of high promise, the 'agricultural policy establishment' – influenced both by the yield-oriented research priorities of international science and by the demands of articulate city-dwellers for plentiful cheap food – tends to place growth, especially of food surpluses, as a policy goal above the stability of rural people's command over food. Health professionals need to explain the health costs of that choice; to help devise methods to reduce them; and to work with agricultural and socio-economic scientists to analyse the case for alternative policies.

Dangerous products: positive risks

Positively dangerous food crops contain elements that endanger life or health. The danger can occur directly, as with *kesari dal*, a variety of lentil that causes perhaps one million current cases of lathyrism in India; or indirectly, following upon some or all methods of storage, processing or preparation, as with the build-up of hydrocyanic acid in many varieties of cassava, which appears to cause health problems (goitre, and sometimes cretinism) only where storage is prolonged but processing is absent or inappropriate (Pachico 1984, p. 32 and sources there cited). In such cases appropriate breeding priorities (Ibid., p. 32) or post-harvest systems can greatly reduce risks. Although testing (e.g. of groundnuts for aflatoxin) normally requires profession-ally supervised laboratory work, field-level health workers may be able to monitor whether the results are readily, inexpensively and punctually available to the poorest growers and consumers. Otherwise they will continue to grow or eat dangerous products, and formal banning orders will be of little avail.

Unfortunately, many health risks from dangerous farm products cannot be dealt with by low-cost varietal or post-harvest innovation. The addictive derivatives of tobacco, opium, and coca are striking cases. As health information and restrictions on advertising and sale are enforced in the developed world, so the pressures increase on growers, processors and intermediaries to push these delayed-action killers in the less safeguarded and sophisticated markets of developing countries. There, populations (being both less educated and younger than in richer countries) provide more receptive audiences, and longer-term supplier profits (Taylor, 1985, chs. 14–15).

The per-acre profitability of all the narcotics to their growers usually so much exceeds that of alternative crops that laws, incentives, or campaigns against cultivation, achieve little. Sometimes even success-ful supply control would not be a 'cheap fix' morally; tobacco – which kills addicts – also saves the lives of many Bangladeshi children, for whose parents it constitutes the only feasible crop to yield an adequate income.

Dangerous products: sins of omission

Negatively dangerous farm products are foods which lack necessary nutrients, or contain potentially damaging features, yet which – especially if they are cheap and/or energy-dense – drive out foods richer in those nutrients, or able to counteract the potential damage. Common causes of illness are staples low in iron, vitamin A, iodine, or absorbable niacine. Where diets contain few other sources of the nutrient, such deficiencies can cause, respectively, anemia, especially with frequent blood loss to hookworm and insects (especially in small children); xerophthalmia; goitre or even cretinism; and pellagra (Mayer, 1985, pp. 5–9). The main remedies – minor crops, food fortification – are of long standing.

Potentially dangerous products include sugar, saturated fats (including coconut and palm oil), and low-fibre foods. None is dangerous in moderation, especially given a lifestyle that reduces other synergistic causes of cancer or ischaemic heart disease. Yet these are increasingly dominant causes of death in many developed and some developing areas – high coconut oil and sugar consumption is almost certainly linked to Sri Lanka's high incidence of degenerative diseases. Here too, there is a case for involvement by health professionals in the design of appropriate supply-side policies to develop healthier varietal and crop mixes.

INPUTS TO OUTPUTS: TECHNOLOGIES AND STRUCTURES

Farm inputs are transformed into outputs through technologies, interacting with structures, and involving public and private choices with major effects on health. Choices in farm *technology* are of five main types: hydraulic, mechanical, chemical, biological, and post-harvest. Health effects of hydraulic, mechanical and chemical alternatives have been considered above. Below, we enquire how health professionals should seek to improve the health impacts of biological research.

Not only *technical* choices determine how farm inputs and outputs affect health. Alternative *structures* of law, custom and power express themselves as control and ownership of, and access to, technologies; land, labour and capital embodying them; and claims on their usufruct. Health professionals could usefully provide more help in making public choices, and influencing private ones, if they could analyse and publicise the health effects, including income effects and hence access to food and health care. However, the training and job descriptions of most health professionals – including social scientists –tend to define them out of influence upon 'structural' decisions, e.g. about how to help a family, a village, or a State to redesign land tenure and inheritance systems.

Health impacts: biological research criteria versus project criteria

Three recent summaries have listed the nutritional impacts of biological research. Pinstrup-Andersen (1984, pp. 14–15) writes:

> Agricultural production research influences human nutrition (via) (1) incomes acquired by households at (nutritional) risk; (2) the prices they must pay for food commodities; (3) the nature of production systems among semisubsistence farmers; (4) risk and fluctuations in food production, storage, prices, and incomes; (5) the nutrient composition of food for malnourished households; (6) intrahousehold income and budget control, and the allocation of women's time; (7) the demand for labour; (8) expenditure of human energy; (9) infectious diseases.

He gives priority to (1), (2) and 'insufficient food', but emphasises that 'using production expansion as a proxy for nutritional effect is ... misleading'. Muscat (1983, p. 3) lists seven nutrition-related questions about agricultural projects that could, as well apply to biological research programmes and outputs; these cover points (1), (2), (4) and (6) only from Pinstrup-Andersen's list, replacing his (3) by a closely related quest for health-linked effects on 'production of foods for home consumption', and specifying seasonal effects in his (4) and effects on women's food preparation and child care in his (6). Reutlinger (1983, pp. 12–21) stresses three questions (corresponding closely to Pinstrup-Andersen's (1), (2) and (3)): does the activity raise or lower at-risk households' incomes, production for own consumption, and purchased food prices?

In appraising alternative technologies for *projects*, health professionals should concentrate on these latter three nutritional effects, giving attention in each case to fluctuations and food requirements, and adding a review of the disease impact of changes in water and pest management. For *research programmes*, especially into crop alternatives, health impact assessment requires a different approach (Lipton and Longhurst, 1985, ch. 5) though the main components of benefit remain as in Reutlinger's list.

The main impact of research into modern cereal and root-crop varieties on poor people's health is via the effects on cereal availability, consumption and prices. If the extra grain adds to grain available from net food imports, cheaper food greatly benefits *consumers*, especially the poor; the poorest group in Colombia in 1970 was 12.8 per cent less poor because extra food supply from modern rice varieties restrained food prices (Scobie and Posada, 1978). Surplus *producers* lose, but the poorest growers eat most or all of their product, gaining as consumers from the new technology (Hayami and Herdt, 1977). A fall of 8 per cent in Philippines rice prices would allow even the poorest to escape undernutrition (Gonzales and Regaldo, 1983). The poor gain even more when modern varieties raise per-person availability of inferior foods, such as cassava meal in Brazil (CIAT, 1981).

Biological research: more output, small health impact

Unfortunately, a rise in *output* does not imply rising per-person *availability*. Most growth in poor countries has favoured the better-off, so, despite the massive extra supply from crop research, real income-per-person has not grown much among the 'vulnerable groups', who alone would tend to use most of any such extra income to buy more cereals. Hence extra food output, due to improved cereals in Asia and Latin America, has (a) matched population growth, (b) built stocks, (c) displaced imports, notably of wheat to India, (d) increased exports, e.g. of cassava chips, but in most countries not (e) raised consumption among those at nutritional risk.

African experiences confirm that lack of appropriate inputs from modern technology – whatever the (very real) gains from on-farm experiment and innovation (Richards, 1985) – is, with population growing at 2.5–4 per cent yearly, far worse for the poor than modern varieties. Health professionals should not 'blame the technology'. However, they can examine research priorities in agricultural technology. The emphasis on high-protein or high-lysine varieties has harmed the poor – who mostly need extra calories, not extra protein – not only by frequent trade-offs between proteins, etc., and yield or stability (e.g. Pachico, 1984, p. 34; Jodha, 1984, p. 111), but indirectly by diverting resources from and delaying development of robust varieties (Lipton and Longhurst, 1985, sec. 5). This diversion is even less justifiable if it aims at nutritional characteristics seldom constant within, or reliably heritable by, a variety (Flinn and Unnevehr, 1984, p. 164–5) or at colour and taste qualities, except in the rare cases where the very poor both grow 'luxury' varieties of cereals at prices enhanced by such research, and use the income to buy low-cost calorie sources. Research should instead focus on achieving energy density (Pinstrup-Andersen, 1984, p. 20), and absorbability by pregnant and lactating women, sucklings, and weanlings, especially those with infections or parasites.

Health, health professionals and the commodity-mix of research

The main issue in the search for better health impact of crops research is the balance among commodities and among regions. Colonial agricultural research – with important exceptions (Arnold and Innes, 1984) – favoured export crops. Health benefits in the colonies were confined to smallish employment effects. Research has partly shifted since independence towards rice and wheat. In most of Africa, and much of Asia and Latin America, however, the poorest, nutritionally vulnerable groups eat mainly cheaper or more locally available staples: sorghum, millet, cassava, yams, and to a lesser extent maize. Maize hybrids have helped their nutrition somewhat in a few countries, but development since about 1970 has been slow.

The true 'green revolution' for the poor since the mid-1970s has been the development and spread in India of drought-resistant high-yielding main-season sorghums and finger millets (Rajpurohit, 1983; Rao, 1982). Major progress in African health largely depends on similar successes (also with cassava and yams (Hartmans, 1985)). Such research depends for nutritional success upon developing varieties and practices, tested as profitable and safe in production and 'child-friendly' in consumption, in the context of traditional poor households and their farming and consuming systems (including intercropping, especially with pulses, and sometimes shifting cultivation (Maxwell, 1985)). Such research – and indeed all bio-research on root crops, sorghum and millet – is much weaker in national research systems, especially in Africa, than in international systems. It is into the former that health professionals need to infiltrate; for success in using international or non-local biological research, where quantified, proves heavily dependent on the scale of national or local research (Evenson and Kislev, 1976) and hence adaptive capacity.

Social structures, agricultural policies and projects, and the poorest

Structural issues affect the health outcome of any agricultural technology. That is why – given the health and agricultural technology – a familiar few countries such as China, Cuba, Costa Rica, and Sri Lanka attain much lower age-specific mortality and morbidity than one would predict from their income levels (Morris, 1979; Sen 1980). The main reason why poor people often fail to gain nutritionally from agricultural projects, and sometimes lose, is that they do not participate in them (Pines, 1983, p. 45; Mason, 1983, p. 93) – or participate too late, so that the big gains have been seized by early participants (Binswanger, 1980, p. 180; Anderson and Pandey, 1985:8; Lipton and Longhurst, 1985, pp. 24–5). They participate late, or not at all, because of the structure of assets, laws or customs which deny non-participants (be they small farmers, tenants, the remote, the low-caste, the female, or just the poor) access to the benefits. Health professionals can seldom change such structures but should describe their effects, and the effects of alternatives, and help agricultural professionals to design and implement projects that allow for, and if possible improve, the impact of current (or changing) structures on project participation by vulnerable groups.

One health-related structure is the 'urban versus rural'. In general, death-rates are much higher in rural than in urban places, often increasingly so. In India, rural infant mortality is about double the urban rate (Mitra, 1979, p. 133; Ruzicka, 1982, p. 29–39). In Africa, profound influences on the urban-rural power balance (Lipton, 1977, 1984) bear a major responsibility for excess rural death and disease, by impeding redirection of resources from lower-priority, but more powerful or articulate, urban users to vulnerable rural groups. Under the banner of 'health for all', many health professionals try to redirect *health* resources (preventive measures, primary care, and family planning) so as to reduce infections and infestations among rural vulnerable groups and thus to lower their nutritional *requirements*. However, there is too little analysis and promotion of the health gains from similarly redirecting *productive* resources to agriculture and rural industry, thereby raising vulnerable groups' income and hence their *command over, and the availability of,* health and nutrition.

Land structure and health

The size of a rural family's operational landholding is usually strongly related to its income, consumption, and hence health status and risks (FAO, 1984, pp. 43–5; for Machakos, Kenya; p. 87 for the Philippines; Pines, 1983, p. 59, for Peru; Vaughan and Flinn, 1983, for El Salvador; Huffman *et al.*, 1983, for Bangladesh; Wijga *et al.*, 1983, and Lipton, 1983, p. 38, for Gujarat, India). The Machakos study shows that low landholding *per person* is linked very weakly to stunting but strongly to wasting. Thus only wasting, corresponding closely to a risk of *severe* undernutrition, is strongly correlated with land poverty.

A major exception to the 'land shortage, poverty, ill-health' nexus arises in areas where land is bad, unreliably watered, and/or not scarce. There, rural nutritional and health status changes very little as the size of a household's agricultural holding increases from zero to 3–5 hectares (Visaria, 1978, 1980; Lipton, 1985), but appears to be raised mainly by off-farm income sources. Tenancy status (e.g. owner or tenant) is related to income and health, if at all, much more weakly than is holding size (Ibid).

Health professionals should therefore not expect major health gains from *tenancy reform*. This is – in the absence of land redistribution – anyway almost impossible to implement either effectively or without damaging side-effects on vulnerable groups (Herring, 1983; Lipton, 1974). On the other hand, *land subdivision* (of large farms into small family-farmed holdings), not only increases many poor peasants' access to income and hence food and health. It also usually raises agricultural output in the medium term (Ibid.; Berry and Cline, 1979), and probably raises the proportion of it comprising food, notably inexpensive foods grown and eaten by vulnerable groups. Wherever land redistribution could be on the political agenda, health professionals should analyse the likely impact on health, especially for landless labourers. Many of these are unlikely to benefit from extra land; and reducing their employment income from the large-farm sector could leave then more vulnerable than before. However, most experience suggests that the much higher labour/hectare ratio of small family farmers outweighs their lower hire/self-employment ratio, leaving the landless at least as much employed after the subdivision as before.

Other asset structures and health

If land is bad, plentiful, or not a major factor of production, vulnerable groups' income (and hence health and nutrition) depends much more upon their access to other assets, such as fishing boats (FAO, 1984, p. 84), or draught animals (Govt. of Botswana, 1975), or small urban capital, often neglected in slum upgrading (Yeh, 1984, p. 59; Cook, 1984, p. 82). Policies for agricultural structure are relevant to all three routes to income and health for the poor, since agriculture is the main income source for over 10 per cent of Third World *urban* workers, and a much larger proportion of the most nutritionally vulnerable families, those headed by female casual labourers.

In country (including plantations) and city alike, many otherwise landless people have a tiny home garden. With appropriate inputs (especially water) research and extension (often for underinvestigated traditional foodstuffs) home gardens could be provided, enlarged or intensified for many of the ultra-poor. They often contribute much more to nutrition, at low cost, even where land is scarce, highly unequal, and politically not reformable. But appropriate water inputs, research and extension are needed (Brownrigg, 1985).

The vulnerable are also more likely to own smallstock – rabbits and backyard poultry, as well as sheep and goats – than cattle. Smallstock, relatively neglected in research and extension, offer urban as well as rural opportunities and could provide substantial extra income, and hence nutrition and health, where most needed.

The policy lesson is simple. Even if land is scarce and structurally unreformable, other agricultural assets can often be created, restructured or redistributed – by changing the incentives and markets, or by more direct State actions – with great benefit to the nutrition and health of vulnerable groups. Notably, smallstock and home gardens provide work and income directly to mothers while they care for children, in many cultures where draught cattle and agricultural land preparation are male-dominated.

Health impact of food price policy: who is at risk?

Two areas of general policy – on prices and on food strategies – raise a key issue for health professionals: that the health impact of a policy is dependent on who the vulnerable groups are. For example, does State action to repress average food prices improve health? If almost all poor households in a typical year are smallish family farmers and net sellers of food, as in much of sub-Saharan Africa, the answer is a plain no. If the great majority of them are net food buyers, as in heavily urbanised Colombia, the answer may well be yes (Scobie and Posada, 1978). If – as increasingly in eastern India – the very poor are dependent, not on urban work or on their own farms, but on employment *by* farmers, the impact of agricultural price repression is complex: they gain temporarily from cheaper food, but lose income in the medium term, as agricultural production (usually labour-intensive) and employment are discouraged relative to other activities. The impact of repression of food prices upon seasonal and year-to-year instability needs review; such instability hits the poor hardest (FAO, 1984, p. 91).

Health professionals seldom feel called upon to explore the link between health provision and food prices. Yet when or where a doctor is most use, or this or that drug is most needed, is *critically* determined – in countries where nutrition–infection–parasite synergisms are the main causes of death and disease – by the level and variation of food prices. Those who form agricultural price policy, too, should be aware of the consequences for the nutrition and health of vulnerable groups. Even 'no policy' is a price policy for food. Even quite widely shared growth, missing out (say) one in four people whether vulnerable or not, will shift first demand, and later supply and investment and research (Pachico, 1984, p. 30), to superior food crops. The medium-term effect – after an initial price fall as demand falls – is probably greater scarcity and *higher* prices for the 'inferior' foods of those consumers who remain poor and vulnerable (Lipton, 1975), for example, as marginal lands shift from coarse cereals to dairy products.

'Food strategy': as if food mattered

Unlike pricing, 'food strategy' (Heald and Lipton, 1984) appears to imply policies favourable to health and nutrition. However, this is only one of four possible goals for a national food strategy. The strategies for Kenya, Mali, Rwanda and Zambia, supported with cash and technical assistance from the EEC, stress above all self-sufficiency (i.e. import elimination) for major food staples; higher farm production; far behind, 'food security'; and much further behind still, reduction or elimination of undernutrition.

The very low priority of nutrition and health in the four *operational* national food strategies, and in IMF and World Bank advice on stabilisation and structural adjustment, reflects doubts about the real impact of such policies on hunger. Yet the massive public support in many rich countries for international assistance to poor countries is heavily focused upon health, nutrition and other humanitarian concerns (as witness the Western popular response to the African famines of 1983–5). On such public support, aid flows ultimately depend, and with them, in part, the salaries of experts in donor and recipient agencies who handle 'food strategies', price policy reform, and structural adjustment. Health professionals should analyse, for these functionaries, the effects of agriculture-related and macroeconomic policies on the health of the poor. Armed with such analyses, they can then reasonably suggest that, since Western popular concern largely pays the functionaries' salaries, major decisions (including macropolicies) affecting agriculture be vetted for their impact on vulnerable groups. By ensuring that decisions are screened – and changed – for their effects on such groups' health and nutrition, health professionals in the development community can significantly contribute to the achievement of the central causes (child welfare, poverty alleviation) to which Hans Singer has so fruitfully dedicated the past forty years of his twin academic and operational careers.

Note

1. This paper is a version of part of my contribution to a joint study, with Emanuel de Kadt, of 'Agriculture-Health-Linkages', to be published by the World Health Organisation. I am grateful to Dr de Kadt for numerous

comments and exchange of ideas, and also to Dr Richard Laing and members of WHO for valuable comments on an earlier draft.

References

ANDERSON, J. and S. PANDEY (1985) 'Assessing impact of agricultural research centres on efficiency and equity objectives', mimeo, Australian Agricultural Economic Society, annual conference. (Armidale).

ARNOLD, M. and N. INNES (1984) 'Plant breeding for crop improvement with special reference to Africa', in D. L. Hawksworth (ed.) *Advancing Agricultural Production in Africa* (Oxford: Commonwealth Agricultural Bureau) pp. 169–174.

BECKFORD, G. L. (1972) *Persistent Poverty* (New York: Oxford University Press).

BERG. A. (1981) *Malnourished People: A Policy View* (Washington DC: World Bank).

BERRY, A. and W. CLINE (1979) *Agrarian Structure and Productivity in Developing Countries* (Baltimore: Johns Hopkins University Press).

BINSWANGER, H. (1978) *The Economic of Tractorization in South Asia* (Washington DC: ADC).

BINSWANGER, H. (1980) 'Income distribution effects of technical change: some analytical issues', *South-East Asian Economic Review*, vol. 1 (3) December, pp. 179–218.

BROWNRIGG, L. (1985) *Home Gardening in International Development* (Washington DC: League of International Food Education).

BULL, D. (1982) *A Growing Problem: Pesticides and the Third World Poor* (Oxford: Oxfam).

BULL, D. (1983) 'Pesticides and the Third World poor', *Social Action*, vol. 33 (2).

CHAMBERS, R. (1982) 'Health, agriculture and rural poverty: why seasons matter', *Journal of Development Studies*, vol. 18 (2).

CHAMBERS, R., R. LONGHURST and A. PACEY (eds) (1981) *Seasonal Dimensions to Rural Poverty* (London: Pinter).

CHIKANZA, I., D. PAXTON, R. LOEWENSON and R. LAING (1982) 'The health status of farmworker communities in Zimbabwe', *Central African Journal of Medicine*, vol. 27 (5), pp. 88–91.

CIAT (1981) *Cassava Programme Annual Report* (Cali).

COOK, D. B. (1984) 'Building codes and regulations in low-income settlements', in Richards and Thomson (eds).

CROOK, N. and T. DYSUN (eds) (1984) *India's Demography: Essays on the Contemporary Population* (New Delhi: South Asia).

DANDEKAR, K. and M. SATHE (1980) 'Employment guarantee and food-for-work programme', *Economic and Political Weekly*, vol. XV (15), 12 April.

DASGUPTA, B. (1977) *Village Society and Labour Use* (New Delhi: Oxford University Press).

EVENSON, R. and Y. KISLEV (1976) *Agricultural Research and Productivity* (New Haven, Conn.: Yale University Press).

FAO (1983) *Community Level Statistics*, Economic and Social Development Paper, no. 33 (Rome).

FAO (1984) *Integrating Nutrition into Agricultural and Rural Development Projects: Six Case Studies*, Nutrition in Agriculture Series, no. 2 (Rome).

FLINN, J. C. and L. J. UNNEVEHR (1984) 'Contributions of modern rice varieties to nutrition in Asia – an IRRI perspective', in Pinstrup-Andersen *et al.* (eds) *International Agricultural Research and Human Nutrition*.

GOLDSMITH, E. and N. HILDYARD (1984) *The Social and Environmental Effects of Large Dams: Vol. 1: Overview* (Camelford: Wadebridge Ecological Centre).

GONZALES, L. A. and B. M. REGALDO (1983) 'The distributional impact of food policies on nutritional intake in the Philippines' (Los Banos: IRRI).

GOVERNMENT OF BOTSWANA (1975) *Rural Income Distribution Survey* (Gaborone: CSO).

HARTMANS, E. (1985) 'Increasing the pace of development in sub-Saharan Africa: the role of IITA', mimeo (Ibadan).

HAYAMI, Y. and R. HERDT (1977) 'Market price effects of technical change on income distribution in semi-subsistence agriculture', *American Journal of Agricultural Economics*, vol. 59 (2).

HEALD, C. and M. LIPTON (1984) *The EC and African Food Strategies*, Working Document, no. 12 (Economics) (Brussels: Centre for European Policy Studies).

HERRING, R. (1983) *Land to the Tiller* (New Haven, Conn.: Yale University Press).

HUFFMAN, S., A. HUQUE and A. ZAHIDUL (1983) 'Pre-school child nutrition in Bangladesh', mimeo (Baltimore: Johns Hopkins University Press).

HUNTER, J. M. (1980) *Disease Prevention and Control in Water Development Schemes*, World Health Organisation, PDP/80.1, mimeo (Geneva).

ICRISAT (1982) *Sorghum in the Eighties* (Patancheru, India)

INTERNATIONAL FUND FOR AGRICULTURAL DEVELOPMENT (IFAD) (1983) *Nutritional Impact of Agricultural Projects* (Rome: UN-ACC-SCN).

JODHA, N. S. (1984) 'ICRISAT research and human nutrition', in Pinstrup-Andersen *et al.* (eds) (1984).

JUL, M. (1979) 'Unexpected benefits from a dairy project', *Food and Nutrition Bulletin*, vol. 1(3).

KUMAR, S. (1977) *Role of the Household Economy in Determining Child Nutrition in Kerala*, Occ. Paper no. 95 (Ithaca, NY: Cornell University Press).

LEHMANN, D. (ed.) (1974) *Agrarian Reform and Agrarian Reformism: Studies of Peru, Chile, China and India* (London: Faber & Faber).

LIPTON, M. (1974) 'Towards a theory of land reform', in Lehmann (ed.)

LIPTON, M. (1975) 'Urban bias and food policy in poor countries', *Food Policy*, vol. 1(1).

LIPTON, M. (1977) *Why Poor People Stay Poor* (London: Temple Smith).

LIPTON, M. (1982) 'Post-harvest technology and the reduction of hunger', *IDS Bulletin*, vol. 13(3).

LIPTON, M. (1983) *Poverty, Undernutrition and Hunger*, Staff Working Paper, no. 597 (Washington DC: World Bank).

LIPTON, M. (1983a) *Labor and Poverty*, Staff Working Paper, no. 616 (Washington DC: World Bank).

LIPTON, M. (1984) 'Urban bias revisited', *Journal of Development Studies*, vol. 2(3).

LIPTON, M. (1985) *Land Assets and Rural Poverty*, Staff Working Paper, no. 744 (Washington DC: World Bank).

LIPTON, M. (1985a) *The Place of Agricultural Research in the Development of sub-Saharan Africa*, Discussion Paper, no. 202 (Brighton: Institute of Development Studies).

LIPTON, M. and R. LONGHURST (1985) *Modern Varieties, International Agricultural Research and the Poor*, Study Paper, no. 2, CGIAR Impact Study (Washington DC: World Bank).

LONGHURST, R. (1984) *The Energy Trap: Work, Nutrition and Child Malnutrition in Northern Nigeria*, Cornell International Nutrition Monograph Series, no. 13 (Ithaca, NY: Cornell University Press).

LONGHURST, R. (1985) 'Agricultural strategies, food and nutrition: issues and opportunities', 15th Annual Conference of McCarrison Society, Oxford (forthcoming in *Nutrition and Health*, 1986).

LONGHURST, R. and P. PAYNE (1979) 'Seasonal aspects of nutrition: review of evidence and policy implications', *Discussion Paper*, no. 145 (Brighton: Institute of Development Studies).

MARGA INSTITUTE (1984) *Intersectoral Action for Health: Sri Lanka Study* (Colombo).

MASON, J. B. (1983) 'Minimum data needs for assessing the nutritional effects of agricultural and rural development projects', in IFAD, 1983.

MAXWELL, S. (1985) *Farming Systems Research*, Discussion Paper, no. 198, (Brighton: Institute of Development Studies).

MAYER, J. (1985) 'Nutrition and health in Africa', 1985 Workshop on Alleviation of Poverty, mimeo (Geneva: Centre for Applied Studies in International Negotiations).

McJUNKIN, F. E., L. REY and D. SCOTT (1982) *Water and Human Health* (Washington DC: USAID).

MILLER, D. (1982) 'Factors affecting energy expenditure', *Proceedings of the Nutritional Society*, vol. 41.

MITRA, A. (1979) *India's Population: Aspects of Quality and Control*, vol. 1 (Delhi: ICSSR).

MORRIS, M. D. (1979) *Measuring the Condition of the World's Poor: The PQLI Index* (Oxford: Pergamon Press).

MUSCAT, R. J. (1983) 'Introduction', in IFAD, 1983.

PACHICO, D. H. (1984) 'Nutritional objectives in agricultural research – the case of CIAT', in Pinstrup-Andersen *et al.* (eds) (1984).

PANIKAR, P. G. K. and C. R. SOMAN (1984) *Health Status of Kerala* (Trivandrum: Centre for Development Studies).

PINES, J. M. (1983) 'Nutritional consequences of agricultural projects: evidence and response', in IFAD, 1983.

PINSTRUP-ANDERSEN, P. (1981) *Nutritional Consequences of Agricultural Projects: Conceptual Relationships and Assessment Approaches*, Staff

Working Paper, no. 456 (Washington DC: World Bank).

PINSTRUP-ANDERSEN, P. (1984) 'Incorporating agricultural goals into the design of international agricultural research – an overview', in Pinstrup-Andersen *et al.* (eds) (1984).

PINSTRUP-ANDERSEN, P., A. BERG and M. FORMAN (eds) (1984) *International Agricultural Research and Human Nutrition* (Washington DC: IFPRI/UN-ACC-SCN).

RAJPUROHIT, A. (1983) 'Recent trends in agricultural growth in Karnataka', *Indian Journal of Agricultural Economics*, vol. 38(4).

RAO, N. (1982) 'Transforming traditional sorghum in India', in ICRISAT, 1982, vol. 1.

REUTLINGER, S. (1983) 'Nutritional impact of agricultural projects: conceptual framework', in IFAD, 1983.

REUTLINGER, S. and M. SELOWSKY (1976) 'Malnutrition and Poverty: Magnitude and Policy Options', *World Bank Staff Occasional Papers*, no. 23 (Baltimore: Johns Hopkins University Press for the World Bank).

RICHARDS, P. (1985) *Indigenous Agricultural Revolution* (London: Hutchinson).

RICHARDS, P. J. and A. M. THOMSON (1984) *Basic Needs and the Urban Poor: the Provision of Communal Services* (London: Croom Helm).

RUZICKA, L. (1982) 'Mortality in India', mimeo, British Soc. for Population Studies, Oxford Conf., Dec. 1982 (reprinted in Crook and Dyson, 1984).

RYAN, J. G. (1984) 'The effects of the international agricultural research centres on human nutrition – catalogue and commentary', in Pinstrup-Andersen *et al.* (eds).

SCHOFIELD, S. (1974) 'Seasonal factors affecting nutrition in different age-groups', *Journal of Development Studies*, vol. 11(1).

SCOBIE, G. and R. POSADA, T. (1978) 'The impact of technical change on income distribution: the case of rice in Colombia', *American Journal of Agricultural Economics*, vol. 60 (1).

SEN. A. K. (1980) *Levels of Poverty: Policy and Change*, Staff Working Paper, no. 401 (Washington DC: World Bank).

TAYLOR, N. (1985) *The Smoke Ring* (London: Sphere Books).

TRIPP, R. (1984) 'Production research at the IARCs and its goals', in Pinstrup-Andersen *et al.* (eds) (1984).

TWOSE, N. (1984) *Cultivating Hunger* (London: Oxfam).

VALLE-RIESTRA, J. (1984) 'The incorporation of nutritional goals into the research design at CIP', in Pinstrup-Andersen *et al.* (eds) (1984).

VAUGHAN, S. and W. FLINN (1983) 'Socio-economic factors associated with undernourished children: El Salvador rural poor survey; June 1977–July 1978' (Washington DC: USDA–USAID).

VISARIA, P. (1978) *Size of Landholding in Rural Western India*, ESCAP–IBRD Working Paper, no. 3 (Washington DC: World Bank).

VISARIA, P. (1980) *Poverty and Living Standards in Asia* (Washington DC: LSMS, World Bank).

WIJGA, A. *et al.* (1983) 'Feeding, illness, and nutritional status of young children in rural Gujarat', *Human Nutrition: Clinical Nutrition*, vol. 37(7).

WORLD BANK, UNDP and GOVERNMENT OF FRANCE (1985) *Study*

on Options and Investment Priorities in Irrigation Development, Project INT/82/001, Annex 3 'The ex-ante Assessment of the Health Impacts of Irrigation Projects' Third workshop on Irrigation Investment Analysis (Washington DC: World Bank).

YEH, S. (1984) 'Urban low-income housing in South-east Asia', in Richards and Thomson (eds).

Part III

Responses

8 Aid for Development: What Motivates the Donors

Raymond H. Hopkins

International aid serves complex and diverse political, economic and humanitarian purposes. The principles that govern aid transactions among states consequently do not constitute a coherent regime; rather they are fraught with tension and contradictions. This is a major reason why the effects of aid as a development tool, ending poverty, underdevelopment and hunger in developing countries, are seldom optimal. Development as discussed here means simply that aid causes a net improvement in the rate of economic growth in recipient countries with attention to efficiency and equity considerations.

Both the givers and receivers of aid have always been motivated by other goals than development. Indeed broad forces shape the size and allocation of aid, and this limits the prospects for development-oriented analysis to be effective. Practitioners and theorists of development do well to recognise these broader forces. They set limits within which development uses of aid may be pursued. They also constitute an arena within which development-minded analysts must work if they seek to affect the general principles and specific practices used in administering aid.

This essay briefly reviews the evolution of the post-1945 aid regime, and then discusses the role that development criteria play in that regime. Development economists, I believe, have influenced changes in aid, especially food aid, a commodity which has been accused of being especially perverse for development. The argument I offer is that some major changes in rules and practices of aid have occurred that cannot be explained by political factors, and instead result from the impact of theories and arguments of development strategists.

REVIEW OF THE AID REGIME

Two unique features mark the relations among states in the forty years

153

since the Second World War. First, thanks to the dangers of nuclear weapons, there have arisen extensive, enduring and interdependent security arrangements. Second, thanks to global economic ties, complex mechanisms have evolved through which rich states transfer resources to poor and weak states. These features have few precedents in international affairs.[1]

The result is that 'co-operation' among peoples of diverse cultures and situations has reached levels unprecedented in world history. This 'co-operation' is, of course, embedded in a framework of East–West power conflicts and North–South economic conflicts. These two overlapping antagonisms, however, merely reinforce the joint interests of states in avoiding the mutual calamities that would be produced by nuclear war, on the one hand, or world depression, on the other hand.

The evolution of economic co-operation and in particular the system of economic aid has both symbolic (principles, norms) and material (cash, food, technical assistance) components. Since the Second World War four major changes have occurred in the evolution of foreign aid. First, mechanisms for transferring resources have moved from *ad hoc* arrangements to institutionalised rules and practices. Second, the flow of aid resources has shifted from war depleted states to poor Third World recipients. Third, principles shaping aid have moved towards giving greater priority to the economic development of recipients. Fourth, multilateral channels for aid have expanded along with recipient power over aid.

Referring to aid as a regime emphasises the symbolic component of aid activity, and focuses on the third aspect of change mentioned above. By 'regime', political scientists refer to the principles, norms, rules and practices which govern aid resource transfers (Krasner, 1983; Hopkins and Puchala, 1979). These features are manifest in the language and words used to regulate aid. Different regime features may be found in the detailed legal language of specific aid agreements, the legislation of various policy bodies, and the philosophical declarations of the speeches by legislators and chief executives. An example of the latter is Robert McNamara's 1973 address to the World Bank's Board of Governors, a signal event in the shift in focus towards making rural poverty a major goal of economic assistance.[2] Such words do more than justify aid; they give it meaning and constrain its uses. These subjective features are as important a factor in aid as its tangible aspects. They have an impact on decisions of who gets aid and they encourage different policies within recipient states. A norm of 'adjustment with a human face', for example, carries with it an implication for welfare consideration not otherwise included in macroeconomic policy and IMF lending.

Unlike the flow of words, the material characteristics of aid are carefully recorded and statistically analysed. Annual reviews by the Development Assistance Committee (DAC) of the Organisation for Economic Co-operation and Development (OECD) make a major contribution here. The DAC's recordkeeping of concessional resource flows is a particularly useful compendium for tracing physical aid transactions and the shifts in these. More generally, the DAC promotes co-ordination and effective use of aid from the major Western donor states. (Its members are shown in Table 8.1.) This committee and the larger OECD body were created in response to the organisational requirements of the original massive economic recovery programme (the Marshall Plan) launched by the United States after the Second World War. The DAC, along with the World Bank, the World Food Programme, the United Nations Development Programme, three regional banks, and a myriad of national and regional aid bureaucracies, constitute a network of donor supported organisations for managing aid. Altogether the historical growth of those bodies has institutionalised the aid mechanism in world affairs.

Let us turn to a review of material aid flows. In 1983 official development assistance (ODA) to the developing world amounted to over 36 billion dollars. Of this, 76 per cent came from DAC members, approximately 15 per cent came from OPEC states and the remaining 9 per cent from the Soviet Union and Eastern Europe (OECD, 1984a, p. 207). In 1970 aid (in constant 1982 dollars) was 21.8 billion dollars; thus the growth to 36 billion in 1983 (Ibid., pp. 64–5) was a rise of 67 per cent. This real growth in aid has been largely contributed by the DAC countries. The major rise (in real terms) occurred in the years immediately after the 1973–4 economic crisis.

A second noteworthy trend in the material aspects of aid has been the decline in the portion of aid provided by the United States. In 1960, the USA provided over half of official development assistance (ODA), but it gave less than 30 per cent in 1983. The decline of the USA as the hegemonic state in the world's economy was paralleled by a few other states. As the figures in Table 8.1 show, colonial and hegemonic states generally, including France, the UK and the USA, have given relatively declining amounts of aid both as a share of all aid, but especially as a share of their national economy. This decline in ODA in the 1960s and 1970s continues a trend of the 1950s. In 1946–8,

Table 8.1 DAC countries' contributions to official development assistance, 1960–83 (shown in millions of US$ and as a percentage of GNP)

	1960		1966		1971		1975		1981		1983	
Australia	59	0.38	126	0.53	202	0.53	507	0.60	650	0.41	753	0.49
Austria			13	0.11	12	0.07	64	0.17	220	0.33	158	0.23
Belgium	101	0.88	76	0.45	146	0.50	378	0.59	575	0.59	480	0.59
Canada	75	0.20	187	0.38	391	0.42	880	0.55	1189	0.43	1429	0.45
Denmark	5	0.09	21	0.13	74	0.43	205	0.58	403	0.73	395	0.73
Finland							48	0.18	135	0.28	153	0.33
France	847	1.38	745	0.75	1075	0.66	2093	0.62	4177	0.73	3815	0.74
Germany	237	0.33	419	0.38	734	0.34	1689	0.40	3181	0.47	3176	0.49
Italy	91	0.27	78	0.14	183	0.18	182	0.11	666	0.19	827	0.24
Japan	105	0.24	283	0.29	511	0.23	1148	0.23	3171	0.28	3761	0.33
Netherlands	35	0.31	94	0.36	216	0.68	604	0.75	1510	1.08	1195	0.91
New Zealand							66	0.52	68	0.29	61	0.28
Norway	5	0.11	14	0.16	42	0.33	184	0.66	467	0.82	584	1.06
Portugal	37	1.46	22	0.59	99	1.42						
Sweden	7	0.05	57	0.19	159	0.44	566	0.82	919	0.83	754	0.85
Switzerland	4	0.04	13	0.09	28	0.11	104	0.19	237	0.24	320	0.32
United Kingdom	407	0.56	486	0.47	562	0.41	863	0.37	2192	0.43	1605	0.35
United States	2702	0.54	3349	0.49	3324	0.32	4007	0.26	5782	0.20	7992	0.24
TOTAL DAC	4718	0.55	5984	0.44	7762	0.35	13,587	0.35	25,540	0.35	27,458	0.36

Source: DAC, Development Cooperation, 1969, '73, '78, '83, '84 (Paris: OECD).

for example, the United States provided resources amounting to 1.78 per cent of its GNP, largely aimed at stimulating world economic recovery. In this period the major multilateral economic institutions of the World Bank and the IMF were founded. After 1950, however, both the US share of total aid and its aid as a portion of GNP declined.[3] The World Food Programme and UN Development Programme (UNDP), which were set up in the early 1960s, did little to arrest the USA's declining role. In 1983, its aid stood at 0.25 per cent of its GNP. Britain, France and other colonial powers also reduced their relative ODA commitments in the 1970s, declining to about half the portion of GNP in 1983 compared to 1960. The Soviet Union, on the other hand, as a rising hegemonic state, began its aid efforts in the 1950s. In the post-war period it had been a net extractor of resources from conquered states. After the late 1960s, however, Soviet bloc aid has been stagnant.

A third set of material changes occurred with respect to the distribution of aid among recipients. This seems to reflect both changing donor motivations and the 'success' of some countries able to 'graduate' from the need for aid. Over the last two decades, the proportion of total aid to Latin America has declined. In addition, and more dramatically, aid has shifted away from the well-off states of this region. Brazil and Peru received over half the region's ODA in 1961, but were accorded less than 3 per cent in 1983 (see Table 8.2). For many states in this area, especially Brazil, commercial borrowing substituted for credit needs previously met by aid. Asian states remained in 1961–83 the largest aid recipients. They were not, however, thanks to their large populations, the largest recipients on a per capita basis. The portion of aid to Asia has in fact also declined – from 49 per cent of ODA in 1971 to 37 per cent in 1983. India, still the largest single aid recipient, has correspondingly seen its share of aid dwindle; it received one-third of all aid in the 1960s, but got less than 20 per cent in 1983. Especially poor Asian states, such as Bangladesh, have enjoyed some increases, as the goal of attacking poverty has come to play a larger role in allocation. Recipients in Africa, the world's poorest region, have commanded heightened attention. It is the only region whose share of aid has grown since 1961. In this region humanitarian emergency relief motives have been a factor. The result is that on a per capita basis aid to twenty-four low-income African states averaged $12.63 in 1982 compared to $1.42 for eleven Asian states. Thus in Asia, Bangladesh, one of the poorest aid recipients, received less than $10 per capita of concessional aid in

Table 8.2   Major recipients of aid from DAC countries, 1960–83 (in millions of US$ of Official Development Assistance, current prices)

	1961	1966	1971	1976	1980	1983
ASIA	2235	3199	3598	5190	12 896	11 162
India	662	1226	997	1321	1915	1722
Indonesia	133	82	588	668	975	739
Philippines	23	68	70	187	376	424
Sri Lanka		32	55	134	378	470
Vietnam	173	509	460	179	242	106
AFRICA	1657	1591	1962	4578	10 572	10 048
Egypt	127	66	39	776	1293	1444
Ethiopia		41	47	141	241	251
Ivory Coast		44	51	108	124	156
Kenya	65	66	67	160	449	397
Nigeria	33	93	107	53	41	47
Senegal		44	53	118	400	314
Tanzania	41	39	61	267	673	577
Zaire	87	90	108	194	394	314
LATIN AMERICA	876	1180	929	1314	3218	3371
Brazil	342	259	120	111	235	98
Chile	130	151	27	8	−7	1
Colombia	66	96	105	77	102	84
Mexico	64	126	16	63	100	131
Peru	−13	66	38	74	233	288
TOTAL	5577	6861	7449	13 374	33 791	29 992

Source: DAC, *Development Cooperation 1965, '69, '75, '78, '84* (Paris: OECD); OPEC Assistance included after 1977.

1982 compared to $27 per capita for Kenya, $54 for Liberia, $64 for Lesotho and $89 for Gabon (OECD, 1984b; Lele, 1981).

Politics also lies behind the rise and fall of aid to particular states and between bilateral and multilateral channels. Note the decline of aid to Vietnam (Table 8.2) following the Communist take-over in 1975. The loss of Western aid was not fully offset by the rise in Soviet bloc aid. Concomitantly, political factors account for the rise of aid to Egypt after 1974 and to Sri Lanka after 1977 as more Western leaning leaders came to power in these states. More culturally based political favoritism is found, for example, in the large amounts of aid going to Israel from the USA, or to Tanzania from Scandinavian countries, or to Gabon from France. The political strength of developing countries as a bloc and their preference for multilateral aid is one part of the story behind the shift of aid toward multilateral channels. The multilateral share of ODA rose from 26 per cent of DAC donors in 1972–4 to 32 per cent in 1981–3. The 'voting' power of groups, such as the Group of 77, is reflected in their capacity to secure changes in the rules and procedures by which multilateral agencies operate. Although Krasner (1985, pp. 127–75) finds regime changes in multilateral agencies solely the result of power interests and power gains by the developing countries, their 'success' has been almost exclusively in areas supported by development analysts, and developing country initiatives that were defeated, such as the NIEO proposals, including the common fund to stabilise commodity trade, were opposed by most analysts. The pattern of success and failure corresponds substantially to the positive and negative assessments of the new proposals by the majority of academic analysts.

The same factors that account for changes in aid flows – a mixture of political, economic, and humanitarian motivations – also alter regime principles and norms. Most notably, there has been a change in the degree to which economic development criteria are found in the norms and rules that affect the allocation of aid among recipients and the acceptability of various end uses. For example, even for countries like Egypt, where aid has strong political motivations, the effects of aid on economic development are a major concern of donors. The invention of policy based lending, the shift in structural adjustment loans to a softer set of conditions, and the targeting of project aid on rural and agricultural sectors have all been ideas put into practice. Such changes in the aid regime point to the role played by development analysts in reshaping regime principles and practices through their research and writings.[4]

The role of analysts has been substantial. Their efforts have provided justifications for maintaining aid as original alliance-maintaining objectives receded and helped set new normative directions. Their intellectual arguments have been an important part of the struggle over allocation outcomes. For example, in cases where aid has become widely perceived as a failure in fostering development, say because it saps initiative, encourages faulty policy or maintains neo-colonial dependency, levels of interest in and support for aid among donors and recipients have been affected. Witness the decline in aid to Tanzania after 1980 although its international political position had not changed. What did change was the evaluation of the effect of aid and the appropriateness of Tanzania's own development policies.[5]

Analysts who are advocates of aid seek to analyse the conditions under which desirable objectives for both donors and recipients can be achieved. Their criticisms promote reform not abandonment. Over the last thirty to forty years, as aid has become increasingly institutionalised, the principles that justify and shape its dispersal have evolved towards the rationale of worldwide development. For example, within bilateral and multilateral agencies, the criteria for preparing and evaluating projects reflect this. Another change in the aid regime is that domestic policies of recipients have become increasingly important, while the tying of aid, for instance food aid, to specific commodities or supplying countries has come to be seen as decreasingly appropriate *per se*. Many of these trends in the aid regime's framework were preceded by analytical arguments. Hans Singer, for example, has argued consistently for the creation of co-ordinated, recipient-specific and policy-based aid provisions as opposed to unilateral, project-tied, or universal criteria (Singer, 1965; Isenman and Singer, 1977).

The changes that have occurred affect the aid regime generally, but have had special significance for the often suspect component of food aid. The food aid component of the major donors' aid contributions ranges from 3 to 20 per cent. Because food aid has had strong ties to domestic farm policy and surplus disposal needs in donor states, and has been extensively used to support political–military objectives, notably by the USA in countries such as Vietnam, Portugal and Egypt, this type of aid has been an especially dubious resource transfer for those aiming to achieve development. In the remainder of this essay these claims will be amplified – reviewing the political–economic motivations that support and shape the allocations of aid, and highlighting changes in the aid regime generally, and in food aid in particular.

MOTIVATIONS OF AID DONORS

Multiple interests support aid. These are expressed through a variety of social and organisational forms in donors, including the economic and foreign policy bureaucracies. The principal goals of these interests have been identified in a number of studies of aid (Wall, 1973; White, 1974; Nelson, 1968; Spero, 1977). Broadly categorised, these are political, economic and humanitarian. Private charitable flows are particularly related to this last motivation, although certain government aid can also be largely humanitarian.

Political goals

In its broadest sense, aid provides legitimacy for the international economic order established after the Second World War. This includes respect for organisations such as the IMF, the World Bank and the United Nations. The rules of aid giving are set by the industrialised North. They have been only partly resilient to changes proposed by the South. As a result facilities for assistance at the IMF and World Bank have expanded, developing countries have been able to encourage new funding programmes such as the UNDP and the International Fund for Agricultural Development (IFAD) and to have altered, more lenient criteria for lending adopted. All this has helped keep a broad constituency of support for international liberal capitalist rules, including rules of debt repayment and accountability of aid.

Particular donors, using bilateral aid, pursue more specific political aims. Most common of these is the cementing of foreign policy accords between donor and recipient, as between the Soviet Union and Cuba, France and Senegal, or the USA and the Philippines. Governments receive support according to particular donors' own predispositions. As a result at present Sudan receives more aid than Ethiopia and Sri Lanka does better than Vietnam. These flows change with changing political relationships, however. In other cases specific *quid pro quos* may be involved. For example, Soviet aid to Vietnam can be associated with the soviet naval base at Camn Rahn Bay, while US aid to the Philippines is closely tied to naval and air bases there. Votes in the UN also count; the USA reduced Zimbabwe's aid in 1984 in response to unfriendly votes, for example. Finally political goals within a recipient country may be pursued through aid. Donors may wish to help avoid domestic turmoil by maintaining middle-class satisfaction or may wish to bolster the power of a particular group, usually the one currently in control of the government, by providing aid designed to enhance that group. These considerations affect the terms under which aid is given and the projects or programmes supported.

Economic goals

The broadest of the economic goals for aid is to stabilise the world's economy and stimulate the general expansion of production and trade.

Aid as a general resource to maintain the 'liberal' trade regime set up after the Second World War is quite important. It both helps pay for trade, and also provides incentives to poor states to accept the existing economic order. As targeted to particular countries, other economic goals of aid usually include insuring that the aid provider's own economy, or particular groups within it, will benefit from exporting their goods to recipients and will secure other trading opportunities in recipient countries. Aid is frequently tied to purchases or personnel from the provider, and, with food aid, to commodities the provider has to export. Aid donors also tend to favour recipient governments which promise stable investment arenas. Not only are aid-funded projects likely to be thought to have a higher rate of return when this condition is met, but also the aid itself can help a recipient's economy to be more attractive for private capital. Aid to Zimbabwe and Kenya, for instance, has helped to induce investment by multinational corporations.

Humanitarian goals

There is widespread recognition of the yawning gap between the high levels of well-being enjoyed by people in northern industrial states and the impoverished conditions of those in poor, less developed ones. Aid is supported by groups who feel a moral obligation to reduce this global inequality. In addition, specific elements of suffering caused by droughts, civil upheaval, or chronic poverty are targets for relief. This occurs when aid is given to help particular categories of people within states, such as refugees, famine victims or mothers and infant children. The basic aim here is redistribution and direct benefit to those visibly suffering. This motivation is reflected in the dramatic increase in food and other assistance to Africa in 1984–5 in response to developing famine conditions. These humanitarian goals led to reprogramming of aid usually available for other purposes and also supported increased aid.

Development as a goal both transcends humanitarian aims and is in competition with them. Hungry drought victims must be fed and rehabilitated before they can participate in economic development. Money to cement a political alliance can still be invested in ways that serve economic goals. If development outcomes occur, marked by increased efficiency of production and equitable distribution, other donor goals are usually also advanced. Development can thus be pervasive, even when other aid goals dictate particular allocations.

Nevertheless, there may be opportunity costs for development objectives when other goals shape behaviour. If development were the only aim of aid, it would certainly be given to different countries and projects than currently. The review of current aid in the first section of this essay, for example, revealed the interplay among these motivations.

A final point regarding aid allocations and development is germane –namely its role as a macroeconomic stabiliser. Aid tied to projects helps poor states maintain key undertakings during periods of economic downturn. More significantly, it has been at least mildly countercyclical to global economic cycles. During the boom of the 1960s aid declined in real terms, but it increased in the seventies after the oil shocks of 1973–4. Furthermore, it has been more stable than private lending. Although it declined as a portion of total transfers as private lending grew in the late 1970s, it became more important in the 1980s as private lending declined, as Table 8.3 illustrates. While private aid proved rather volatile, ODA in real terms did not decline but grew modestly in the 1980–3 period. Over the longer haul, the volatility of private flows can be seen. They expanded dramatically in the late 1970s. In 1965, ODA was 57 per cent of resource flows to developing countries; but by 1981 it was only 28 per cent. The periods of stagnation and growth in aid not only have a modest countercyclical association with global economic conditions, they also correspond to changes in the political climate. When East–West detente rose in the 1969–74 period, aid fell; as tensions rose after 1979 following the shift in the Carter administration's military policy and the Soviet Union's invasion of Afghanistan, Western support for aid grew, albeit modestly. Thus broad economic and political motivations arising from a desire for world stability and/or competition in Third World regions seems to affect the expansion and contraction of aid resources, and yet can do so in ways congruent with many development objectives.

To summarise, the patterns of aggregate aid levels over time and their distribution among recipients reveal the effect of the major political, economic and humanitarian concerns of the donor states. They also reflect pressure from recipient states. As sketched out these factors motivate aid givers. They shape allocations and are reasons for donors to support the aid system, but they do not eliminate the centrality of seeking economic development. This point is frequently made; see, for instance, Chenery and Strout (1966). To repeat the argument, development is a goal that pervades all motivations.

Table 8.3 ODA and private capital flows from DAC countries as a resource for LDCs (in millions US$, as a % of US GNP, and as a % of net resource flows from DAC countries to LDCs)

	1961	1965	1969	1973	1975	1977	1981	1983
Net ODA	5197	5916	6622	9378	13 846	15 733	25 540	27 458
ODA as % GNP	0.53	0.44	0.36	0.30	0.35	0.33	0.35	0.36
Net private flow					25 706	29 899	57 235	34 300
Total net flows	9249	10 320	13 799	24 655	44 810	51 526	91 387	69 131
Total flows as % GNP	0.95	0.77	0.75	0.79	1.08	1.09	1.25	0.91
ODA as % of total flow	56.2	57.3	48.0	38.0	30.4	30.5	27.9	39.7

Source: DAC, Development Co-operation, various years (Paris: OECD).

TENSIONS IN PURSUING DEVELOPMENT

Development principles are a source of support for aid in many states, especially in Scandinavia. However, organised interests in donor countries, including commodity groups, hunger lobbies, banking and foreign policy organisations compete for setting priorities in aid use. This reality limits the desirability and possibility of development goals being applied in some automatic or deductive fashion. In addition, there are serious disagreements about how to achieve development. Over the years views have changed. Especially with reference to 'late developing' states, arguments to guide aid uses and evaluations have shifted from an emphasis on industrialisation projects to efforts to achieve equitable rural transformation.[6] As the war-recovery aims of aid dwindled, and the system focused principally on Third World states, the initial norms that emphasised the use of advanced technology and rapid industrialisation have waned, albeit only slowly.

The general principles of using foreign aid for development emerged in the effort to assist European and Japanese recovery from the war. As this effort neared completion, and the independence of colonial states accelerated, the development principle came to be applied to recipients with different circumstances. At that time development and political principles agreed that aid was to cement continuing political ties of newly independent states to the donor states (usually Western), to foster state-building, to subsidise economic ties, and to promote industrialisation. Import substitution industrialisation was the major economic approach to the particular targeting of aid 'investments'.

The result of this orientation was support for import substitution industrialisation in many cases. The standard notion was that recipients knew best how to allocate the additional resources that aid provided, but that committing aid to specific projects insured adequate rates of return on investments tied to loans. It also justified technical assistance to planning ministries and projects. This approach, and the analytical assumptions used in it, shaped economic planning. Planning was a common government activity among aid recipients; an implicit donor principle was that planning should occur along lines that supported the commitment to a global division of labour and freer trade, the key economic principles of Western donors. Recipients, however, exhibited an urban bias in allocating investment funds which increasingly clashed with goals of increased productivity. Political considerations often dominated the funding of major projects, such as the Aswan high dam in Egypt built with Soviet aid, the Tanzania-to-Zambia railway supplied by the Chinese or the Volta river project supported by Western states.

The tendency toward an 'urban bias' and other 'distortions' were criticised in a continuing stream of analyses of aid and development, largely by economists (see Ohlin, 1965 and Chenery and Strout, 1966). As a result, alternative principles for guiding aid have been proposed. Foremost among these is the rise in policy-based lending in the 1980s especially in IMF and World Bank loans, but also in some bilateral donor behaviour. The policy context of a recipient is considered to be of paramount importance in achieving development effects. Aid is increasingly conditional on policy reforms or the maintenance of a conducive policy environment. External criteria of donors are thus coming to be accepted as legitimate, at least among donors. An emphasis on rural and agricultural transformation has replaced the original emphasis on the manufacturing and industrial sector. Finally, the distinction between the purposes pursued in bilateral and multilateral aid has become blurred as donor co-ordination has grown. An early instance of the combining of bilateral and multilateral aid, and of cash and food aid, occurred in aid to India in 1965–7 as donor agencies combined to exert pressure on India to emphasise agriculture (Paarlberg, 1985). Instances of combined funding and common objectives have emerged more recently in the African context.

All these changes, whatever the precise constellation of forces promoting them, represent an evolution of regime principles in directions prescribed by academic critics. They also reflect a growing convergence of purpose among donors, one prodded by reports and recommendations of multilateral bodies, which support the need to co-ordinate aid in order to enhance its development impact.

FOOD AID AND DEVELOPMENT AS A PRIORITY

Food aid, originating as a marriage of surplus disposal and humanitarian goals, best exemplifies the ascendance of development principles in aid. Food aid as a special subset of aid has long been criticised as especially flawed as a development tool. It has been accused of being doubly tied (to both origin and commodity), of discouraging local production of food, of disrupting commercial trade and of causing distortions and dependency within recipient economies (Maxwell and Singer, 1979).

The food aid regime has in fact experienced a significant shift towards development principles. This occurred most notably after the 1973–4 period of panic in world food markets. Resolutions of the 1974 World Food Conference, new legislation in the United States and other donor countries, and the relative decline in power of farm interests *vis-à-vis* humanitarian and hunger lobby organisations are all factors in this shift.

Basically the food aid regime began operating on the principles that food would be provided from donor country surpluses as additional imports, on an *ad hoc* bilateral basis, to feed hungry people and serve political goals. Thanks to the criticisms of this system pinpointed by analysts, the guiding principles have shifted significantly to include ones of efficiency and development effectiveness. The older principles, while not completely abandoned, have been superseded by newer ones. These propose that food aid should be provided by the most efficient source (including purchases by donors from developing countries) should substitute for commercial imports and avoid disincentive effects, should be committed over a multiyear period and should aim for development impacts, either through project use or support for policy reforms (see Hopkins, 1984).

A good test of the potency of these newer principles may be found in the contrast between the behaviour of food aid in the 1960s and the 1980s. During the 1960s, a period of large surplus stocks in the USA and costly government price support programmes, food aid ranged from 13 million to 17 million tons of cereals. When costs and surpluses were equally large in the 1980s, however, surplus disposal goals did not take over food aid flows. In spite of a devastating drought and famine conditions in Africa, total food aid flows rose only modestly in reaction to this (roughly doubling to Africa) and showed little prospect of returning to the surplus disposal mode. The changes in food aid which make it a more limited but developmentally targeted resource, one increasingly integrated with other financial resources, were not envisioned by its political designers twenty years ago. These changes were prodded by the continuing appraisals and recommendations of studies including a classic work, *Development Through Food*, prepared by a group of distinguished experts chaired by Hans Singer.[7] Bureaucratic rules and national legislation now require that officials managing food aid design projects, allocate aid and insure its end use in ways that conform to development criteria.[8]

Food aid can be particularly biased toward benefits for those most in need of food. For development purposes, food aid is appropriate for countries with overall food trade deficits and with unemployment problems. What Singer and others have done by fostering the 'food for development' approach is to integrate criteria for using food aid into prescriptions addressed at overall problems in LDCs. The need for employment growth, especially through labour-using techniques, fits well the prescriptions that food aid be integrated with financial resources and used where disincentives are avoided, such as in food-for-work projects (Singer, 1975 and 1984). Using food aid to support research, pilot experiments and investments in human capital is another set of avenues associated with the newer approach to food aid as a development tool. All these uses require that food aid is not subject to swings between surplus disposal needs and shortfalls in donor states, but is rather tied to long-term undertakings in developing countries with variability in aid occurring in response to changes in recipients' needs. Although surplus disposal motivations continue to explain variation in food aid availabilities, the size of the flows, given the large surpluses in the USA and the EC in 1984–5, are well below what they would be if the 'principles' of the food aid system of the 1960s had remained unchanged.[9]

IMPLICATIONS FOR THE FUTURE

The institutionalisation of a system of foreign assistance is a remarkable development in light of the historic pattern in which powerful states most often collected tribute from defeated and weaker states. Participation in economic assistance activities, while largely an undertaking of Western powers, has also been adopted by socialist and OPEC states as an important mechanism of their international behaviour. The 'co-operation' that aid symbolises, however, continues to be shaped by the rivalry among states. Its character, however, has increasingly been targeted towards economic goals in the last forty years. What began as defensive, *ad hoc*, and short-term measures, often designed to bolster regimes threatened by internal subversive communist movements, has become a major tool of international economic management and humanitarian efforts. Co-operative moves have been induced by mutual strategies of reciprocity in fulfilling international lending and trade agreements. This contrasts sharply with the period of mutual defection in economic action of the 1930s (see Oye, 1985).

What are the implications for development of current political forces shaping aid? Given the rise in East–West tensions and the economic recession of the early 1980s, the aid regime's emphasis on development is threatened. Domestic economic priorities of donors and international political uses of aid seem to be on the increase. Two lessons from the past thirty years provide some reassurance for development advocates. First, once allocational pressures from non-development interests have worked their will on aid, there remain complex rules and procedures for dispensing aid that allow for development considerations to have a major effect. Second, the development analysts' shift towards emphasising contextual, policy-based criteria for aid is quite compatible with the concerns and objectives of many of the political forces shaping the aid framework. Thus we can expect a continued refinement of designs for end use that rest upon analyses of the best contextual impact for aid and a linking of aid to policy changes.

Tensions between short- and long-term commitments, between donor budgets and revenues, and between donor and sectoral needs and fluctuating needs of recipients, will surely continue. The rise of symbols such as 'food security', however, may constrain states from capricious international aid behaviour since such a concept implies an effort to integrate welfare needs and macropolicy, both in developing countries and in policy-linked aid commitments from donors.

Finally, the share of aid going through multilateral agencies, presumably somewhat immune from narrow political and economic interests, has not grown as a proportion of total aid since the late 1970s. Shifts to greater multilateralism by some donors have been offset by retreats by others, notably the United States. The Reagan administration represents a coalition with few multilateral sympathies or economic interests. The bilateral–multilateral distinction is becoming increasingly moot as donor co-ordination expands and as multiple donors contribute to complex policy related projects on a bilateral basis. The Mali restructuring project, aimed at liberalising the grain market, is a good case in point. Moreover, the IMF and World Bank have taken a lead role in shaping broad development policy negotiations with developing states, bringing donor actions further into concert. This is largely the result of the greatly expanded indebtedness LDCs face in the 1980s as compared to earlier decades. Debts, even debt servicing, cannot be faced without achieving higher rates of growth than experienced in the 1975–85 period. This pressure, related to the broad political–economic commitment of donor states to an open, capitalist-oriented international economy, should help insure that the aid regimes' principles remain committed to achieving development impacts, and not merely to responding to political–military short-term factors. The role for economists in pinpointing preferred uses for aid remains secure.

Notes

1. There is considerable debate among political scientists as to whether international affairs since the Second World War have been truly unique in any sense. Some argue that nothing novel has occurred. Others, including myself, believe that historical similarities to earlier epochs are only partial. For an argument favouring uniqueness see Mandelbaum, 1981; for the more classic eternal features view see Gilpin, 1981; Krasner, 1985.

2. On McNamara's speech and the subsequent effort to implement the principle directing resources towards the world's rural poor, see Ayres, 1983, pp. 4–6, 93–147.

3. According to USAID, 1978, the total of all US bilateral economic assistance averaged $4.184 billion per year in 1946–8, while the total economic assistance given in 1977 amounted to $5.591 billion, indicating a considerable drop in real-dollar terms. Comparing these figures with Commerce Department figures for US GNP, reported in *The Economic Almanac 1964* and *Encyclopedia Britannica Year Book 1979*, US bilateral aid dropped from 1.78 per cent of GNP over the years 1946–8 to 0.30 per cent in 1977. Still, the latter figure is higher than the one reported by the DAC (OECD, 1981), which gives US net official development assistance for 1977 as $4.682 billion, and as 0.25 per cent of GNP. (Differing accounting procedures are responsible for the difference in figures between USAID and the DAC.) The decline was continuous over the thirty-year period but fastest in the 1950s.

4. For example, a major contribution to the thinking of development economists was the volume by Chenery *et al.* (1974). Many themes in this volume summarise convergent recommendations and analyses among those in the development community. An earlier report on Kenya by a team of experts led by Hans Singer (ILO, 1972) exemplifies this rising concern for equity in development.

5. For a critical review of Tanzania, see Coulson, 1982.

6. Some argue that these emphases are compatible. Certainly agricultural transformation and industrialisation should be complementary. Nevertheless, earlier aid neglected integrating the two, and tensions remain. See Singh, 1979.

7. (FAO, Rome, 1961). The other experts were M. R. Benedict, J. Figures, V. K. R. V. Rao, P. N. Rosenstein-Roden. The FAO has recently reissued this report as the third part of a volume of works on food aid written in prelude to the major changes in the regime that occurred with the establishment of the World Food Programme. See FAO, 1985; the

experts' report is on pp. 223–343. This study projected US surpluses available for aid at 15.4 million tons of wheat per year and 2.5 million tons of coarse grains. Indeed, in 1965–7 US food aid came close to these levels, but in 1983–4, when supplies were again of a similar size absolutely, US food aid was about one-third this level.

8. In the USA during the 1970s legislation was passed that required food aid to be targeted to poor countries (food aid to Israel thus ended), food for development uses were required, and disincentive effects on local production and marketing were proscribed. In addition, bureaucrats launched policies to give priority to development over 'welfare' projects.

9. This claim rests upon work by Panos Konandreas at the FAO using surplus disposal and recipients' needs to predict food aid flows (personal communication) and on regression parameters obtained from US food aid from 1955 to 1977 in my own research. The equation explaining US food aid as a function of large US stocks and low grain prices for the 1964–77 period (R2 of .93) yields parameters that predict much higher grain food aid for 1983–5 than was in fact supplied. This reflects, I believe, the greater consequence of surplus disposal on levels of food aid in the earlier period and the difficulty of using food aid as an avenue to reduce stocks in the 1980s. This difficulty arises from opposition and laws requiring that food aid does not have a disincentive effect. See Hopkins, 1980.

References

AYRES, R. C. (1983) *Banking on the Poor: The World Bank and World Poverty* (Cambridge, Mass.: MIT Press).

BHAGWATI, J. and R. ECKAUS (eds) (1970) *Foreign Aid* (Harmondsworth: Penguin Books).

CHENERY, H. B. *et al.* (1974) *Redistribution with growth* (London: Oxford University Press).

CHENERY, H. B. and A. M. STROUT (1966) 'Foreign assistance and economic development', *American Economic Review*, vol. 41, pp. 679–733.

COULSON, A. (1982) *Tanzania* (London: Oxford University Press).

Economic Almanack (1964) (New York: Newsweek).

Encyclopedia Britannica Year Book (1979) (Chicago).

FAO (1961) *Development through Food: a Strategy for Surplus Utilisation* (Rome: Food and Agriculture Organisation).

FAO (1985) *Food Aid and Development: Three Studies by Gerda Blau, Mordecai Ezekial and B. R. Sen* (Rome: Food and Agriculture Organisation).

GILPIN, R. (1981) *War and Change in World Politics* (Cambridge: Cambridge University Press).

HOPKINS, R. F. (1980) *Political Economy of International Policy Formation* (Swarthmore, Penn.: Swarthmore College).

HOPKINS, R. F. (1984) 'The evolution of food aid towards a development first regime', *Food Policy*, vol. 9(4), pp. 345–62.

HOPKINS, R. F. and D. J. PUCHALA (eds) (1979) *Global Political Economy of Food* (Madison: University of Wisconsin Press).

ILO (1972) *Employment, Incomes and Equality* (Geneva: International Labour Organisation).

ISENMAN, P. J. and H. W. SINGER (1977) 'Food aid: disincentive effects and their policy implications', *Economic Development and Cultural Change*, vol. 25(2), pp. 205–38.

KRASNER, S. (1983) *International Regimes* (Ithaca, NY: Cornell University Press).

KRASNER, S. (1985) *Structural Conflict: The Third World Against Global Liberalism* (Berkeley, Cal.: University of California Press).

LELE, U. (1981) 'Rural Africa: modernization, equity and long-term development', *Science*, 6 February pp. 551–2.

MANDELBAUM, M. (1981) *The Nuclear Revolution* (Cambridge: Cambridge University Press).

MAXWELL, S. J. and H. W. SINGER (1979) 'Food aid to developing countries: a survey', *World Development*, vol. 7 (3).

NELSON, J. (1968) *Aid, Influence and Foreign Policy* (New York: Macmillan).

OECD (1981) *Development Cooperation Review* (Paris).

OECD (1984a) *Development Co-operation Review* (Paris).

OECD (1984b) *Geographical Distribution of Financial Flows to Developing Countries 1979–82* (Paris).

OHLIN, G. (1965) 'The evolution of aid doctrine', in *Foreign Aid Reconsidered* (Paris: OECD) reprinted in Bhagwati and Eckaus (eds).

OYE, K. (1985) 'Co-operation under anarchy', *World Politics*, vol. 38(1).

PAARLBERG, R. C. (1985) *Food Trade and Foreign Policy: India, the Soviet Union and the United States* (Ithaca, NY: Cornell University Press) pp. 143–70.

SINGER, H. W. (1965) 'External aid: for plans or projects', *Economic Journal*, vol. 75, pp. 539–45, reprinted in Bhagwati and Eckaus (eds).

SINGER, H. W. (1975) *The Strategy of Development: Essays in the Economics of Backwardness* (London: Macmillan).

SINGER, H. W. (1984) *Development Through Food: Twenty Years' Experience*, Report of the World Food Programme/Government of the Netherlands Seminar on Food Aid (Rome) pp. 31–46.

SINGH, A. (1979) The 'basic needs' approach to development versus the New International Order: the significance of Third World industrialisation', *World Development*, vol. 7(6), pp. 585–606.

SPERO, J. (1977) *The Politics of International Economic Relations* (New York: St Martin's Press).

US AGENCY FOR INTERNATIONAL DEVELOPMENT (1978) *US Overseas Loans and Grants, and Assistance from International Organizations, 1 July, 1945–30 September 1977* (Washington DC).

WALL, D. (1973) *The Charity of Nations: The Political Economy of Foreign Aid* (New York: Basic Books).

WHITE, J. (1974) *The Politics of Foreign Aid* (New York: St Martin's Press).

9 Food Aid for Food Security and Economic Development*

John W. Mellor

Food aid plays an important role in the economies of the developing countries of the world. Total food aid to the developing countries currently amounts to about $2.5 billion a year, and accounts for 9.4 per cent of all official development assistance.[1]

The purpose of this paper is to examine food aid's contribution to the dual objectives of food security and economic growth in the developing world. It begins by reviewing the statistical record of food aid since the early 1960s. The paper then analyses the important contribution that food aid can make to food security, economic development, nutrition and employment in the low-income countries of the world. In these sections particular emphasis is placed on the role of food aid in Asia and Africa. The paper concludes that food aid can, and does, help provide the means needed to protect (and raise) the consumption status and labour productivity of the poor.

STATISTICAL RECORD OF FOOD AID

While cereal imports by developing countries have increased dramatically over the last twenty years, food aid has declined, both absolutely and on a per capita basis. According to Table 9.1, total cereal food aid for ninety-nine developing countries dropped from 11.6 million metric tons in 1961–3 to 8.4 million tons in 1981–3. During this period of time, the share of food aid in total imports of cereal dropped from nearly 40 per cent to less than 10 per cent. On a per capita basis, food aid dropped by about 55 per cent (Table 9.2).

It is rather striking to note that since the early 1960s food aid per capita has declined for three of the four major regions of the developing world. This decline has been particularly pronounced in the regions of Asia and Latin America. Since the early 1960s a number

Table 9.1 Volume of commercial cereal imports, total cereal imports, and food aid received by ninety-nine developing countries[a] grouped by region, 1961–3, 1976–8 and 1981–3

Region	Year	Commercial cereal imports	Food aid[b]	Total cereal imports
		(million metric tons)		
Asia (including China)	1961–3	11.4	5.7	17.1
	1976–8	22.2	4.2	26.4
	1981–3	36.9	2.7	39.6
Latin America	1961–3	3.7	1.9	5.6
	1976–8	14.2	0.4	14.6
	1981–3	21.6	0.9	22.5
North Africa/Middle East	1961–3	1.9	3.9	5.7
	1976–8	14.6	2.5	17.1
	1981–3	27.6	2.7	30.3
Sub-Saharan Africa	1961–3	1.5	0.1	1.6
	1976–8	4.1	0.9	4.9
	1981–3	6.4	2.1	8.5
Total developing countries	1961–3	18.5	11.6	30.0
	1976–8	55.1	8.0	63.0
	1981–3	92.5	8.4	100.9

Sources: 1961–3 and 1976–8 data from Huddleston (1984, p. 22).
1981–3 data from 1983 FAO Trade Yearbook (1984) and FAO (1985).
Notes
[a] The 99 developing countries include those covered by the Huddleston study (1984). Nineteen of these countries are in Asia, 24 in Latin America, 17 in North Africa/Middle East and 39 in sub-Saharan Africa.
[b] Food aid total for 1976–8 does not include approximately 700 000 metric tons reported by FAO, most of which went to Indochina and Portugal.

Table 9.2 Per capita volume of total cereal imports and food aid in ninety-nine developing countries[a] grouped by region, 1961–3, 1976–8 and 1981–3

Region	Year	Food aid per capita[b]	Total cereal imports
		(kilograms)	
Asia (including China)	1961–3	3.82	11.54
	1976–8	2.06	12.98
	1981–3	1.18	17.14
Latin America	1961–3	8.31	25.00
	1976–8	1.17	43.26
	1981–3	2.30	60.80
NorthAfrica/Middle East	1961–3	24.13	35.81
	1976–8	10.22	70.96
	1981–3	10.19	112.72
Sub-Saharan Africa	1961–3	0.62	7.87
	1976–8	2.89	16.21
	1981–3	5.85	23.29
Total developing countries	1961–3	5.59	14.49
	1976–8	2.74	21.59
	1981–3	2.55	30.50

Sources: 1981–3 population data from World Bank (1984); all other data from sources listed in Table 9.1.
Note: See Table 9.1.

of large-scale recipients in these two regions – such as India and Pakistan in Asia, and Brazil, Chile and Colombia in Latin America – have drastically reduced their receipts. Although some of these countries continue to receive food aid, the volume received by these five countries dropped by 5.0 million metric tons between 1961–3 and 1981–3.

Over the years the geographic distribution of food aid has shifted dramatically to Africa. As the data in Table 9.2 show, sub-Saharan Africa is the only region of the developing world to record an increase in per capita food aid. Between 1961–3 and 1981–3 per capita food aid to sub-Saharan Africa increased from 0.62 kilograms to 5.85 kilograms per person. Much of this increase is due to recurrent food shortages in this area of the world.

Table 9.3 Per capita volume of food aid to thirty-one low-income developing countries,[a] 1961–3 and 1981–3

Region	Year	Food aid per capita (kilograms)
Asia	1961–3	3.78
	1981–3	1.04
Latin America	1961–3	7.37
	1981–3	17.52
North Africa/Middle East	1961–3	1.62
	1981–3	4.36
Sub-Saharan Africa	1961–3	0.97
	1981–3	7.50
Total low-income developing countries	1961–3	3.52
	1981–3	1.73

Sources: Same as Tables 9.1 and 9.2.
Notes:
[a]According to the World Bank (1984), low-income developing countries are those with 1982 gross national product (GNP) per person at less than US $410. Such a classification yields a total of 34 low-income countries: 11 in Asia; 1 in Latin America; 1 in North Africa/Middle East; and 21 in sub-Saharan Africa. Data on 31 of these 34 low-income countries are included in this table.

The shift in the geographic distribution of food aid becomes even more pronounced when attention is focused on the low-income developing countries of the world.[2] According to Table 9.3, between 1961–3 and 1981–3 food aid per capita declined for thirty-one low-income developing countries. Yet a closer look at the data in this table shows that food aid per capita actually *increased* in three of the four regions of the developing world. The low-income countries of sub-Saharan Africa, for example, recorded a particularly large increase in food aid per capita during this twenty-year period. Only in Asia did food aid per capita decline, largely because of reductions in the levels of assistance to two very populous countries: India and Pakistan.

In recent years, important changes have also been taking place in the donor community. Whereas the United States once supplied nearly all food aid, it now supplies only about 50 per cent of the total.

Canada, Australia and the European Economic Community have emerged as other significant suppliers. Moreover, an increasing share of food aid, now about 25 per cent, is being channelled through international agencies like the World Food Programme.[3]

FOOD AID AND FOOD SECURITY

In the developing contries of the world food aid can play a pivotal role in improving food security. In many of these countries food supplies fluctuate widely, depending on the degree of production variability and the extent to which this variability is compensated by changes in imports and stocks.

It is important to realise that such fluctuations in supply have an immense impact on the poor. Research in India (Mellor, 1978) indicates that the poor spend between 60 to 80 per cent of their increments to income on food. Thus, as food supplies decline and prices rise, it is the poor who must bear the brunt of the burden. The poor suffer in two ways. First, as food prices rise, the poor suffer a reduction in their real purchasing power. Second, as food prices increase, the wealthier classes tend to reduce their consumption of those labour-intensive goods and services that provide employment for the poor. With fewer employment opportunities, the poor suffer a decline in their ability to procure food at any price.

In recent decades the food security problem of the poor has been the product of two important forces: chronic food insecurity in most developing countries, and widespread fluctuations in annual food production in many other developing countries. The first is a long-term problem of aggregate food supply, a problem that focuses attention on the need to use food aid to increase rates of food production growth throught the Third World. The second problem is a more short-term one that requires the extension of food aid in order to iron out those weather- or price-induced fluctuations in food production that have such a negative impact on the poor.

The pressing nature of these two problems is easily demonstrated. With respect to the first problem, in recent years aggregate food production in the developing world has just barely kept pace with the rate of population growth. Between 1961 and 1980 food production in the Third World increased at an average rate of 2.6 per cent a year (Table 9.4). This was only slightly faster than the average annual population growth rate of 2.4 per cent. On a per capita basis, food

Table 9.4   Population and major food crop production[a] in the developing world, 1961–80

Country group	Average annual population growth rate, 1961–80 (per cent)	Average annual major food crop production growth rate, 1961–80 (per cent)
Developing countries[b]	2.4	2.6
Asia (including China)	2.3	2.8
North Africa and Middle East	2.7	2.5
Sub-Saharan Africa	2.8	1.7
Latin America	2.7	2.8

Source: Paulino (forthcoming).

Notes:

[a]Includes cereals, roots and tubers, pulses, groundnuts, bananas and plantains. Rice is in terms of milled form.

[b]Includes a total of 105 Asian, African, Middle Eastern and Latin American countries.

production in the Third World as a whole increased by only 0.2 per cent. However, this aggregate figure covers sharply different rates of food production growth in various regions of the developing world. For example, while per capita food production in Asia increased by a strong 0.5 per cent per year, in sub-Saharan Africa it fell by a shocking 1.2 per cent. In both these areas, as well as throughout the Third World, accelerated rates of food production growth are needed to meet the pressing food needs of the poor.

With respect to the problem of fluctuations, in recent years the modest rate of growth of world food production has been accompanied by a steadily increasing degree of production variability. According to recent research by Hazell (1984), between the periods 1960–1 to 1970–1 and 1971–2 to 1982–3 the coefficient of variation of total world cereal production increased from 2.8 per cent to 3.4 per cent. This represented a net increase in production variability of 21 per cent.

Preliminary analysis suggests that the major source of this increase in production variability lies in increases in yield co-variances between crops and regions. This may well be because of factors associated with the new seed/fertiliser technologies. For example, if all of a country's production of a crop – such as maize in the United States – has a single parent, that crop might be more vulnerable to pestilence. This is a problem that crop scientists are currently analysing. Yet in the meantime, another problem still remains. In many developing countries policies affecting the availability of fertiliser, electricity and water inputs change from year to year. Such policy changes may have a large, and unfavourable, effect on agricultural production as that production becomes more dependent on the supply of those water and fertiliser inputs that are associated with the new technology.

In recent years, the steady growth in world food production has also been accompanied by a rising degree of price variability. While international grain prices were relatively stable in the 1950s and 1960s, since 1971 they have become highly variable. According to research by Valdes (1984), the coefficient of variation for wheat export prices was more than eight times as high in the 1970s as it was in the 1960s. For rice, the coefficient of variation for export prices more than doubled between the two decades.[4]

What could food aid do to mitigate the impact of these fluctuations in production and price? Most obviously, food aid could be used to meet the more immediate food security needs in the developing world. In general, food aid could represent a more efficient means of meeting temporary food needs than any type of domestic stocking programme. Stocks held at the national level tend to be very large (and expensive) because of the random occurrence of poor crop years and the potential for a sequence of bad years. Reutlinger and Bigman (1981), for example, have estimated that a 6 million metric ton domestic stock would cost between $59 and $82 million a year to operate.

Food trade (and hence food aid) between countries represents a far more cost-effective approach to food security than such domestic stocking arrangements. Such use of food aid would allow developing countries to avoid many of the diseconomies associated with stocks and to concentrate more of their scarce resources on the critical goal of increasing domestic food production. We know, of course, that food aid has not typically been used in such a countercyclical manner. Indeed, during the global food crisis of the mid-1970s total food aid declined. The benefits from more attention to a counter cyclical use of food aid would be immense.

Helping developing countries meet their immediate food security needs was the basic principle behind the creation in 1981 of a cereal import facility at the International Monetary Fund.[5] This facility is designed to provide financing to countries facing short-term problems of domestic food production shortfalls or high international prices. By loaning the funds needed to ship food to points of immediate need, the IMF cereal facility is supposed to provide food security to countries at rates cheaper than those associated with domestic storage. In concept, the facility is also able to provide low-income countries with the financial means to procure food in times of fluctuating food aid supplies or worldwide food shortages. It can then help make up for the deficiencies of food aid in meeting food security needs.

However, in the five years since its creation, the IMF cereal facility has provided financing for excess cereal imports for only a handful of developing countries.[6] This suggests that there is a need to broaden and extend the coverage of the facility. On the one hand, there is a need to liberalise the rules regarding drawings from the facility so as to make it accessible to more countries.[7] At the same time, the coverage of the facility needs to be broadened to include *all* food items – cereal and non-cereal – consumed by low-income people in the developing world. Recent research by Huddleston, Johnson, Reutlinger and Valdes (1984) indicates that non-cereal items account for a considerable percentage of total food imports in many developing countries.

FOOD AID AND ECONOMIC DEVELOPMENT

A large body of literature argues that food aid has no appreciable effect on economic development.[8] According to this literature, factor proportions are technologically fixed during the development process, and food supplies do not represent a major constraint on growth. In this view, existing food supplies can easily support a labour force that is expanding at a rate consonant with the limited capital stock.

In fact, both the main assumptions of this literature are wrong. On the one hand, factor proportions are not fixed during the development process. Whereas there may be no efficient alternatives to highly capital-intensive processes for making steel or petrochemicals, labour-intensive processes can be used to produce a wide range of consumer goods and simple industrial tools. At the same time, wage goods – particularly food – do place a significant constraint on labour mobilisation. Since the marginal propensity of the poor to spend on food is so high (i.e., 0.6 to 0.8), any growth strategy that leads to a rapid increase in employment will necessarily generate an increased demand for food. In the absence of sufficient food supplies, such increased demand will tend to restrict the mobilisation of labour, as rising real food prices reduce the demand for labour (Mellor, 1976; Isenman and Singer, 1977).

It is now clear that the process of labour mobilisation for economic growth depends on the working of two interacting markets – the labour market and the food market.[9] As labour is mobilised and receives a larger share of the total wage pool, it spends most of that increased income on food. Additional supplies of food are therefore needed to prevent the type of increases in food prices and wages that would reduce the demand for labour. In countries where foreign exchange reserves are limited, food aid can play a critical role in relieving the resulting pressure on food supplies.

The dynamics of these relations can be easily seen in food-for-work programmes, which link employment and payment of food directly. Such programmes are attractive to donors because their benefits for the poor are highly visible. These programmes assure that the food will be given where it is needed, and that highly labour-intensive activities will be pursued.

In Asia, south Asia in particular, there is a large stock of labour that can be mobilised readily for growth. The addition of wage goods would pull that labour from agriculture with little or no decline in agricultural production. In Africa, however, the situation is more complex. In most African countries, one can expect a nearly proportionate decline in agricultural output as labour is withdrawn from agriculture. This is because the agroclimatic and technological conditions that dominate African agriculture tend to cause low labour productivity and a scarcity of labour in seasonal peaks. Thus, in the short-run withdrawal of labour from food production causes a much more substantial decline in food production in Africa than in Asia. In such a situation, food aid can be used to support the increased consumption and the decreased production. Of course, one of the effects of such a process should be provision of infrastructure and other investment that will raise food production in the long run.

There is currently a widespread view that food aid is particularly deleterious in Africa. This view tends to overlook the fact that the basic development strategy pursued in much of Africa assigns a very low priority to agriculture. For example, during the period 1978–80 the median annual public expenditure on agriculture in fifteen African countries was only 7.4 per cent of the total government budget (Table 9.5). By comparison, during the early 1960s the central government in India allocated approximately 20 per cent of its budget to agriculture (Lele, 1981).

Table 9.5   Percentage of central government expenditures to agriculture in selected African countries, 1978–80

	1978	1979	1980	Average all years
Ghana	12.2	10.4	12.2	11.6
Rwanda	10.3	12.7		11.5
Madagascar	11.5	11.4	10.2	11.0
Sudan	9.0	11.3	9.4	9.9
Botswana	10.5	9.2	9.7	9.8
Somalia	12.6	10.6	5.6	9.6
Kenya	8.5	8.4	8.3	8.4
Tanzania	9.3	7.0		8.2
Niger	7.1	8.9	6.8	7.6
Liberia	9.0	2.7	3.1	4.9
Cameroon	4.1	4.3	4.2	4.2
Sierra Leone	4.2	4.1		4.2
Upper Volta	4.2	3.9		4.1
Ivory Coast	2.9		3.4	3.2
Nigeria	2.6	1.4	2.5	2.2

Source: International Monetary Fund (1982).

In Africa, the underinvestment of public resources in agriculture has produced a poorly developed rural infrastructure, little research on food crops and a weakly staffed agricultural extension service. All these factors have played a far more important role in curtailing the rate of food production growth in Africa than food aid. Food aid is more the symptom of this underlying malaise than its cause. Correcting these problems goes way beyond the use of food aid to include establishing more reasonable government priorities in the use of public resources and commercially earned foreign exchange. Throughout Africa the need for road, credit, water and agricultural research systems is immense. Given the character of such needs, a far more constructive view of the potential benefits of food aid is sorely needed.

FOOD AID AND NUTRITION

Food aid can have a major impact on nutrition in two ways: first, by reducing the market price of food; and second, by providing the means to pursue market intervention policies designed to improve the nutritional status of the poor.

According to Indian data (Mellor, 1978), food grains comprise more than half the total consumption expenditure of people in the lowest two income deciles. Thus, while a 10 per cent increase in food grain prices reduces the food grain consumption of the two lowest income deciles by 5.9 per cent, it decreases the food grain consumption of the upper half of the tenth decile by only 0.2 per cent. The absolute real expenditure on food grains is reduced ten times as much for the lowest two income deciles as it is for the upper half of the tenth decile.

As these data show, in a developing economy like India the bulk of the adjustment to reduced supplies of food staples is made by poor people. Thus, food aid that adds to total supplies of food grains has a major effect on the incomes, consumption, and nutritional status of low-income people. Yet an important caveat is in order here.

In India, those in the top 5 per cent of the income distribution spend more than two-and-a-half times as much per capita on food grains as the lowest 20 per cent. Thus, the upper income group experiences twice as large an effect on its overall income from a change in food grain prices as does the lower income group. Whereas food grain consumption varies little in the upper income group in response to changes in food grain prices, consumption of other goods and services varies substantially. Such changes in consumption by the rich may have an important indirect impact on the poor, who find many of their employment opportunities in the production of labour-intensive goods and services.

The need to improve both the nutritional status and the employment opportunities of the poor calls attention to various types of market intervention policies that target the benefits of food aid more directly to the poor. Two basic types of market intervention programmes can be distinguished here: food-for-work programmes and supplementary feeding schemes.[10]

Food-for-work programmes were originally designed to provide income-generating employment opportunities and to improve infrastructure in the rural areas. As the name implies, wages in food-for-work projects are paid in part or in full with food, some of which is often supplied by food aid. According to Maxwell (1978), about 16 per cent of all food aid is used for food-for-work programmes.

On the whole, food-for-work programmes have been quite successful in increasing employment. Brundin (1978), for example, reports that the food-for-work programme in Bangladesh has increased the person-days of work by 45 million, provided employment for 1.5 million people, and used 160 000 metric tons of grain. Similar results have been reported in other countries (World Bank, 1979).

While food-for-work programmes have also contributed significantly to the development of better rural road and drainage systems, much still needs to be done to improve the effectiveness of these programmes in contributing to rural infrastructure development. The food must arrive in a timely manner; the projects planned must have sound engineering and effective local input if they are to be efficiently built; and considerable financial support is needed for complementary materials, such as culverts. All too often these requisites are missing or inadequate, thereby reducing the effectiveness of food-for-work programmes.

Because of the employment provided, food-for-work programmes seem to have a very favourable impact on the income of the poor. In Bangladesh, for instance, it has been estimated that the net income of participant households increased by 10 to 11 per cent of the annual wage income, and by a much larger percentage during the season of their food-for-work employment (BIDS/IFPRI, 1984).

The effect of food-for-work programmes on the consumption and nutritional status of the poor is, however, more complex. Given the significant impact of these programmes on the incomes of those people who tend to spend so much of their income on food, it should follow that food-for-work programmes have a very positive effect on the nutritional status of the poor. However, the actual relationship seems less clear. Some of the food in these programmes is sold by recipients, thereby diffusing the benefits to others through lower prices, but perhaps reducing the direct nutritional benefits to the recipients. The BIDS/IFPRI study in Bangladesh shows a preference of recipients for mixed payments (in kind and in cash) but little support for payment only in cash. This is an important issue with many ramifications that requires further study. In addition, food for work generally provides income for only a short season. While that season is frequently one of particularly low income, the recipients must plan ahead to other seasons. The BIDS/IFPRI study shows a reduction of indebtedness during the food-for-work period, suggesting less improvement in diet in that time, but a better ability to deal with later periods of acute food purchase needs. All this suggests that there are important areas of food-for-work programmes that still require much work and analysis if improved policies are to materialise.

With regards to the use of food aid to support supplementary feeding programmes, it is logical to focus on those programmes catering to pregnant and lactating women and infants. These programmes are among the most common in developing countries.

Recent reviews of more than 200 supplementary feeding projects indicate that such projects have had a positive effect on prenatal and child participants.[11] Studies conducted in India, Colombia, Mexico and Canada show that supplementation during pregnancy improves perinatal outcome. In India, for example, birth weights of infants born to women who received a daily protein supplement were significantly higher than those of infants born to a non-supplemented control group (Iyenger, 1967).

Despite the positive effects found in India and elsewhere, the benefits of most supplementary feeding programmes are usually modest. Increments in birth weights attributed to such programmes typically run in the range of 40 to 60 grams. Similarly, the increases in growth observed in preschool children are generally small.

The reasons for these relatively modest growth effects are still not fully understood. However, one reason appears to be that only a part of the food given actually reaches the targeted population. 'Leakages' of the supplemented foods occur when the food is shared by non-target family members, or when the food is substituted for other food. On the one hand, these 'leakages' need not be regarded as inefficiencies in the system, since they are often being used to improve the nutritional status of other malnourished household members. Yet on the other hand, as a result of such 'leakages', supplementary feeding programmes are generally only able to fill 10 to 25 per cent of the apparent energy gap in the target population (Kennedy and Pinstrup-Andersen, 1983). Given this small net increment in energy, it is not surprising that the observed effect on growth is small. It is also notable that the administrative costs of such targeted programmes are quite high, because they require a large component of trained manpower resources.

FOOD AID AND EMPLOYMENT GROWTH

While it is easy to conceive of an increase in the labour intensity of production, to achieve such an increase is much more difficult. Yet in most cases technological change in agriculture can do much to facilitate such an increase in labour intensity. Technological change in agriculture increases the income of small landowning peasants, who, in Asia, typically spend 40 per cent of their increments to income on locally produced, non-agricultural goods and services (Hazell and Roell, 1983). Since these goods and services are highly labour intensive, their production provides new sources of employment and income growth for the poor.

Past research indicates that the employment and income linkage effects of technological change in agriculture are much weaker in Africa than in Asia (Ibid.). This is partly because incomes of peasant producers in rural Africa are lower than in Asia, partly because the infrastructure in Africa is poorer, and partly because the agroclimatic environment in Africa results in lower average labour productivity and a more even distribution of a low level of income.

While both food aid and domestic agricultural production add to the supply of wage goods, the latter tends to stimulate the creation of new employment and income opportunities. Its contribution to growth is, therefore, far superior to that of food aid. For this reason, it is important that food aid encourages – rather than inhibits – the rate of growth of domestic agriculture.

In the past, discussions on the disincentive effects of food aid on agriculture have usually focused on its impact on local agriculture through the price mechanism. Yet empirical studies now suggest that the disincentive effects of food aid on domestic agriculture tend to be overemphasised.[12] For instance, Maxwell and Singer (1979), in their review of twenty-one studies on the impact of food aid, found only seven cases reporting 'significant' disincentive effects on either prices or production. On this basis the two authors conclude that any disincentive effect of food aid on local agriculture 'can be and has been avoided by an appropriate mix of policy tools' (Ibid., p. 231).

On the whole, policy tools designed to avoid the small, direct disincentive effects of food aid need to meet two conditions. First, employment must be created for low-income people with a high propensity to spend on food. Second, food aid must be tied to other forms of assistance in such a way so as to facilitate long-term agricultural development. An important disincentive effect of food aid occurs when that aid is used to solve short-run problems of food supply, thereby allowing politicians to turn their attention to matters other than those pertaining to agricultural development. Thus, linking food aid positively to other assistance may be more effective than simply attaching conditions to food aid alone.

In any case, food aid can be used directly to facilitate growth in agriculture. Through the mechanism of food-for-work programmes, food aid can help meet one of the most pressing agricultural development needs in many developing countries: the lack of rural infrastructure. One of the principal contributions to date of food-for-work programmes has been the building of better roads, irrigation and drainage systems, and communications networks. In effect, food-for-work programmes to build rural infrastructure can decrease the cost of food production more than the potential depressing effect of food aid on producer prices. At the same time the very positive impact of these programmes on the rural infrastructure helps pave the way for the multiplier effects of agricultural growth to expand income and employment in other sectors of the economy.

CONCLUSION

Food aid can, and has, made an important contribution to food security and economic development in the Third World. In the short run, food aid has provided developing countries with the means to protect the nutritional status of their citizenry during periods of domestic production shortfalls. In the long-term, food aid has also helped a number of countries to pursue the type of employment-oriented agricultural strategy of development that is needed to stimulate domestic food production. By supporting the creation of food-for-work and other programmes in the countryside, food aid has helped lay the administrative and institutional structures for accelerated food production growth. In most cases such increased food production growth represents the only long-term solution to the problem of chronic food insecurity in the Third World.

If food aid is to make its maximum contribution to food security and economic growth, three demands need to be met by the food donor and two by the food aid recipient.

The donor must: (1) provide reliable amounts of food aid so that long-term development programmes can be built; (2) provide large amounts of food aid – a significant effect on employment cannot be expected unless some measurable percentage of the country's existing food supplies is added; and (3) recognise the conditions of effective food aid use so that, for example, efforts can be made to provide other resources needed for the effective use of labour.

The recipient, in turn, must: (1) give priority to agricultural development in order to minimise the disincentive effects of food aid and to ensure the feasibility of a high-employment strategy of growth; and (2) pursue policies that spread capital supplies as evenly as possible over the labour force in order to maximise employment growth. These two demands require attention to investment policies, pricing policies and to the type of technological changes in agriculture needed to stimulate growth.

These requirements for both donor and recipient demand high analytical skills in technical departments developing and administering such a food aid strategy. Given the important role that food aid has played in the past, and the potentially favourable impact of such aid on most developing countries in the future, a commitment to such a strategy should be attractive to donor and recipient alike.

Notes

*I appreciate the assistance of my colleagues at the International Food Policy Research Institute, and particularly Richard H. Adams, Jr for his substantial work directly on this paper.

It is particularly fitting that this paper be presented in honour of Hans W. Singer, the person who played such a seminal role in the early intellectual articulation of food aid and modern development assistance.

1. These figures represent average figures for the period 1981–3, as recorded in World Food Programme (1985).
2. For a definition of low-income developing countries, see note to Table 9.3.
3. For more on this point, see Wallerstein (1980).
4. The major reason for this sharp increase in price variability lies in the changed character of the agricultural support policies pursued by the United States and Canada. Prior to 1971, these two governments either owned or controlled large stocks of grain, which contributed greatly to international price stability. Since 1971 these two governments have generally been unwilling to hold such large stocks.
5. For an analysis of the functions of the IMF cereal import facility, and an examination of the factors that led to its establishment, see Adams (1983).
6. Between 1981 and 1985 a total of seven developing countries made drawings from the IMF cereal import facility. These drawings totalled 962.5 million special drawing rights (SDRs).
7. For a detailed examination of possible ways in which the rules governing the use of the IMF cereal import facility might be liberalised, see Ezekiel (1985).

8. For a sampling of this literature, see Srinivasan (1965) and Chakravarty (1969). For a more detailed critique of this literature, see Mellor (1974).
9. For more on the way these markets operate, and the implications for employment growth and other variables, see Lele and Mellor (1981).
10. Much of the information in the foregoing paragraphs comes from Kennedy and Pinstrup-Andersen (1983).
11. See Anderson *et al.* (1981) and Beaton and Ghassemi (1979).
12. See, for example, Isenman and Singer (1977) and Islam (1972).

References

ADAMS, R. H. (1983) 'The role of research in policy development: the creation of the IMF cereal import facility', *World Development*, vol. 11 (7), pp. 549–63.
ANDERSON, M. *et al.* (1981) *Nutrition Intervention in Developing Countries, Study 1: Supplementary Feeding* (Cambridge, Mass.: Oelgeschlager, Gunn and Hain).
BANGLADESH INSTITUTE OF DEVELOPMENT STUDIES (BIDS) and INTERNATIONAL FOOD POLICY RESEARCH INSTITUTE (IFPRI), Washington (1984) *Results of the Household Survey of the Food-for-Work Programme*, Prepared by Siddiqur Rahman Osmani (Dhaka: BIDS; Washington DC: IFPRI).
BEATON, G. H. and H. GHASSEMI (1979) *Supplementary Feeding Programs for Young Children in Developing Countries* (New York: United Nations Childrens Fund).
BRUNDIN, H. (1978) *Food for Work Saturation Level and Constraints to Expansion Study* Dhaka: US Agency for International Development).
CHAKRAVARTY, S. (1969) *Capital and Development Planning* (Cambridge, Mass.: MIT Press).
EZEKIEL, H. (1985) *The IMF Cereal Import Financing Scheme*, Report prepared for the Food and Agricultural Organisation, Rome and the International Food Policy Research Institute, Washington DC.
FOOD AND AGRICULTURAL ORGANISATION (1984) *Food Aid Bulletin*, no. 1 (Rome: FAO).
FOOD AND AGRICULTURE ORGANISATION (1984) *FAO Trade Yearbook*, vol. 37 (Rome: FAO).
FOOD AND AGRICULTURE ORGANISATION (1985) *Food Aid in Figures, 1984* (Rome: FAO).
HAZELL, P. (1984) 'Sources of increased variability in world cereal production since the 1960s', *Journal of Agricultural Economics*, vol. 36(2), pp. 145–59.
HAZELL, P. and A. ROELL (1983) 'Rural growth linkages: household expenditure patterns in Malaysia and Nigeria', *Research Report*, no. 41 (Washington DC: International Food Policy Research Institute).
HUDDLESTON, B. (1984) 'Closing the cereals gap with trade and food aid', *Research Report*, no. 43 (Washington DC: International Food Policy Research Institute).
HUDDLESTON, B. *et al.* (1984) *International Finance for Food Security* (Baltimore: Johns Hopkins University Press).

INTERNATIONAL MONETARY FUND (1982) *Government Finance Statistics Yearbook* (Washington DC).

ISENMAN, P. and H. W. SINGER (1977) 'Food aid: disincentive effects and their policy implications', *Economic Development and Cultural Change*, vol. 25(2), pp. 205–37.

ISLAM, N. (1972) 'Foreign assistance and economic development: the case of Pakistan', *Economic Journal*, vol. 82, pp. 502–30.

IYENGER, L. (1967) 'Effect of dietary supplementation late in pregnancy on the expectant mother and her newborn', *Indian Journal of Medical Research*, 55 (January).

KENNEDY, E. and P. PINSTRUP-ANDERSEN (1983) *Nutrition-Related Policies and Programs: Past Performances and Research Needs* (Washington DC: International Food Policy Research Institute).

LELE, U. (1981) 'Rural Africa: modernization, equity and long-term development', *Science*, vol. 211, pp. 547–53.

LELE, U. and J. W. MELLOR (1981) 'Technological change, distributive bias and labour transfer in a two sector economy', *Oxford Economic Papers*, vol. 33(7), pp. 426–41.

MAXWELL, S. J. (1978) 'Food aid, food for work and public works', *Discussion Paper*, no. 127 (Brighton: Institute of Development Studies).

MAXWELL, S. J. and H. W. SINGER (1979) 'Food aid to developing countries: a survey', *World Development*, vol. 7(3), pp. 225–47.

MELLOR, J. W. (1974) 'Models of economic growth and labour-augmenting technological change in foodgrain production', in N. Islam (ed.), *Agricultural Policy in Developing Countries* (New York: Wiley).

MELLOR, J. W. (1976) *The New Economics of Growth* (Ithaca, NY: Cornell University Press).

MELLOR, J. W. (1978) 'Food price policy and income distribution in low-income countries', *Economic Development and Cultural Change*, vol. 27(1), pp. 1–26.

MELLOR, J. W. (1984) 'Food aid: reflections on a decade of action', *Food and Nutrition*, vol. 10(1), pp. 91–104.

PAULINO, L. (forthcoming), *Food in the Third World: Past Trends and Projections to 2000* (Washington DC: International Food Policy Research Institute).

REUTLINGER, S. and D. BIGMAN (1981) 'Feasibility, effectiveness and costs of food security alternatives in developing countries', in A. Valdes (ed.) *Food Security for Developing Countries* (Boulder, Col.: Westview Press).

SINGER, H. W. (1984) 'Success stories of the 1970s: some correlations', *World Development*, vol. 12(9).

SRINIVASAN, T. N. (1965) 'A critique of the optimizing planning model', *Economic Weekly*, Annual Number (February).

VALDES, A. (1984) 'A note on variability in international grain prices', unpublished paper prepared for IFPRI Workshop on Food and Agricultural Price Policy (Washington DC: International Food Policy Research Institute).

VALDES, A. and P. KONANDREAS (1981) 'Assessing food insecurity based on national aggregates in developing countries', in A. Valdes (ed.), *Food Security for Developing Countries* (Boulder, Col.: Westview Press).

WALLERSTEIN, M. (1980) *Food for War – Food for Peace: United States Food Aid in a Global Context* (Cambridge, Mass.: MIT Press).

WORLD BANK (1979) *Draft Report of an International Comparative Study of the Performance of Employment-creating Public Works Programs* (Washington DC).

WORLD BANK (1981) *Accelerated Development in sub-Saharan Africa: An Agenda for Action* (Washington DC).

WORLD BANK (1984) *World Development Report, 1984* (Washington DC).

WORLD FOOD PROGRAMME (1976) *Interim Evaluation Report: Bangladesh 2197 Q-Relief Works Program for Land and Water Development* (Rome).

WORLD FOOD PROGRAMME (1985) *Review of Food Aid Policies and Programmes*, Committee on Food Aid Policies and Programmes, WFP/CFA: 19/5 (Rome).

10 The Effectiveness of Aid as a Problem of Bureaucratic Management

Jens H. Schulthes

PUTTING THE LAST FIRST – THE MESSAGE AND THE MEDIUM

Concern with aid effectiveness is not new,[1] but recently the debate seems to have taken a new turn, and one which is particularly alarming to aid bureaucrats, among whom this writer counts himself. As the purpose of aid is being more closely articulated – changing the condition of the poorest – the task of aid administrations is becoming correspondingly more ambitious. However, recognition is also growing that this task is not being accomplished: that the poorest are seldom reached, and sometimes even harmed by aid; that methods of evaluating the effects of aid, perhaps even of distinguishing success from failure, are inadequate; and that, in general, both the conceptual basis of development aid, and the organisational structures which govern its delivery, are of a nature that makes its effectiveness uncertain. There is a growing sense of failure,[2] and it is taking hold even within the aid organisations themselves.[3] Aid bureaucrats begin to ask themselves whether their task is not perhaps too difficult, 'the game too tough' (Elliot Berg).

Just how difficult the task is, comes out clearly in two recent books: Robert Chambers' *Rural Development – Putting the Last First* (1983), and Brigitte Erler's *Tödliche Hilfe – Bericht von meiner letzten Dienstreise in Sachen Entwicklungshilfe* (1985).[4] The two books could not be more different in style and quality: the first is as rich in experience, nuanced and constructive as the second is superficial, sweeping and bitterly polemic. Both authors, however, look not at aid programmes, but at the people who implement them, and both share the same preoccupation: that there are powerful biases at work throughout all aid systems making it almost impossible that the last are indeed put first. Chambers is stronger in the analysis of the reasons and conflicts of interest which produce such biases; Ms Erler is more outspoken in demonstrating where they are located – within the aid bureaucracies, of donors and recipients alike.

This approach is still exceptional.[5] Most aid organisations continue to view the problem of effectiveness from the conceptual and procedural angle: refinement of programming methodology and of the 'project cycle',[6] food policy analysis, development of food strategies, donor co-ordination and more recently a shift in emphasis from project to programme aid (see World Food Council, 1985), policy dialogue and structural reform (for example World Bank, 1984), to mention only a few of the major variations on the same theme.

Refinements of approach are certainly important elements in the efforts to increase aid effectiveness. Yet, in the absence of other changes, one must doubt whether they will make the decisive difference any more than did previous efforts of the same kind (e.g. the UN Capacity Study of 1969). On the contrary, by further refining the conceptual framework of aid, or by perfecting the techniques of programming and delivery, these efforts may well add to the complexity of the task and in the end simply aggravate further the discrepancy between 'reality and rhetoric' (Bauer, 1984).

It is the thesis of this paper that the problem of aid effectiveness is not primarily one of 'approach', but that its roots reach deeper: into the very nature and limitations of bureaucracy itself. To borrow from Marshall McLuhan: the 'message' of aid – i.e. putting the last first – must pass through the 'medium' of bureaucracy, and so must necessarily be affected, perhaps transformed, certainly conditioned by it. Too little attention has so far been given in the literature to this interaction, and aid organisations, not surprisingly, do not reflect much about it. Perhaps the subject is so general in scope that it seems to defy any attempt at drawing practical conclusions. On the other hand, the fact that so great a variety of aid programmes have all experienced similar types of failure suggests that the problem must have a common origin. This paper argues that a better understanding of bureaucracy can provide some explanation of that common origin.

The paper attempts to describe development aid in terms of a bureaucratic function; and to identify some of the specific constraints by which bureaucratic aid management is almost inevitably flawed. It attempts to propose areas in which changes in current practices could perhaps bring some measure of improvement. On the other hand, it may be that the management of international aid on the current scale simply goes beyond the kind of task with which bureaucracies can effectively cope. The game may indeed be too tough.

MUST AID BE BUREAUCRATIC

The term 'bureaucratic' is today used unthinkingly in a pejorative sense and is applied typically to the international or national aid organisations when contrasting them with the voluntary agencies and non-governmental organisations, which are considered as non-bureaucratic alternatives. Lord Bauer (1984, p. 61 and preface) goes as far as to exclude 'the work of voluntary agencies' from his definition of aid. For the purpose of this paper, the term 'bureaucracy' is used in the sense in which Max Weber has developed and indeed praised it.[7] As his analysis of bureaucracy is essential to this paper, a brief summary of it will probably be helpful.

Weber's starting point is the observation that the possible types of legitimate authority ('Herrschaft') are finite, and in fact limited to three: the traditional, based on the everyday belief in the sanctity of tradition and the legitimacy of the acts of the traditional ruler; the charismatic, based on the exceptional and voluntary trust in the order established by an exceptional and heroic leader; and the rational, based on the acceptance of the legality of statutory order and of the authority of government acts emanating from it, irrespective of persons. Weber goes on to show how rational government, with its emphasis on objective, non-personal authority (law, statutes, rules and procedures), functions through bureaucracy, i.e. a staff corps constituted on the basis of continuing employment, salary, pension, advancement, formal education and professional background, division of labour, firmly defined terms of reference, documented proceedings (dossier), hierarchical order; in other words, people of professional qualification, adhering objectively to rules and procedures, but – within the standards of professional ethics – motivated by legitimate self-interest rather than 'enthusiasm' (Weber, 1976, p. 129), and not personally involved in a 'cause'. The idea of legitimate self-interest on the part of bureaucrats and, beyond the individual, on the part of bureaucratic systems, is important in Weber's concept of bureaucracy and is, therefore, emphasised here. Weber recognises it as a flaw, but one which is inevitable: when conflict arises, bureaucrats and bureaucracies will, at a certain point, put themselves first.

Weber's most important conclusion is that of the inescapability

(Unentrinnbarkeit) of bureaucratisation: because of its rational and impersonal professionalism, it is more reliable and objective, faster, technically more effective and, therefore, historically superior to all other forms of government. Thanks to this superiority, it develops its own power and self-interest. Consequently, all sectors of public life, not only government, but also industry, political parties, trade unions, churches, and indeed all administrations of any size become progressively bureaucratised. What is more, once bureaucratisation has been achieved, it is irrevocable. Eventually, bureaucracy becomes universal.

If bureaucratisation is the fate of all forms of modern administration, aid organisations cannot expect to be exempted from it. All large aid organisations, national or international, are today thoroughly bureaucratised, and new programmes are following the same inescapable trend as they grow. Voluntary or non-governmental organisations may resist this trend, as long as they are clearly based on personalised responsibility and other than purely professional motivation (typically religious missions), but they will remain in this state only as long as they remain very small. It should be noted also that recipient governments end up by exercising control over the programmes carried out in their countries by voluntary agencies or non-governmental organisations as soon as these programmes attain any size; and that the aid bureaucracies of the recipients are, of course, no less bureaucratic than those of the donors. As long as billions of dollars worth of resources are to be transferred as aid from donor to recipient countries, there is no alternative but bureaucracy (again Max Weber 'The alternative to bureaucracy is dilettantism' (Ibid., p. 128). If bureaucracies cannot perform it, then the task cannot be performed.

CAN BUREAUCRACIES PERFORM THE TASK?

One hesitates even to ask this question, since there is in any case no alternative. Max Weber, writing in 1913, counted welfare, allocation of public funds to target groups and, in general, 'social pacification' (Ibid., p. 561), (incidentally: also 'overseas expansion', p. 560) among the areas into which, because of their complexity and need for professionalism, bureaucracy would naturally extend. For him, complexity was an argument for, rather than against, bureaucratisation. He did not foresee that a legitimate public task could go beyond the technical capacities of the bureaucracy to which it was assigned, although he did foresee that it could exceed the capability of its political leadership (see below). Modern development aid, however, may be just such a task. This paper examines three aspects which distinguish bureaucratic aid management from the functions of the classical bureaucracies and which, taken together, indeed make the task of aid bureaucracies a formidable one: lack of authoritative policy, too great a complexity and a particular exposure to conflict.

POLICY: HOW AUTHORITATIVE CAN IT BE?

Bureaucracy, although it has its legitimate role, power and dignity, is, in the eyes of Max Weber, only an instrument for the implementation of policy. Policy is determined not by the bureaucracy itself, but by an external political authority. Weber's concept of bureaucracy would be incompletely described without reference to the non-bureaucratic, that is political, leadership which determines policy, controls its implementation and ultimately assumes responsibility for its success or failure (Ibid., pp. 832–7).

May one consider aid bureaucracies from this aspect? If one does, the conclusion appears inescapable that their first, and perhaps greatest, difficulty lies in the absence of politically responsible leadership and in the resulting uncertainty of authoritative policy, authoritative in the sense of political legitimation. The problem is as obvious as it is unsolvable: different from the classical bureaucracies, which function on their own national territories, aid bureaucracies, by definition, deal with issues that affect both donor and recipient countries, and there exists no supra-national authority for development. While it is often deplored that aid has become 'too political', it is, at least in this sense, not political enough. This is one of the conclusions of a stimulating paper, *Effectiveness of Aid in Support of Food Strategies*, recently published by the World Food Council, the international body with the clearest political mandate in the field of aid. There the point is made that effectiveness of aid requires 'the explicit delineation of the policy conflicts and resource trade-offs' which are inherent in the support of food strategies, without, of course, being able to say who should be the ultimate arbiter of these conflicts.

While the problem is unsolvable in principle, in practice there are important nuances between different aid bureaucracies in respect of their access to, and support from, policy guidance. Certain donor governments and parliaments provide stronger and more informed leadership to their aid agencies than do others. Certain recipient countries are more selective in their acceptance of aid than others, and aid selectivity on the part of recipients is a strong element of policy (this point is also made in the World Food Council paper quoted above). Certain international 'governing bodies' provide more effective leadership than others and in this connection, structured voting rights can have a strong influence (World Bank). The subject requires more detailed study, which goes beyond the scope of this paper. Here, the point to be made is that lack of authoritative policy is one of the sepcific handicaps of aid bureaucracies.

COMPLEXITY: A BEWILDERING MULTIPLICITY OF CONCERNS

The classical national bureaucracies of, say, justice, finance or even welfare have behind them a wealth of legal and administrative tradition; they are embedded in a rich social context; they function under the daily scrutiny of, and response from, their clientele and, beyond that, of the local and national information media; and this within a framework of established supervision and guidance by leaders who are ultimately responsible to parliament. Over time, their tasks have become known and the approaches and techniques to be used in performing them have become defined by law and tradition, usually in great detail. This applies in particular to those national administrations allocating welfare or subsidies: they are neither invited nor permitted to make gifts. They are not dealing in 'free goods'.

Development aid, is, alas, precisely that: a 'free good', free in the sense of the absence of much of that supportive framework which, in the classical bureaucracies, tradition and legislation provide. Were they to be handled in the context of a classical bureaucracy, all development interventions, from a World Bank loan to a bilateral emergency food donation, would not only have a background in tradition but would also be required to have a solid legal basis. The development bureaucrat has, however, little guidance of this sort. Depending on the standards of his organisation, he will have collected whatever supporting social and economic data he could find, but these will often not be more than a fraction of what would be needed to back up a similar project for consideration by a national administration. Moreover, even if statistical information can be found, this does not necessarily mean that the cultural and social context of the project is being understood in terms of local customs, power relations and general human environment. No other type of bureaucracy faces this problem of understanding, and in no other bureaucracy is the discrepancy so great between theoretical prescriptive pronouncements (basic needs, integrated rural development, food security, popular participation, advancement of women, etc.) and the limits of understanding in practice.

Consider three simple examples of projects assisted by the World Food Programme (WFP): the first in the field of mother and child health care, the second in agricultural development, and the third in a case of drought emergency. These are among the most common types of activity suited to food aid intervention, and WFP alone supports over one hundred such projects at any one time, at a cost of several hundred million dollars annually. And yet the decision to commit resources even to such common projects is anything but simple. It assumes, for example, that satisfactory answers can be given to questions such as these:

Mother and child health care

Does malnutrition constitute a public health problem in the project area? How can this be known? Is food aid an adequate response, or would the problem be more effectively addressed by other measures such as nutrition education, or simply by the provision of clean drinking water? Will the project reach those most in need? Who are they? How effectively are the most needy targeted? At what cost? Will the distribution of food take too much of the technical staff's time and thereby affect the public health functions of the centres? Will collecting the food be too time consuming for mothers because of long distances to health centres? Is there a danger that the food supplied will act as a disincentive to breast feeding? What purpose precisely will the food serve, i.e. will it provide additional consumption for the beneficiaries and thereby directly improve their nutritional status? Or will it serve as an incentive for mothers to visit the health centres? If so, is this a legitimate incentive from the public health point of view? Or will it replace food that households would otherwise have purchased, and thus constitute additional income? In the latter case: are the rations sufficient to make any noticeable difference in the family budget? And can it be expected that such additional income will be spent on food and that this food will have a nutritional effect on the target beneficiaries (remember that the project was supposed to improve the nutrition of poor mothers and children)? Is it necessary to know what the households in the project area will actually do with the additional income? And if it is considered necessary to know this, how can it be known? And how can the nutritional effect or any other effect of the project be observed? At what cost? Will the government continue the programme after the aid has terminated?

Agricultural development (irrigated rice production)

Is rice a suitable crop for the country, ecologically, economically, nutritionally? Is production through irrigation cost-effective, given the energy requirements? Will rice produced in this way be competitive with imported rice? If not, is there justification for subsidising it? Is the additional labour available that will be necessary for work in the new fields or for the production of two crops instead of the previous one? Do the farmers want to work for two crops? During which season will the work be required and will it conflict with other seasonal employment of the beneficiaries? Who will provide the labour, men or women? If women, what effect will this have on their workload (household tasks, child care)? Or on their income (from work in their own fields or gardens)? Is the government approach of encouraging large mechanised perimeters appropriate or should priority be given to small village schemes? What is the land tenure system, and who will ultimately benefit from the project? Is the government organisation which will operate the project effective? Is it working in the interest of the rural poor? More specifically in regard to the food aid input: are the works labour-intensive and suitable for food aid, or should they be carried out with heavy equipment? Assuming that the beneficiaries will be improving their own land, is food really needed as an incentive? For how long? What kind of food? And in what quantity? Based on nutritional requirements or on local retail value? How are households going to use the food? Will they sell it? Does it matter?

Drought emergency

What is the overall crop shortfall likely to be? Can this be reliably estimated? When will it be known with sufficient certainty to justify aid commitments by donors? How many people are or will be affected, and where are they? Can food reach them, how, at what cost, and by when? Considering the inevitable delays in the donor procurement system, is it realistic to expect that food will arrive before the next harvest? If not, what additional arrangements would have to be made for putting it to good use? How many of the affected people really need outside assistance? All? One half? One third? How will the need be ascertained? Should food be provided free, or against payment, or in return for labour? For how long? In the case of nomads or other pastoral populations, what is to be done about their animals? Should they also be fed? What will happen to the beneficiaries after food aid comes to an end? Will those who have been in camps wish to return to nomadic life after a year or more of free food distribution, health service, and perhaps schools for their children? Will nomads be able to leave the camps if they have no animals? Should they be forced to leave? If the beneficiaries have been farmers, will they have seeds etc. to start production again? Can the emergency operation be phased into a development project? Who will do that?

This is a somewhat breathless presentation of issues, to be sure. But it serves to demonstrate the variety of concerns that even the most common aid intervention unavoidably raises. Nor does it attempt to be complete. Any good project analyst would quickly point to important omissions; and comparable lists of technical issues quite different from these would of course have to be made for projects in other fields: rural infrastructure, community development, settlement, education, energy, not to mention sectoral programmes like the restructuring of a cereal production and marketing system. The above examples have been taken from project food aid merely because of the author's more immediate familiarity with this field. Any other type of aid gives rise to a similar number of issues. Aid bureaucracies have to build up knowledge in a greater variety of fields than the classical bureaucracies are expected to deal with.

Moreover, while specific technical problems can be solved and their solution applied in other projects, there are more general aid issues which, although they surface regularly with each new project, remain unresolved. Taking examples again from food aid, these are typical issues: the relative importance of malnutrition as an impediment to development is not fully understood. The disincentive effects (creation of beneficiary dependency, displacement of local production, retardation of policy adjustments) are difficult to observe, and even more difficult to demonstrate to the satisfaction of all parties concerned. The problem of fungibility remains today as unresolved as it was when Hans Singer pointed to it in 1964: a large portion of aid goes to projects which the recipient government would have undertaken in any case, and thereby in effect provides budget support to the government not for the project for which it is intended, but for a different and usually unknown one, which, for the donor, would probably have a lower priority. The problem is particularly acute for medium-size programmes, whose contributions remain below the threshold at which government planning can be made the subject of meaningful conditions and dialogue. In the case of smaller programmes, there is often no other alternative than to ignore the problem and simply assume that their assistance is, in fact, additional.

In short, aid is not self-targeting, and in administering it, aid bureaucracies are invariably faced with a 'bewildering multiplicity of concerns' (Bauer, 1984, p. 162). Nor is this multiplicity even finite, or such that an organisation could eventually and over time fully master those concerns peculiar to its own particular field. New ones (priorities, strategies, approaches) are continuously being added. Aid bureaucracies are expected to develop a much greater learning capacity than is required from the classical bureaucracies.

THE WEAKNESS IN ADDRESSING CONFLICT

Unless provided with specific codes and procedures, as for instance in the case of magistrates or tribunals, bureaucracies are not effective in dealing with conflict. Conflict arises over a 'cause' and bureaucrats have no 'cause'. This point was made earlier, but it is central to the thesis of this paper and is, therefore, made again here: bureaucracies are necessarily and inescapably made up of functionaries who, within the bounds and standards of professional quality and ethics (which can be high), are motivated by self-interest. To perceive, and then settle, conflict requires more: it requires 'enthusiasm' (Weber), that is, willingness to take a stand, to accept risks, to cross boundaries and assume responsibilities beyond the formal terms of reference of a given position in the hierarchy; and it requires all this not only in the person of one individual, but collectively: to be effective, the individual needs the loyalty and support of the higher echelons and of the organisation as a whole. This support tends to be forthcoming only up to a point, beyond which the 'conflict-conscious' individual in a bureaucracy tends to be isolated. All bureaucracies have a deeply rooted aversion to conflict and a keenly developed sense for eliminating it as soon as it occurs.

In the case of classical bureaucracies, this is not fatal because, as pointed out earlier, conflicts can be settled by external authorities, the settlements then providing the policy for the executing bureaucracy. This applies typically to those areas which, in a national context, are comparable to development aid, e.g. the allocation of subsidies in favour of specific groups or regions.

Aid bureaucracies do not have this recourse, although of course, development aid is fraught with conflict. The allocation of scarce resources in favour of specific groups excludes, by definition, other groups. Aid programmes favour the least developed countries, or the poorest sectors of a given population, or landless labourers, or women, or children. It is only the extreme degree of abstraction (Erler, 1985, p. 97) inherent in the term 'development' which conveniently hides the fact that, by definition, these programmes signify change, i.e. that they run counter to established systems and structures and that their implementation in practice will invariably affect hard-won positions and vested interests, meaning conflict. Every aid administrator knows what Brigitte Erler has called 'the unholy alliance' (Ibid., pp. 83–6): the need to accommodate the interests of the donor or recipient establishment, or both, against one's own better professional judgement and against the interest of the intended project beneficiaries.

Moreover, conflicts do not only arise as a kind of 'end product' in the developing countries and within the confines of a specific programme or project. Conflict is inherent in all relations of the aid bureaucracy with donors, recipient countries, other agencies, and internally. The adoption of doctrine, the selection of programmes or projects, the organisational structure, and, not least, the personnel policy: none of these remain untouched for long. The entire fabric of an aid bureaucracy is affected by the basically conflictual nature of its aims and *raison d'être*; and, not least, by the fundamental discrepancy, never admitted, between its altruistic purpose – aid – and the egoistic principle of its organisation – self-interest. Putting the last first is, for a bureaucracy, an extremely hard task.

Faced with this task, and the massive amount of conflict inherent in it, and in the absence of authoritative policy, one would expect aid bureaucracies to develop ways to avoid conflict, diffuse it, patch it over, or elevate it to a higher and non-controversial level of abstraction – and thereby neutralise it. And that is, of course, precisely what they do. The enormous investment by the aid community in conferences, committees, *ad hoc* consultations, symposia, workshops, task-forces, further studies; the never-ending attempts at greater integration and co-ordination, the frequent resorting to consultancies, to say nothing of the endless procession of missions to developing countries is, much of it, the bureaucratic response to conflict. Organisational distinction between planning and implementation, or reference of problems to further study or other fora, to new procedures and systems, and, generally, to a higher level of abstraction, is the typical way of avoiding decision. It is the 'escape from responsibility'.[8]

If conflicts arise on the theoretical issues of doctrine and programme, they arise even more sharply on the practical question of aid effectiveness. Because they are less supported by law, tradition and known social context, aid interventions necessarily involve a higher level of assumption, speculation and hence risk than do the acts of classical bureaucracies, and continuous evaluation is, therefore, crucial. Aid bureaucracies, more than others, depend on their willingness and capacity to learn from their own errors. Here again, the situation of classical bureaucracies is different: their effectiveness is judged by outside authorities and these authorities then draw conclusions and, if need be, impose sanctions. Aid bureaucracies have no recourse to this type of authority and, therefore, have no alternative but to evaluate themselves.

This statement may come as a surprise, particularly to those who advocate 'independent' evaluation of aid programmes and who expect significant improvement to derive from it.[9] The fact is that independent evaluation is largely a myth. Evaluation of aid is an extremely costly and complex undertaking. Even if the sources of financing could be found fully from the outside (which is the exception), organisational arrangements would still have to be made in collaboration with the programme to be evaluated, and would have to accommodate bureaucratic concerns at some point. But what is more important, independent evaluation is only valuable to the extent that it assumes responsibility for the consequences of its findings. There has to be an authority which declares the findings valid and imposes their application. Early on in this paper, the point has been made that such authority does, for most aid bureaucracies, not exist.

Considered in this light, the evaluation efforts of many aid organisations are respectable, and, in some, the institutional arrangements, as well as expenditures, made for them are impressive. Even these, however, stop short of going into the type of investigations (and findings) that could cast serious doubts on a particular programme, and perhaps even endanger the existence of the organisation itself. The professional ethics of bureaucrats, individually or collectively, simply do not require, nor does their environment allow them to push evaluation to a point at which the system itself is called in question. In the case of the evaluation of development assistance, this point is often uncomfortably close. Aid bureaucracies, therefore, have particular difficulties in learning from their own errors.

ARE CHANGES POSSIBLE? – WHAT MAKES SUCCESS?

While this analysis is not an optimistic one, it does not apply equally to all forms of aid. Many non-governmental or voluntary organisations, although individually small, provide aid which not only is signficant in its total volume, but which also sets examples and standards for the aid community as a whole. A large sector of financial aid relies on the established know-how and criteria of banking. Other types of aid intervene directly at the political level, involving more than the usual political responsibility of the decision makers. The tripartite development of labour relations promoted by ILO can fall into this category, as can sectoral restructuring programmes that are of sufficient size and importance to encourage the corresponding policy reforms by recipient governments. Yet another type of aid can be purely humanitarian, as for instance multilateral and bilateral emergency aid. These forms of aid, although of course executed by bureaucracies like all others, are, to a certain extent, guided by non-bureaucratic (commercial, political, moral) considerations, which can support bureaucratic decision-making. Technical or food assistance to integrated rural development, education, nutrition, participation of women, etc. does not benefit from the same concrete guidance or government interest. There are also differences between multilateral and bilateral aid organisations in respect of their political responsibility; or between recipient countries in respect of the quality of their aid administrations. All these are differences of nuance rather than principle, but nuance in development aid can be the essential ingredient. Nevertheless, the phenomenon of low effectiveness is sufficiently common to warrant the search for a common explanation. All aid organisations have experienced the frustration of finding that, when searching for their own success stories, these tend, upon reflection, to diminish in number. Unqualified successes are very rare.

If one reflects further about the reasons and conditions that have made a particular project successful, one is invariably led to the individual: a courageous political leader in the recipient country, an experienced desk or field officer in the aid organisation, a perceptive technical expert, an enthusiastic project director in the government department – all of them members of a bureaucracy, but all with that extra element of understanding, imagination, intelligence, self-critic-ism, experience, meticulousness; and initiative, willingness to take a stand and assume responsibility; in short, with that extra element of professional, managerial and perhaps also human calibre which it takes to master complexity and to face conflict; and which within their own organisations, mark then as exceptional. It seems that successful aid interventions require exceptionally good people.

THE IMPORTANCE OF THE INDIVIDUAL

While there are, obviously, a large number of objective factors – material, conceptual and procedural – required for the success of any development undertaking, they all seem to converge on the human factor. Policies, resources, institutional knowledge, systems, proce-dures, all these are important, but in the ultimate analysis, all have to be applied by individual people. Norman Borlaug has made the point that, in order to increase agricultural production in the developing countries, the scientific knowledge was already available in various places and disciplines, but that what was lacking was 'that rare bird, the integrator' who would bring this fragmented knowledge together. This is true in a much wider sense than just that of agricultural science and technology: complexity in general has to be understood before it can be reduced to manageable essentials, and conflict has to be articulated before it can be addressed and resolved. Both require a power of intellectual and managerial integration, which only indivi-duals can provide in a responsible manner.[10]

If the emphasis on the individual appears to the reader as perhaps a little banal or as a truism, a moment's reflection will show that it nevertheless aims at the field in which bureaucracies face their greatest challenge, and in which contrary forces are most powerful: personnel management. There are many reasons for this.

Among the most important of them, and initially to the credit of bureaucracies, is their restraint in providing themselves with the necessary manpower, or put more technically, in establishing positions. Conscious of the inherent trend, described above, towards expansion and buildup of power, responsible bureaucracies develop mechanisms for checking it.[11] As a result, creation of new staff positions is among those items of expenditure which are most suspiciously considered, jealously reviewed and rigidly controlled. To take the concrete example of the World Food Programme, we find that expenditures for material goods – food, ocean transport, computer systems, documentation – although by orders of magnitude higher than personnel costs, are much more freely delegated to middle management than is the creation of the lowest level secretarial position. A more detailed analysis would probably reveal a similar situation in many other aid bureaucracies, international or national. There are, of course, other factors which contribute to this restraint, including the currently widespread criticism and suspicion of aid, and the lack of familiarity with its requirements on the part of national budget authorities. As a result, no other type of bureaucracy, except the military, handles a comparable volume of public funds, through a comparable number of projects, with so few people. Among the most serious problems facing many aid bureaucracies is their sheer lack of staff.[12]

A second major constraint, this one not to the credit of aid bureaucracies, is their failure or neglect to develop systematic knowledge of what exactly characterises a good aid manager. The professional profile of 'that rare bird, the integrator' is simply not known and very little effort is made by aid bureaucracies to improve their understanding of it. All aid organisations have developed elaborate rituals for the selection and promotion of staff, but a more detailed study of their perceptions in respect of desired qualifications, and of the procedures adopted to assure compliance with these, would probably reveal an astonishing lack of focus – astonishing, if considered in the light of the volume of resources later to be entrusted to that staff. The failure to develop first a theoretical basis, and then an operational system for staff selection is all the more serious because of the strong counter-forces to be found in all bureaucracies, which inevitably militate against the efforts made to put the right man in the right place: seniority, hierarchy, continuing employment, knowledge of languages and national representation, to say nothing of a multitude of outside pressures. No matter what they proclaim, bureaucracies are not geared to imaginative personnel management and consideration of personal qualities. Admittedly, aid bureaucracies have a particularly difficult task here because of the wide range of functions which do not correspond, and cannot, therefore, be referred to more traditional professional profiles and career paths. However, the problem should not be entirely insurmountable, particularly if more attention was to be given to the personality profile of the good aid manager. Provided that the requirements are clearly perceived, and that sufficient priority and resources are devoted to the task, bureaucracies can successfully manage even very complex personnel selection requirements, for instance, those used for selecting airline pilots.

Airline pilots are personally responsible for the success or failure of their job. Although the example is an extreme one, it throws light on a general problem, which affects all bureaucracies: their tendency to reduce personal responsibility. Bureaucracies elaborately spread over as many functions as possible what good management would try to concentrate in a single person: responsibility. In a bureaucracy, there are as a rule no sanctions for failure or rewards for success because neither is attributable to the individual. Bureaucratic organisation does not favour the role of 'integrator'. Responsibility of individual officers covers only specific components of a project, and not the project as a whole. A striking illustration of this is the apparently irrepressible growth in the reliance on consultants: the regular 'line' officer in aid organisations of any size is less and less expected to master the diversity of concerns covered by a project or to assume ultimate responsibility for the project as a whole. Aid bureaucracies have, in general, followed the trend to build up 'staff' to the detriment of 'line', and project concerns have become more and more the domain of consultants or special advisors who, by definition, provide advice which is free from managerial responsibility.

PROFESSIONAL QUALITY AND PERSONAL RESPONSIBILITY – THE IMPORTANCE OF PERSONNEL MANAGEMENT

This then would seem to be one area in which improvements in aid effectiveness ought to be sought: in the improvement of the professional quality of staff and in the recognition and strengthening of personal responsibility. In the view of the writer, this is the area which promises the greatest 'room for manoeuvre' (see Clay and Schaffer, 1984). However, it would also require a much more effective and determined management of personnel. This is a large field, and anything that can be said here can only indicate a direction, not specific actions. Time-honoured personnel and budget systems would have to be called in question. Professional requirements would have to be very much better understood than is now the case; and they would then have to be defined and translated into reliable selection procedures, including examinations and tests specifically designed for different kinds of tasks. This would be particularly important in international organisations which have to respect requirements of national representation. Perhaps even more important, continuous professional on-the-job training would have to be provided at levels which would be orders of magnitude higher than what is currently available. New types of contracts would have to be introduced in order to attract highly qualified managers from the outside for limited periods of time. Budget procedures in general would have to be made more responsive to changing personnel management needs. Levels of delegation would have to be examined and in particular the relationship between an organisation's headquarters and its field stations. There is currently a strong 'headquarters bias' in many aid administrations, which would have to be reversed. Use of consultancies would have to be viewed more critically in the light of how their outcome would be integrated into actual decision-making. The necessity for more and higher qualified staff, as well as arrangements to phase out less suitable staff, would have to be examined. The budgetary consequences of these measures would have to be faced. Above all, very much more time and attention would have to be given to the sector of personnel throughout all aid bureaucracies. High professional quality of staff and their willingness to assume personal responsibility have their price.

OUTLOOK

Greater attention to the personnel management in aid bureaucracies: is this a convincing course of action that could lead the way out of the dilemma of low effectiveness? Max Weber, who has inspired much of the effort of this paper, would probably not be impressed. He would readily agree with the emphasis on greater professional quality. Professionalism is one of the corner stones in his concept of bureaucracy, and there can be little doubt that, for many reasons, the professional quality of the staff of today's aid administrations leaves much to be desired. Improvements here would make an important difference, although Weber himself would point to the inherent limitations, among them the fact that in the interest of universal recruitability, bureaucracies tend to sacrifice excellence. This is evident in the international aid administrations, but it is to a less visible degree common to all bureaucracies. The insistence, on the other hand, on greater personal responsibility, Weber would probably not accept, because he would not see a place for it in the basically hierarchical structure of bureaucracy. He would argue that personal responsibility – both the burden and the privilege that went with it – belonged not to the professional staff of bureaucracies but to their political leaders, or else, to the entrepreneur.

This leads naturally to the question whether bureaucracies can in fact learn and benefit from the principles of modern business management, with its emphasis on action rather than systems, i.e. informal communication, delegation, team work, motivation, leadership, in short: individual people.[13] The subject is too wide to be pursued in more detail in this paper. Much effort has been, and continues to be, made to introduce modern management techniques into bureaucratic processes. If the personal observations of the writer were to be any guide, it would appear that the outcome has so far remained uncertain. The question is not only of applicability. Management principles are highly applicable to bureaucratic tasks, and upon their first introduction, their relevance is usually immediately perceived. Over time, however, the hierarchical structures of the bureaucracy seem to reassert themselves and the new management practices seem to be absorbed into the more traditional style, thereby losing their initial effect. Convincing evidence that bureaucratic administrations can adopt modern management techniques, particularly in the personnel sector, is still awaited.

Notes

1. No detailed review of aid criticism is intended in this paper, and a few names may therefore stand for many: P. T. Bauer (1971) and (1984); T. Hayter (1971); K. B. Griffin and J. Enos (1970); Hans Singer (1984), among others, has pointed to the convergence of dissent which may originate from quite different political leanings. A particularly helpful guide through the critical aid literature up to 1984 is found in L. de Silva (1984).
2. Most prominently evidenced in the case of Gunnar Myrdal (1982), see for instance 'The bucks stop here', article co-authored with Dudley Seers.

3. Aid organisations do not easily publish critical analyses of their own programmes, an exception being the EEC's 'Pisani Memorandum'; a critical analysis of aid effectiveness within the US System was presented by the Executive Director of the World Food Council in preparation for the WFC eleventh ministerial session (1985). See also R. Jolly's Barbara Ward Lecture, which, although personal, reflects a gloomy analysis of current aid effectiveness. The manuscript of this paper was completed before M. Bertrand of the UN Joint Inspection Unit published his very critical analysis of the effectiveness of the UN System. Although the main thrust of the report is towards structural reform, and although the main emphasis is on the political, in particular the peace-keeping function of the UN, there are some striking parallels in the analysis of the current constraints of the UN development bureaucracy (absence of political guidance, complexity of the task, inability to address conflict and bring about consensus, and above all, inadequacy of professional staff and recruitment/training practices). An area of possible disagreement with Bertrand would be whether these constraints are specific for the UN, as Bertrand seems to imply, or whether they are not, as this author believes, characteristic of all aid bureaucracies, international and national alike.

4. This book led to a wide discussion in the German language media, see for instance reviews by W. Böll (*Frankfurter Allgemeine Zeitung*, no. 155, 9 July 1985); O. Matzke (*Neue Zürcher Zeitung*, no. 104, 8 May 1985); J. Mayer-List (*Die Zeit*, no. 20, 10 May 1985; U. Holtz (*Vorwarts*, 8 June 1985); E. Haubold (*Frankfurter Allgemeine Zeitung*, 10 October 1985).

5. Included here should be a stimulating collection of essays edited by Clay and Schaffer (1984); individual essays will be referred to later on.

6. Well documented and, therefore, instructive is the case of the World Food Programme (WFP). See its *Review of Proposals for Improvement of WFP's Project Cycle*.

7. Although written in 1913, Weber's analysis of bureaucracy has remained a classic in Germany, and it seems to be gaining ground outside Germany, judging from the fact that major translations are recent (Italy, 1961; USA, 1968; France, 1971). Yet, turning to Max Weber for the purpose of this paper needs an explanation, because, obviously, much study has been devoted since to bureaucratic decision-making and the behaviour of bureaucrats. However, this is precisely the point: while a behaviourist approach is certainly useful for the understanding of individual bureaucratic decisions, it is not a good point of departure for a debate on bureaucratic aid management in general. Such a debate cannot lead anywhere, unless one is willing to recognise not only the flaws, but also the legitimacy and ethics of bureaucracy. This Weber does more explicitly than do subsequent writers.

8. This is one of the central themes of *Room for Manoeuvre* edited by Clay and Schaffer, quoted earlier. See, in particular, essays by M. Evans, 'Policy and Change: The Asian Development Bank' (pp. 75–100) and B. Schaffer, 'Towards Responsibility: Public Policy in Concept and Practice' (pp. 142–90).

9. One of the strongest advocates of independent evaluation continues to

be O. Matzke, who has been influential particularly in Germany and Switzerland through his continuous reporting on FAO and WFP in the daily newspapers *Neue Zürcher Zeitung* and *Frankfurter Allgemeine Zeitung*.

10. This point is made by S. D. Biggs, in Clay and Schaffer (1984), in his 'Awkward but Common Themes in Agricultural Policy'. Biggs contrasts the 'normative institutional engineering approach' with the real understanding of the local institutional context; and he emphasises in this connection the role of 'selectors', 'rejectors', 'adaptors' and 'innovators', i.e. of certain types of people as a necessary condition.

11. The motivating forces here are obviously complex and would merit more detailed consideration, particularly in light of the phenomenon that budgetary growth invariably tends to favour a buildup of 'staff' to the detriment of 'line'. Crozier (1964) (p. 194) has certainly touched on one important aspect of the problem when he explained it as a 'vicious circle': the rigidity of the bureaucratic task structure as well as the human relations network in bureaucracies results in lack of communication with the environment and among the organisation's groups; the resulting difficulties, instead of imposing a readjustment in the model, are utilised by individuals or groups for improving their position in the power struggle within the organisation; thus, a new pressure is generated for impersonality and centralisation, the only solution to personal privileges.

12. This point is strongly made by W. Böll in his critical, but in the last analysis concurring, review of B. Erler's book; Böll, who was a high official in the German Ministry of Co-operation, calculates the amount of resources that individual heads of country desks have to commit each year and finds that the amount – about $20 million – is too high. Amounts in certain UN organisations – WFP for example – can be far higher.

13. The literature on this subject is very large and growing. A typical but exceptionally readable and instructive recent example is T. Peters and R. Waterman, *In Search of Excellence* (New York, 1982).

References

BAUER, P. T. (1971) *Dissent on Development* (London: Weidenfeld & Nicolson).

BAUER, P. T. (1984) *Reality and Rhetoric – Studies in the Economics of Development* (London: Weidenfeld & Nicolson).

BERTRAND, M. (1985) *Some Reflections on Reform of the United Nations* (JIU/REP/85/9) (Geneva: UN Joint Inspection Unit).

CHAMBERS, R. (1983) *Rural Development – Putting the Last First* (Longman: London; New York: Lagos).

CLAY, E. J. and B. B. SCHAFFER (eds) (1984) *Room for Manoeuvre – An Exploration of Public Policy in Agriculture and Rural Development* (London: Heinemann).

CROZIER, N. (1964) *The Bureaucratic Phenomenon* (London: Tavistock).

DE SILVA, L. (1984) *Development Aid – A Guide to Facts and Issues* (Geneva: Third World Forum).

ERLER, B. (1985) *Tödliche Hilfe – Bericht von meiner letzten Dienstreise in Sachen Entwichkungshilfe* (Freiburg: Dreisam-Verlag).

EUROPEAN COMMUNITIES COMMISSION (1982) *Memorandum on the Commission's Development Policy* (COM(82)640 final) Brussels (The Pisani Memorandum)).

GRIFFIN, K. B. and J. ENOS (1970) 'Foreign assistance: objectives and consequences' *Economic Development and Cultural Change*, vol. 18, pp. 313–27.

HAYTER, T. (1971) *Aid as Imperialism* (London: Penguin).

JOLLY, R. (1985) *Adjustment with a Human Face* (The Barbara Ward Lecture) (Rome: Society for International Development).

MYRDAL, G. and D. SEERS (1982) 'The bucks stop here', *The Guardian*, 2 July (London).

PETERS, T. and R. WATERMAN (1982) *In Search of Excellence* (New York: Warner Books).

SINGER, H. W. (1964) *International Development – Growth and Change* (New York: McGraw-Hill).

SINGER, H. W. (1984) 'The ethics of aid', *Discussion Paper*, no. 195, p. 9, Institute of Development Studies, University of Sussex.

WEBER, M. *Wirtschaft und Gesellschaft – Grundriss der verstehenden Soziologie*, Fünfte, Revidierte Auflage, besorgt von J. Winckelmann, J. C. B. Mohr (Paul Siebeck), Tübingen, 1976.

WORLD BANK (1984) *Toward Sustained Development in Sub-saharan Africa: A Joint Program of Action* (Washington DC).

WORLD FOOD COUNCIL (1985) *Effectiveness of Aid in Support of Food Strategies* (paper for the Eleventh Ministerial Session) WFC/1985/3 (Rome).

WORLD FOOD PROGRAMME (1984) *Review of Proposals for Improvement of WFP's Project Cycle* (WFP/CFA:17/10) (Rome).

11 The Roles of Non-Governmental Organisations in Development

Larry Minear

A review of the roles of non-governmental organisations (NGOs) is appropriate in a volume on Poverty, Development and Food to honour one whose approach over the years has reflected the commitment of NGOs to place human beings, particularly the impoverished, at the centre of the development enterprise. Those roles as I see them are basically three: to assist the poor as operational development agents, to educate people to development imperatives, and to influence governments through advocacy of more appropriate public policies (Minear, 1983).

NGOs AS DEVELOPMENT AGENTS

NGOs have been around for a long time, pre-dating the organised efforts of governments to address human need. Reflecting perhaps a fundamental instinct of people to help each other, informal and, eventually, formal groupings have taken shape in communities on every continent. As communities have expanded and interdependence has become more planetary, local self-help efforts have assumed a more international character.

'In the last twenty to thirty years,' observes a recent study of NGOs by the Development Assistance Committee (DAC) of the Organisation for Economic Co-operation and Development (OECD), the development activities of NGOs 'have increased impressively: close to 2000 NGOs are now mobilising private financial and human resources in DAC-Member countries and channelling them directly, or indirectly, through some of the 6000–8000 [developing country] NGOs, toward development activities in more than 110 developing countries' (OECD, 1985, p. 1). DAC figures place NGO development grants from privately contributed funds in DAC-member countries at about $2.4 billion annually, supplemented by well over $1 billion in government funds.

There is more general awareness, no doubt, of this impressive scale of NGO resource mobilisation efforts than of the private agencies and networks engaged in carrying out development activities. The outpouring of private contributions to Africa stimulated by public events such as We are the World and Live Aid is far better known than the plethora of private agencies through which those contributions are ultimately channelled. Yet people-to-people channels do exist and are, with varying degress of success, assisting people in need.

The new-found prominence of NGOs reflects several realities. First, NGOs are the beneficiaries of widespread and growing scepticism about the effectiveness of official development assistance. While the critiques take varying form, most embody the view that development assistance, including food aid, has simply not accomplished its objectives.[1] The scepticism is typified by a recent US Senate report which, in recommending special funding for the African emergency, at the same time called for 'a thorough examination of longer-range developmental efforts for Africa'. Noting that official development assistance to sub-Saharan Africa during the past six years has topped $50 billion – the highest per capita allocation of any region – the report observed that 'it is necessary to ask why these very sizeable aid flows have been by and large ineffective' (US Senate, 1985a, p. 4).

Aid practitioners themselves acknowledge the limited success of governments in advancing equitable development. A 1970's review of World Bank project experience in Africa acknowledged that 'increased consciousness of the equity issue and the perceived impotency of the donors to deal with it' had led to rising criticism of official development agencies. However, it questioned not the validity of that judgement of World Bank loans but the view that the Bank should even be expected 'to improve incomes of the very poor and the landless through its projects' (Lele, 1979, pp. 240–1). Reflecting the concern of many governments that current aid approaches are in need of major revision, the World Food Council's ministers at their 1985 meeting urged a 'fresh appraisal of the theories and practices of international aid' (World Food Council, 1985, p. 32).

Second, popular and professional disillusion with governmental aid has been matched by a general belief in the effectiveness of people-to-people efforts. The public feels that NGOs can be counted on to go where the need is, roll up their sleeves and, with a minimum of administrative expense and bureaucratic folderal, get the job done. A United States congressional report credits American NGOs with 'contributing mightily to putting a human face on US foreign aid throughout the world (US Senate, 1985b, p. 35). While the public doubtless underestimates the extent to which NGOs depend on the co-operation of governments and overestimates the extent of their engagement with the very poor, experienced observers by and large locate the NGOs' major strength at the point of government aid programmes' major weakness: a failure to take account of the needs, aspirations, and potential for involvement of the poor at the community level.

The OECD (1985) study referred to above observers:

It is widely believed that the unique features of NGOs – or their 'comparative advantages' – are their ability to deliver emergency relief or development services at low cost to many people; their rapid, innovative and flexible responses to emerging financial and technical assistance needs at the grass-roots level; their long-standing familiarity with social sector development and poverty allevia-tion; their experience with small-scale development projects as well as with those requiring a high degree of involvement by, and familiarity with, the concerned target groups.

The paper goes on to observe that 'These are the very features frequently absent in LDC Governments'. The characterisation might well have been extended to external aid agency efforts as well. In the DAC Secretariat's view, the absence of the strengths represented by NGOs helps explain the 'inadequate ... progress [toward] reaching poverty alleviation objectives' which is in turn related to inadequate attention to 'the basic developmental issue of sub-Saharan Africa today, namely the low rate of return on investment'. A major opportunity is missed in that 'NGO efforts typically result in improving overall resource use within developing countries through helping to resolve human resource, institutional and absorptive capacity issues, by their provision of technical skills and organisational know-how' (OECD, 1985, p. 15).

The discovery of NGOs during the last decade by governments and official aid agencies – whether because of the limitations of their own effectiveness or the complementary nature of NGO activities – is something of a mixed blessing for NGOs themselves. First, governments naturally seek to integrate NGOs into their own programmes, an expectation which creates tensions on several scores. The number of NGOs alone is formidable. The Dutch aid agency during the years 1980–3 received co-financing requests for some 3500 projects by 2200 NGOs. (It funded many of them through four NGO consortia.) The field in the USA seems crowded with almost 170 individual NGOs registered with the Agency for International Development, plus many which are not.

Even if the diversity and heterogeneity of NGOs is somehow accommodated as part of a host government or aid agency country development plan – no mean accomplishment in itself – many NGOs do not visualise their contribution as lying in what the DAC Secretariat above termed 'their ability to deliver emergency relief or development services'. They seek instead to carry out individual projects, to demonstrate in selected communities that a given approach is workable, to organise local people to take charge of their own lives and avail themselves of their due from governments. It is too facile for governments to expect simply to plug NGOs into the gap between themselves and local communities.

Second, channelling governmental aid agency funds through NGOs can be a recipe for disaster unless both parties are clear in their expectations. United States government policy, for example, now views US NGOs as both 'independent [development] entities in their own right' and 'intermediaries in conducting AID programs' (USAID, 1982, p. 2). Yet as an operational development agency, and one which deals primarily in a government-to-government mode, AID tends to emphasise NGO activities as an extension of itself and to play down the extent to which private and voluntary agencies have – and need to protect – an existence and constituency independent of their relationships with government.

The DAC comments upon 'the need for donor governments to ensure that ... NGO autonomy can be maintained – and even strengthened' in the face of the substantial amounts of government resources frequently entrusted to these organisations (OECD, 1985, p. 11). However, all too easily NGOs gravitate into a similar dependence on government resources and direction to that which has undermined efforts towards self-reliance by recipient communities and nations in the developing world. Even from the United States government NGOs receive mixed signals. Given the disaffection with official aid programmes and official reluctance to entrust United States development funds to governments like those of Ethiopia,

Haiti, and the Philippines, NGOs have received more AID resources and direction – yet, at the same time, they are required to give more attention to maintaining their private characteristics. Some governments and aid agencies have been more successful than others in providing resources without hobbling the NGOs' unique contributions to development. The DAC's interest in assessing and promoting the best arrangements among member governments is encouraging.

Protecting the distinctive nature of NGOs even figures in a current discussion of their name. NGOs involved in the November 1984 World Food Assembly, an event they designed to review critically the decade since the World Food Conference, were generally agreed 'that "NGO" is a negative and inadequate definition, [quite] apart from the fact that it embraces many groups which are in no way concerned with people's development' (World Food Assembly, 1985, p. 4). The Assembly network is now being consulted about replacing 'NGO' with 'PDO' (Peoples Development Organisations), though there is some talk of scrapping the term 'development' as well in favour of a more explicitly equity- and solidarity-oriented tag.

Third, NGOs themselves have a great deal to learn from the way governments, aid agencies, and development institutes wrestle with issues. To be sure, NGOs can resist integration into countrywide development plans, can insist on accepting only those resources which will not compromise their autonomy, and can define themselves without reference to governments. Nevertheless, the fact remains that national development plans are increasingly seen to be indispensable to more effective efforts to improve the quality of life of the poor, and government resources appropriately provided can enhance the ability of change-oriented people's organisations to assist more effectively the dispossessed.[2]

A continuing weakness of many NGOs – and one which government aid agencies are increasingly seeking to address – is a lack of historical wisdom and expertise on development policy and strategy issues. A recent article in the *Washington Post* reviewed sympathetically the judgement of a seasoned professional that 'disaster relief is the last great [p]reserve of the professional amateur'. The old relief hand found adequate management capacity lacking not only in NGOs but in multilateral agencies, and donor governments as well.

Similar criticisms have been levelled at the development activities of NGOs, although the situation may be improving. There are probably fewer instances now than ten years ago, for example, of NGOs operating major food aid programmes in certain countries without the necessary in-country economic expertise available to them. However, some seasoned observers still fault NGOs for being more concerned with self-satisfying inputs than cost-effective outputs, for not matching a passionate concern for the poor with a hard-headed knowledge of economic and political realities.

There is surely some validity to the view that, just as NGOs rightly call on the major aid institutions to pay more attention to the microeffects of government policies on local communities, they themselves need to become more knowledgeable about macrofactors, even those they have little ability to influence. Economic factors and forces, international and national alike, affect not only the quality of life of the poor but ultimately the success of individual NGO projects as well. Particularly at a time of economic recession, NGOs dare not carry out their own activities in a policy vacuum nor assume the ability of governments to replicate their management-intensive efforts, irrespective of cost.

Whatever their views of governments and official aid agencies, NGOs have an interest in more effectively empowering the poor. Towards that end, there is clearly more room, well short of being taken over, for NGOs to share information, perceptions, and experience with governments. After all, as someone from government has pointed out, NGOs are the eyes and ears of the development system in the field. They tell us what rural people are thinking, doing, needing. Conversely, NGOs can also learn from governments in developing countries as they wrestle within the constraints of resource scarcity and political will to deal with the needs of their citizens. A clearer, more rational and more mutual division of labour would be a major step towards improved development effectiveness overall.

NGOS AS AN EDUCATIONAL FORCE

At a recent board meeting of a US NGO, a visitor from a Central American colleague agency reported on the situation in his country and on his agency's use of privately donated food and medicine, blankets and clothing from the United States. Against the backdrop of national civil strife and international East–West tension, he described withering government pressure on private organisations, such as his own, to make humanitarian aid a highly politicised instrument and to harass and intimidate private relief workers engaged in its provision.

Asked by a board member what more might be done by concerned outsiders, the visitor encouraged him to inform his American contributors about the nature of the situation and to apply pressure on the United States government to modify its policies. 'Was there not a need for more material resources?' the board member asked again. The answer came back the same. The exchange recalled the comment of an earlier day: 'Your government is speaking so loudly that we cannot hear what your missionaries are saying.'

NGOs are more aware these days than when Hans Singer first addressed development issues of the need to press beyond overseas projects to the related and indispensable tasks of global education and public policy advocacy. Some operational agencies have taken on those functions themselves, using their experience as practitioners to lend credibility to their efforts. In fact some agencies have found that, as their overseas activities have become more supportive of Third World colleague agencies rather than seeking to mount programmes administered by expatriate staff, they have been able to devote more attention to what only they can do: educate and mobilise their own constituencies at home.

Rather than developing expertise in education and advocacy themselves, some NGOs have charged consortia of which they are members with carrying out such work on their behalf. Still other NGOs, which are not themselves development practitioners, are devoted fulltime to educating citizens to the realities of global interdependence and to influencing their government towards more sensitive policies. The permutations are myriad and reflect the philosophy, objectives, constituency, and country setting of the particular NGO.

In one sense, there is nothing new about NGOs functioning as educators. Cultivating broad awareness of the need for the kind of assistance they can provide has always been a necessary part of nurturing a durable base of financial support. However, the role of NGOs as educational agents is something quite different from self-promotion. As US NGOs have recently formulated their task:

Development education has as a primary goal the building of a committed constituency for development both at home and abroad. It begins with a recognition of global interdependence and the continuing need for justice and equity in the world. Its programs and processes convey information, promote humanitarian values, and stimulate individual and community action aimed at improving the quality of life and eliminating the root causes of world poverty.[3]

As the statement suggests, the educational role of NGOs as it has developed in the last decade is based on a global approach to poverty and underdevelopment. Reflecting on what had been learned in the decade since the 1974 World Food Conference, North American NGOs submitted a document to the Tenth Ministerial Session of the World Food Council in Addis Ababa, in June 1984. In it they commented on the now clearer perception that wherever it exists, in developed as well as in developing countries, 'hunger has similar causes. Industrialised food-exporting countries no less than developing food-importing countries are wrestling with common issues such as assuring fair incomes to food producers, protecting small-farm agriculture, producing food in environmentally sustainable ways, and improving the quality of rural life'.

What has happened, of course, is not just that the common causality of hunger has been realised but that the impacts of an increasingly global world food economy are being felt. The document points out that

as food trade has increased among countries, agricultural self-reliance has been dealt a serious blow in many nations. Foodstores in developed and many developing countries have become global supermarkets. Many countries have increased their dependence on the international market-place for export earnings and for food imports. [Thus] the decade has witnessed not only a maturing perception of the global nature of agriculture but also a progressive internationalisation of many aspects of national economic life.

In this context, the burdensome agricultural abundance of food-exporting countries and the debilitating food shortages of poorer nations are signs not that some countries are doing better at implementing rational agricultural policies than others, but rather that both situations betoken an international food economy in serious need of repair. Overproduction and underproduction alike reflect the inability of governments to provide the proper context within which producers can flourish. The fact that the context is now no longer simply national, and therefore controllable, but rather one in which any government, however well-endowed its treasury and productive its producers, is vulnerable, provides a major educational challenge.

Food aid is a specific case in point. From the standpoint of sub-Saharan African countries, it is now increasingly indispensable to their very survival. From the standpoint of North America and the EEC countries, it is a major contribution to a life-and-death crisis. But from the standpoint of world food security, steadily rising food aid tonnages signal 'trends of growing external food dependence – and client state status ... [which] can and must be reversed' (Williams, 1985, p. 1). Chronic overproduction can never be the solution to chronic undernutrition. Western agricultural abundance can help Africa, but so too can changes in Western agricultural policies. African farmers can grow more food, but not in no-holds-barred competition with the highly protected farming and heavily subsidised exports of wealthy country producers. A world food system which pits some farmers against others and leaves 500 million people without basic food security is not in anyone's best interest.

The educational challenge faced by NGOs is thus formidable. At a time when it is tempting to see problems in isolation, NGOs need to be pointing out how interconnected hunger is. At a time of paralysing politicisation along East–West lines, NGOs need to be staking out the importance of North–South issues. At a time when faith in international problem-solving is low, NGOs need to be emphasising the need for multilateral approaches and institutions. At a time of scepticism about the effectiveness of development assistance and food aid, NGOs need to be affirming that some types of assistance are more successful than others and cautioning against throwing out the baby with the bathwater.

The fact that underdevelopment and hunger are manifestations of structural dysfunctions in national and international systems suggests that NGO activities as educators will frequently need to be critical of the status quo. The difficulties already inherent in the complexity of issues are, in one sense, further complicated by the availability in recent years of government funds for use in development education by NGOs. Where such grants are made explicitly to build a more extensive and articulate constituency for governmental aid programmes, the integrity of the educational effort may be compromised. On the other hand, where a government is prepared to make an investment in the long-term value of expanded public awareness of global interdependence, accepting criticism of its own policies as part of the process, its funds may well contribute to a broader understanding of the fundamental issues – and eventually even to greater support for effective government aid programmes.

One development education venture which has blossomed in recent years is World Food Day. First observed on 16 October 1981 by a smallish company of development stalwarts, the fourth such occasion last year involved countless people in some 150 countries. Myriad international, national, and local events have been planned by NGOs in co-operation with governments and the United Nations, particularly the FAO, whose founding the day marks.

The breadth of participation in the planning of World Food Day activities assures that a wide range of issues is addressed in World Food Day events. Each year the FAO suggests several themes including, in 1984, women in agriculture and, in 1985, the relation between poverty and hunger. Other subjects are world food security, food and health, law and food justice, protecting family farms, food and peace, food waste, food surplus, food/energy links, environmental protection, food trade and food aid.

The breadth of NGO involvement is suggested by the membership of 350 groups on the United States Committee for World Food Day, to mention a country example. Among the groups are major food, farm, nutrition, consumer, educational, religious, and overseas development and relief organisations, including such diverse groups as the American Academy of Pediatrics, the American Associations of Bakers, Home Economics, and Retired Persons, the Consumers Union, Cooking for Survival Consciousness, Farm Labor Organizing Committee, Friends of the Earth, Global Tomorrow Coalition, Lions International, Millers National Federation, New England Small Farm Institute, Overseas Development Council, Partners of the Americas, Planetary Citizens, Population Crisis Committee, Southern California Interfaith Hunger Coalition, US Catholic Conference, the Urban League, Worldwatch Institute, and the YM and YWCAs. Membership contributions to the committee's budget are supplemented by funds from AID's development education account.

The United States National Food Day Committee's inclusive approach reflects the strategy endorsed in the NGO Framework for Development Education in the US noted earlier (note 3). 'Working in coalition with affinity groups is essential for effective [NGO] development education activities. The general public often views [NGO] concerns as precious, even arcane. To reach beyond such barriers and to achieve outreach, impact and consensus, [NGOs] should make common cause with related movements: human rights, peace, environment, women's rights, nuclear control.' World Food Day is thus making an increasingly important contribution to expanding the common understanding throughout the world of the importance of food and development issues.

NGOs AS PUBLIC POLICY ADVOCATES

There is increasing consensus throughout the international community that hunger will not be eradicated nor food security achieved until there are fundamental changes in the world food system and in the policies on which it is based. NGOs are increasingly exercising a constructive role in advocating such changes in the policies of governments, a role generally complementary to their work as development agents and educators.

NGO advocacy has been directed both towards international organisations and individual governments. Its imprint on the resolutions of United Nations gatherings and their implementation has been real and continuing. For example, one of the provisions of the World Food Conference resolution on food aid, adopted in 1974 with active NGO support, states that 'food aid should be provided in forms consonant with the sovereign rights of nations, neither interfering with the development objectives of recipient countries nor imposing the political objectives of donor countries upon them'. The World Food Council has reiterated that view regularly, as for example in reaffirming in 1985 its belief that 'food should not be used as an instrument of political and economic pressure'. The fact that governments continue to violate their pledge – it was United States economic sanctions against Nicaragua which underlay the Council's debate in 1985 – simply points to the need for continued advocacy by NGOs.

Major NGO interest in international conferences on the Environment (1972), Women (1975, 1980, and 1985), and Agrarian Reform and Rural Development (1979), had a major bearing on their outcome. NGOs helped such gatherings function as international consciousness-raising exercises on urgent human topics. Sometimes NGO sessions running parallel to official conferences have confronted difficult issues more forthrightly. The vitality of discussions among thousands of NGOs – outside the formal sessions at the July 1985 World Conference to review and appraise the achievements of the UN Decade for Women – cannot but have put pressure on the deliberations of official government delegations and influenced the seriousness with which governments approach the unfinished task.

On occasion NGOs raise difficult issues which might otherwise be ignored. At the 1984 World Food Council meeting in Addis Ababa, the NGO spokesman told the ministerial plenary that 'continuing and increasing friction between international organizations' – he named the FAO on the one hand and the World Food Council and World Food Programme on the other – 'is highly disturbing and can only impair efforts to reduce world hunger as well as undermine public faith in the United Nations system' (World Food Council, 1984, p. 42). It remains to be seen whether the modest steps taken in 1985 to give WFP more control over selected administrative and personnel items previously handled by the FAO will make a significant difference.

NGOs have also come to function as significant, if not yet totally awesome, advocates *vis-à-vis* individual governments. In the United States, their imprint on development and food aid policy legislation is clear, both through the offering of congressional testimony and through the lobbying of individual committees and members. A number of changes in United States food aid policy, for example, owe enactment in part to the efforts of such groups. These include the creation of a food aid reserve to backstop PL 480, the assurance of a certain minimum tonnage of grant food aid year in and year out, and payment by the government of certain inland transport and administrative costs in recipient countries. Interestingly the advocates involved include both operational NGOs (such as CARE and Catholic Relief Services) and those without activities in developing countries (such as Bread for the World and Interfaith Action for Economic Justice).

As in their functioning as development educators, NGOs as advocates have a difficult task, particularly to the extent that they are also development practitioners. They are caught in the tension between advocacy for government resources which they themselves administer (financial and food aid grants, for example) and advocacy of improved government policies and programmes for which they are not the intermediaries (such as more poverty-oriented allocations of aid among countries and a larger proportion of human needs aid as against military aid). If they lobby for only their own programmes, they are as self-serving as any other interest group. Yet if they take on broader issues with major impacts on the poor, they risk allegations of being 'political' and may jeopardise their own government grants and constituencies. Whatever path NGOs take, however, the issue today is no longer whether or not they should function as advocates, but what they should advocate, on what basis, for whom, and at what risk.

The requirement of export licences from the United States government for sending funds or material to colleague agencies in countries with which the US is at odds presents an interesting case in point. Humanitarian items enjoy certain statutory protection, though the licensing process itself can be administered so as to discourage response. Immediately following Typhoon Nancy in 1982, several NGOs applied for licences to send emergency food and medical supplies to Vietnam. After a lengthy interval, several were granted; one was denied five months later on the grounds that the emergency no longer existed!

The protections afforded to humanitarian aid are sometimes not extended to reconstruction or development inputs. One NGO decided to withdraw its licence application for shipping a tractor to a Kampuchean vegetable seed multiplication farm in 1983 when told it would not be granted. (The capriciousness of the process is suggested by the fact that in the same year another NGO was granted a licence to export a tractor for use at a Kampuchean fertiliser-producing phosphate plant.) While the economic sanctions recently imposed by the United States against Nicaragua allow emergency humanitarian shipments, NGO requests in support of development activities – e.g. through the provision of livestock – are in jeopardy.

Some of the NGOs, concerned beyond their own projects about the situation of people in such countries and seeking to build people-to-people bridges across governmental divides, sometimes use the frustrations of the licensing process as a point of departure for educational and advocacy activities. In 1981, the Mennonite Central Committee was denied a licence to ship schoolkits assembled by American and Canadian children to their counterparts in Kampuchea. The shipment was allowed to proceed after they deluged President Reagan with pencils to dramatise the absurdity of the decision.

NGOs as advocates are discovering natural allies within the international community. Many are finding, for example, that some multilateral agencies are more compatible partners in policy or operations than others, whether because of their mandate, approach, or style. UNICEF over the years has succeeded in establishing close links with operational NGOs and in many countries has enlisted its private contributors in advocacy functions. More recently, IFAD has begun to command a substantial NGO following based on its affinity with the development philosophy of many NGOs. If it receives a long overdue three-year lease of life, it may become a more operational partner with NGOs. The non-operational World Food Council, in exercising its role as 'untiring advocate for the poor and hungry' (OECD, 1985), has won the respect of many NGOs and enlisted them in its mission of generating political will to end hunger. Ironically, several UN agencies which have established formal processes for cultivating NGO relationships have yet to establish a broad NGO following.

Some NGOs have been rather categorical in their assertions that all government aid by its very nature reinforces existing inequalities and is inimical to the interests of the poor. It is, therefore, noteworthy that the World Food Assembly follows its thorough-going critique of aid with some sympathetic reference to work being done by selected official agencies. The Assembly resolved that its member groups 'join in a united campaign to expose the gaps between the rhetoric and the reality of "aid"' including food aid, in order to demand greater accountability and to highlight the adverse social effects of much so-called foreign assistance'. The Assembly resolved 'at the same time, however, to stress the positive efforts and achievements of some agencies, whether independent [i.e., NGO] or at the official level' (World Food Assembly, 1984).

The development prospect which attends Hans Singer at his 75th birthday is doubtless much more grim than that which he encountered a quarter of a century ago, as a member of the Expert Group reviewing possibilities for an expanded programme of surplus food utilisation. However, if the challenges appear more formidable now, there may be some encouragement in the growing involvement in development during that period of the non-governmental community.

The enhanced NGO roles in development, to be sure, cannot and should not displace the responsibilities of governments acting alone or together. However, a more experienced and policy-oriented NGO community has begun to emerge and is increasingly prepared to work together with others, including governments, in a more clearly defined joint effort to help assure that hunger and poverty do not have the last word.

Notes

1. The debate about the limited effectiveness of aid in assisting the poor is reviewed in the author's 'Reflections on Development Policy: A View from the Private Voluntary Sector', in Gorman (1984).

2. Examples of government-funded aid projects which empower the poor are cited in Minear (1984).
3. Joint Working Group on Development Education: *A Framework for Development Education in the United States* (p. 3). The two consortia which joined to produce the strategy – the American Council of Voluntary Agencies for Foreign Service and Private Agencies in International Development – have since merged into a single consortium, Amercian Council for Voluntary International Action (Interaction), which has an active development education interest.

References

GORMAN, R. F. (ed.) (1984) *Private Voluntary Organizations as Agents of Development* (Boulder, Col.: Westview Press).

JOINT WORKING GROUP ON DEVELOPMENT EDUCATION (1984) *A Framework for Development Education in the United States* (Washington DC).

LELE, U. (1979) *The Design of Rural Development: Lessons from Africa* (Washington, DC: World Bank).

MINEAR, L. (1983) 'Development through food: some non-governmental reflections', Paper for the World Food Programme/Government of the Netherlands Seminar on Food Aid, The Hague (Rome).

MINEAR, L. (1984) 'Reflections on development policy: a view from the private voluntary sector', in R. F. Gorman (ed.) *Private Voluntary Organizations as Agents of Development*.

OECD (1985) *Aid Agency Co-operation with non-Governmental Organisations* (Paris: Development Assistance Committee Secretariat).

'Toward redoubled efforts to end hunger and malnutrition: some non-governmental organization recommendations' (1984), Paper presented to the Tenth Ministerial Session of the World Food Council, Addis Ababa, 11–15 June 1984. (Privately printed).

US AGENCY FOR INTERNATIONAL DEVELOPMENT (AID) (1982) *AID Partnership in International Development with Private and Voluntary Organizations* (Washington DC).

US SENATE (1985a) *Report of the Committee on Foreign Relations on the African Famine Relief and Recovery Act of 1985*, no. 99–4 (Washington DC).

US SENATE (1985b) *Report of the Committee on Foreign Relations on the International Security and Development Cooperation Act of 1985*, no. 99–34 (Washington DC).

Washington Post (1985) 'African relief efforts hit for lack of pros', 14 July, p. A–27.

WILLIAMS, M. J. (1985) *Food and Hunger Issues before World Food Council Ministers*, Paper presented to the Eleventh Ministerial Session of the World Food Council, Paris, 10–13 June (Rome: World Food Council).

WORLD FOOD ASSEMBLY (1984) *Manifesto* (London).

WORLD FOOD ASSEMBLY (1985) *Bulletin*, April–June (London).

WORLD FOOD CONFERENCE (1974) *An Improved Policy for Food Aid*, Resolution XVIII, E/CONF/65/20.

WORLD FOOD COUNCIL (1984) *Report on Tenth Ministerial Session*, General Assembly Official Records: 39th Session Supplement 19 (A/39/19).
WORLD FOOD COUNCIL (1985) *Communique of the Eleventh Session* (Rome).

12 Normal Professionalism, New Paradigms and Development*

Robert Chambers

Probably the single most prevalent claim advanced by the proponents of a new paradigm is that they can solve the problems that have led the old one to a crisis.

Kuhn, 1962, p. 152

THE SETTING

In 1985 the morbid preoccupations of development studies looked more than ever justified. There had been some big gains, especially in health and education; but the scale and awfulness of deprivation among the poorer people on the planet, and especially the rural poor in the Third World, remained an outrage. As more countries, and perhaps more people than ever before in recent history, were trapped in downward drifts, development studies, theories and practice were caught off their guard. The rate of obsolescence of fashions and ideas had accelerated. Some passed so fast that, as with the unsuccessful mountaineers on Rum Doodle (Bowman, 1956), high altitude deterioration set in before acclimatisation was complete: prescriptions and policies were abandoned before they had time to work, or to adapt and adjust and improve in the light of mistakes and experience. We seemed never to get there, or get there in time. We were always late, and always out-of-date. But against the gloom and frenetic rise and fall of fashions, could be set one steady trend which augured well in the long term: the gradual emergence of a new set of ideas about the theory and practice of development, especially, but not only, in rural development. These were cohering into a new pattern. They generated new agendas for research and action, and demanded and

229

supported a new professionalism.

These ideas I shall call the new paradigm. I use the word paradigm to mean a coherent and mutually supporting pattern of concepts, values, methods and action, amenable to wide application. Some of the 'new' in this paradigm is old, having been part of the currency of development thinking for some time. What is new is that hitherto disparate strands and tendencies are now fitting into an increasingly clear and powerful, though not fully recognised, pattern. The old development paradigms have left much to be desired. The question now is whether the new one can succeed in those domains where the old ones have failed.

DEVELOPMENT PROFESSIONS AND PARADIGMS

Any discussion of paradigms invites reference to Thomas Kuhn's illumination of normal science. He used 'paradigm' in a restricted sense, to mean 'universally recognized scientific achievements that for a time provide model problems and solutions for a community of practitioners' (Kuhn, 1962, p. x). Kuhn's universe of sciences was consciously limited to the physical ones such as astronomy, physics and chemistry. In development, however, these are either entirely or largely irrelevant, whereas biology, engineering, medicine, and the social sciences are involved in both research and in action. Three contrasts between the development professions and sciences and Kuhn's physical sciences are worth noting:

a changing reality: for the physical (and also biological) sciences there is a strong, though not unchallenged (see Sheldrake, 1981) assumption that the basic reality does not change, whereas in the development social sciences not only does the reality constantly change (compare sub-Saharan Africa 1970 with 1985), but the rate of change seems to be accelerating.

new ideas derived from experience: the driving force for change in the physical sciences comes from anomalies and from technologies for observation, measurement and reductionist analysis. In the development field the driving force comes much more from changing reality and from action and experience.

tolerance of competing ideas: in the biological and social sciences competing paradigms can co-exist more easily over long periods

(Lamarckian and Darwinian, and neo-Lamarckian and neo-Darwinian, theories of evolution; Marxist and neo-classical theories in economics) whereas in the physical sciences paradigm shifts normally take place within a generation.

In such fluid conditions, the use of the word paradigm, with its sense of formal and stable relationships, may be questioned. In the social sciences it is more customary to talk of networks and discourses which accommodate shifts of meaning and content. I shall retain the word paradigm because my argument is that underneath or alongside the sudden switches of vocabulary and the lurches of policy, a new, coherent and consistent set of ideas about development and especially about rural development practice has been emerging almost independently, as though in another dimension; and that its gathering support and influence have been partly concealed by the overlays of rhetoric and transient policy debate at the macro level.

It is also overlaid and hidden by another, more powerful, stable continuity which survives passing academic fashions and rapid changes in policy wisdom. This is to be found in the practical professional side of development and its teaching. This stability has links with academic disciplines and is entrenched in and sustained by the development professions working in government departments. It is part of what I shall call normal professionalism, where each profession can be said to have its normal paradigm.

NORMAL PROFESSIONALISM

Normal professionalism refers to the thinking, values, methods and behaviour dominant in a profession or discipline. In the development professions, it is concerned not just with research, but with action; and its actors are not just in research institutes and universities, but also in international and national organisations, most of them in specialist departments of government (administration, agriculture, animal husbandry, community development, co-operation, education, finance, fisheries, forestry, health, irrigation, justice, planning, public works, water development, and so on). Normal professionalism is a worldwide phenomenon, and has built-in stability from its links with knowledge and power, its reverence for established method, its capacity to reproduce itself, and its defences against threat. It is sustained by the core-periphery structure of knowledge and knowledge generation, by education and training, by organisational hierarchy, and by rewards and career patterns. Let us examine these last in turn.

The core-periphery structure of knowledge and knowledge-generation is so universal that it is habitually overlooked. Those who seek advancement in life seek education and training, and look upwards and inwards for enlightenment and reward. In their careers they move geographically inward to urban cores, and simultaneously upward in organisational hierarchies. Professional rewards (the Nobel prizes being the most extreme example) stem from and reflect the values of the cores, and attract and orient peripheral aspirants like iron fillings to their magnets. At the university stage, textbooks are the stone tablets of normal professionalism; later, journals and the real or supposed policies of journal editors become more significant, together with promotion boards and professional associations.

Conservatism
The process is conservative. The diploma disease (Dore, 1976) drives students to seek degrees or certificates as tickets for jobs and upward movement. Value is placed on methods for doing things. Wherever possible, in deference to the hard sciences and the power of mathematics, these involve numbers. Where methods are mathematical and lend themselves to ritual repetition, they are easily accepted and perpetuated. They survive both because they are useful and because they provide psychological security for those who practice them. So economists learn social cost-benefit analysis; civil engineers learn rules of design; sociologists learn to prepare and analyse questionnaire surveys; argicultural scientists learn to design and lay out experimental plots; psychologists learn to test intelligence and other psychological attributes. Those who pass upwards in the system then feel confident that they know what to do; and assume that the exercise of their learnt skills will establish truth, if they do research, or lead to right actions, if they are involved in development.

Conservatism also takes the form of peripheral fossilisation. This is built into the core-periphery relations and hierarchy of training. Sometimes teachers lecture to their students from their own old notes. They hang on to their old textbooks for security. Teaching is then reproduced through successive generations. Staff from Third World universities are trained in the West (or East) and return home with the ideas, orthodoxies, and fashions of those particular years, which some then reproduce for the remainder of their academic lives. Some

Departments of Extension Education in Indian Agricultural Universities teach the concepts and concerns about diffusion of innovations that were current in the late 1950s and 1960s when their now senior staff spent time in American Universities. Today, the book and journal famine in much of sub-Saharan Africa is having a similar effect, for different reasons. It is reported that the University of Nairobi was last able to order books five years ago, the University of Dar es Salaam seven years ago, and the University of Makerere thirteen years ago.[1] The tragic irony of these effects is that new debates about development become incestuously North–North, and conservative normal professionalism itself develops a core-periphery gradient: the poorer the country and the more isolated its professionals from the rest of the world, the more behind the times (as defined by some in the core) and the more normal its professionals are liable to be.

Defences
Normal professionalism also maintains itself through a repertoire of defences against discordance and threat.

The first defence is narrow specialisation. Foresters stick to trees, and moreover to trees in the forests and plantations which they control. Agricultural scientists stick to crops, those in which they have specialised. Civil engineers in irrigation stick to design and construction, with a little maintenance, and hold back from operation and management. In such ways, only the familiar is faced.

Simplification is also a defence that limits concerns and criteria. It often takes the form of a single measure or criterion: the single numeraire that consummates cost-benefit analysis; or the single objective of 'production' so often proclaimed by agriculture scientists. But as Oscar Wilde once said: 'Truth is never pure and rarely simple': the real world is complex; objectives are multiple; paths of change are not undirectional, and they cannot be predetermined. So other defences are also needed.

One of these is rejection, taking various forms, including ridicule and even persecution. The best known examples come from the history of science: the persecution of Galileo; the scorn poured in our time by geologists on Wegener's theory of continental drift. The major comparable rejection by the development professions is of the validity of the knowledge of rural people, or indigenous technical knowledge (ITK) (Chambers, 1979). Wegener's theory was rejected by geologists partly because Wegener was a meteorologist; ITK is rejected because those who possess it are worse, not even professionals, but illiterate, low status and poor.

A final normal professional defence against a threat is to assimilate it through extension of the normal paradigm, using familiar methods to modify, describe and often put some sort of number to the discordance. Thus economists respond to the challenge of differential social effects through weightings and shadow pricing; irrigation engineers respond to poor performance on canal irrigation systems by extending physical works, which they know how to construct, to lower and lower parts of the system; doctors respond to the charge that they serve only urban élites by expanding health clinics to provide curative services to rural areas.

In all these instances, the response is 'normal'. It does not threaten the paradigm; rather it extends and even reinforces it. Thus, irrigation engineers have more work to do but it is of the same kind. Doctors have larger networks of curative institutions to manage, and armies of health workers to train, but they fit into a hierarchy of medical competence and specialisation in which each level deals with what it can, and refers the more professionally exacting cases upwards, reaffirming and reinforcing professional authority. Normal professionalism is very stable.

Weaknesses
Normal professionalism has virtues. Civil engineers do build dams, usually very successfully; doctors do cure the sick. But much is wrong. Three weaknesses illustrate parts of a larger syndrome: gaps; misuse of methods; and prior bias.

There is a core élitist assumption that if enough disciplines are mustered and put to study a rural situation or problem in their normal professional way, it will be fully covered. Like searchlights, they will, if there are enough of them, shed dazzling light on all of the target. But this is not so. One example can suffice. Agroforestry – the growing of trees in interaction with crops and/or animals – is a major component in the farming systems of hundreds of millions of poor farmers. But professional forestry is concerned with trees in forests, agricultural sciences with crops, and animal sciences with animals. There is no discipline or recognised profession of agroforestry. The journal *Agroforestry Systems* is only a few years old. ICRAF – the International Council for Research on Agroforestry – has been denied membership of the Consultative Group for International Agricultural Research, and has only some eighteen scientists for the whole world.

Agroforestry is a low status activity, the responsibility either of a junior forester isolated in a Ministry of Agriculture, or of a junior agricultural scientist in a Ministry of Forests, or of no one at all. As with agroforestry, so in general, disciplines, professions and departments are so organised and interlocked that many gaps are left unilluminated.

Misuse of methods is another weakness of normal professionalism. Often misuse makes it possible to manage political pressures; often, too, misuse represents the exercise of informal power under the guise of technical objectivity. Thus, those responsible for social cost-benefit analysis often face political pressure to produce an acceptable internal rate of return so that a project can qualify for funding. It is easy (though not in the textbooks) to alter assumptions about speed of implementation, volume of future production, and future prices, to produce whatever internal rate of return is required. 'First I decide whether the project is good and worth funding; then I do the cost-benefit analysis', are typical words of an experienced practitioner. Economists appraising projects are thus able to bend to political pressures, while at the same time, through the inaccessibility of their calculations and assumptions, maintaining some autonomy and power.

According to the law of prior bias, what comes first stands highest, gets most, and sets patterns. This has been enormously influential in development thinking, with mutual reinforcement between overlapping sequences: industrialisation before agriculture in early post Second World War development theory and practice; infrastructure before agricultural and rural development in the evolution of priorities of the World Bank; and the sequence of appraisal, design and construction before operation in every project, even in agriculture. Thus we have hardware before software; and construction before operation. Mathematical skills are also more needed and more used in these earlier stages than in the later ones. Much of this is necessary and inevitable, but the effects are profound and lasting. For methods and patterns developed for the early (hardware, construction, physical) activities persist into and dominate the later (software, operational, social) stages.

But these limitations of normal professionalism are only what is revealed by a core-periphery, centre-outwards view. There is another, reversed, periphery-core, outside to centre, view which reveals much more. To understand this we need to examine polar contrasts between what is core or 'first' and what is peripheral or 'last'.

Table 12.1   Deep preferences

Core or First	Peripheral or Last
power	weakness
comfort	discomfort
wealth	poverty
core location	peripheral location
urban	rural
industrial	agricultural
things	people
clean, odourless	dirty, smelly
uniform	diverse
tidy	untidy
controlled	uncontrolled
certainty	doubt

Polar paradigms: first and last

Power, wealth, knowledge and professionalism are intimately linked. The poles which professionals normally embrace I shall call 'core' or 'first', and those which they normally reject I shall call 'peripheral' or 'last'. I am positing these deep biases (Table 12.1) not as universal laws, but as general tendencies.

Linked and partly overlapping with these are preferences for technology, as in Table 12.2.

These preferences are embodied in a basic ideology in which development is seen as the spread of core conditions into peripheries. So industry has been valued more than agriculture, large-scale agriculture than small-scale, coffee than cassava, tractors than bullocks or human power, exotic cattle than indigenous, and cattle more than goats, hens or bees.[2] Development has been seen as a process of growth stimulated by transfer of technology, a transfer in one direction, from rich and powerful to poor and weak, from first to last.

Research approaches and methods are similarly polarised, between those that are formal and respectable, with a strong statistical and mathematical content, and those that are informal and looked down

Table 12.2 Preferences for technology

Core or First	Peripheral or Last
large-scale	small-scale
capital-intensive	labour-intensive
modern	traditional
hardware	software
inorganic	organic
market-oriented	subsistence-oriented
mechanical	human or animal-powered
developed in core	developed in periphery
'high' technology	'low' technology

upon, which are more qualitative and judgemental. The contrasts are shown in Table 12.3.

NORMAL AND NEW PROFESSIONALISM

This brings us to a central tension in the development professions in their normal guise. They are, or are meant to be, concerned with people, and at the level of rhetoric for over a decade they have been concerned with poorer people, especially the rural poor. In reality, most are drawn away from those who are poor, peripheral and last by deep preferences for whatever is core or first, for whatever is high status within professions, for respectable methods of investigation, and for manipulating and measuring things rather than meeting and serving people. Where they are concerned with people, it is usually with those who are richer, more powerful, of higher status, and male, rather than those who are poorer, weaker, of lower status and female. Other biases also operate, of class, caste and colour. Most normal professionals adopt attitudes towards the poor which range from rejection, hostility and blame, through indifference, to benevolent superiority.

In sharp contrast, small numbers of what I shall call 'new professionals' have reversed these values and put those who are last first. They see poor people as active and knowledgeable, professional colleagues as much as clients, people from whom to learn and whom to serve in a role of consultant. The contrasts of preferred clients, and

Table 12.3   Preferred research approaches and methods

	Core or First	Peripheral or Last
basic logic	reductionist	holistic
learning mode	data collection	gaining experience
	'objective' analysis	'subjective' judgement
information accepted and admitted	'hard'	'soft'
	quantified	qualitative
	precise	imprecise
	visible	invisible
methods used	precise measurement	visual assessment
	formal surveys	Rapid Rural Appraisals (RRAs)
	formal questionnaires	semi-structured interviewing
experimental conditions	few variables	many variables

	controlled laboratory conditions, holding
	    much constant
		uncontrolled, real conditions allowing much
		    to vary

location	on-station, in-laboratory, in office	in field
priorities determined by	professionals	user-clients
evaluation by	peers, research sponsors	user-clients

Table 12.4   Normal and new professionals: preferred contacts, perceptions and roles

	Normal professionals	New professionals
Contacts preferred with people who are	'first'	'last'
	powerful	weak
	high status	low status
	educated	illiterate
	male	female
	adult	child
	light-skinned	dark-skinned
'last' clients seen by professionals as	obstinately conservative	rationally risk-averse
	passive	active
	ignorant	knowledgeable
	to blame	victims
	beneficiaries	collaborators
	inferiors	colleagues
	dependent adopters	autonomous innovators
roles of professional	teacher	learner
	expert	consultant

how professionals see clients and their own roles, are presented in Table 12.4.

The new professionalism reverses power relations – 'puts the last first' – in choice of clients, professional values, research methods, and roles. Such reversals may appear extreme. If all professionals adopted them, the modern world as we know it might cease to hold together. There is, though, little danger of that. Professional systems are so powerfully biased that a balance will never be achieved unless many professionals resolutely make the reversals. New professionals have already done much, for example in community medicine, nutrition, agricultural economics, and agricultural research. But most of the need remains unmet and most of the potential untapped. There are many reasons of convenience, convention and incentive for this. But the reason of respectability is weaker now than in the past, for these reversals fit and are reinforced by the emerging new development paradigm which is commanding more and more support.

THE NEW DEVELOPMENT PARADIGM

No short statement can do justice to the new paradigm. Nor can I do more than provide a personal sketch, starting with some of its origins in both negative and positive experience.

On the negative side, there is the long-standing failure of first–last approaches for poorer people, especially the rural poor. It has been well documented that first–last biases which are variously urban, industrial, capital-intensive, centralised, high technology, and planned top-down have often left poor people out or made things worse for them. Curative medicine, on-station agricultural research, parastatals, co-operatives, subsidised agricultural equipment, centrally administered credit programmes – these and many other initiatives have favoured the less poor.

But there have been many positive experiences: the World Health Organisation's 'health for all' programme and UNICEF's 'GOBI' (growth charts, oral rehydration, breastfeeding and immunisation), both of which explicitly seek to reach and empower the poorer people, especially women and children; avant-garde agricultural research (e.g. Matlon *et al.*, 1984; Ashby 1984; Rhoades and Booth 1982; Rhoades 1984a, b) which seeks to enable poor farmers to identify research priorities and to retain the initiative as collaborators in the technology development process; voluntary, and some government, agencies have encouraged the formation of groups which can exercise effective demands. Perhaps the most significant and influential experience, though, has been in south and south-east Asia with the initiatives which generated the idea of the learning process approach to development (D. Korten 1980, 1984; Bagadion and F. Korten 1985).

The new development paradigm has four interacting levels: normative; conceptual; empirical; and practical. The *normative level* is simple: development should be people-oriented (Korten and Klauss 1984; Cernea 1985). People should come before things, and poorer people before the less poor. It is right to give priority to those who are most deprived and help them to demand what they want and need and to change their conditions.

The normative level supports the reversals of the new professionalism. Women come before men, and children before adults. The weak come before the strong. Professionals become not experts but learners and poor people their teachers. Priorities are not those projected by professionals, but those perceived by the poor. The goal of development is not growth but well-being. Poor people will define their well-being in different ways. Many are likely to want sustainable livelihoods more than employment (Chambers 1983, 1985), meaning a decent and secure stock and flow of food and cash, and security against impoverishment; and they are likely to emphasise both health and consumption.

At the *conceptual level*, development is not progress in a single direction, but a process of continuous adaptation, problem-solving and opportunity-exploiting under pressure. Causality is complex and circular, not simple and lineal (Jamieson, 1985, p. 5). Development is not movement towards a fixed goal but a continuous adaptation to maximise well-being in changing conditions.

At the *empirical level*, there are four verifiable elements:

conditions are diverse and complex. Physically, many environments contain much variation. Resource-poor farms contain, create and exploit microenvironments. Resource-poor farming is usually more complex and diverse in its crop–livestock–tree interrelations and its use of biomass than resource-rich farming. Poorer people are often 'foxes' with many different enterprises with which they cobble together a livelihood, doing different things at different seasons, in contrast with better-off people who are more often 'hedgehogs', with one major life support. Diversity and complexity are usually greater for the poorer than for the less poor.

rates of change are accelerating. The rates of ecological change in many parts of the Third World have been insidiously accelerating. The crisis of the Sahel is the outcome of a long decline. The population growth rate in sub-Saharan Africa of 3.2 per cent per annum, with a doubling time of twenty-two years, implies unprecedented rates of change in agriculture, livelihoods and social relations; and in other continents too, ecological, economic and social change appear to be more rapid than before.

poor rural people know a lot (Brokensha *et al.*, 1980; Chambers, 1979; Richards, 1985). Indigenous technical knowledge (ITK) is now respected more, and valued not only for its validity and usefulness, but because it is part of the power of the poor. ITK is strong on knowledge of local diversity and complexity, precisely where outsiders' knowledge is weak. In rapid change, its advantages over outsiders' knowledge are even greater.

rural people are capable of self-reliant organisation. This gross generalisation cannot be universal. But that most rural people are more capable of self-reliant organisation than most outsiders are conditioned to believe is supported by much evidence.[3]

The *practical level* of the paradigm integrates the other three. A practical approach to development embodies reversals, not just of normal professionalism, but of normal centripetal tendencies. Decentralisation and empowerment are the central thrusts. Resources and discretion are devolved, turning back the inward and upward flows of resources and people. Empowerment means that people are enabled to take more control over their lives. Ownership and control of productive assets are a key element. Decentralisation and empowerment enable local people to exploit the diverse complexities of their own conditions, and to adapt to rapid change. Core programmes spread standardisation over diverse realities: the same crops and treatments are recommended in totally different eco-systems; but in the new paradigm, diverse ecological and socio-economic conditions and personal needs generate their own tailored innovations.

Decentralisation, empowerment, and adaptation to and exploitation of diverse complexity fit and are part of the clearest, most authoritative and most convincing articulation of the practical aspects of the new paradigm, by the Kortens and Bagadion (D. Korten, 1980, 1984a,b; Bagadion and F. Korten, 1985). David Korten has contrasted a 'blueprint' and a 'learning process' approach to development. These correspond closely with normal and new professionalism, except that new professionalism, as advocated in this paper, gives more explicit attention to the poorer. Drawing on various Korten sources (including personal communications), and with additions, the two paradigms are contrasted in Table 12.5.

Managerially, the blueprint approach fits the type of organisation which Burns and Stalker (1961) call mechanistic – with clear and fixed definition of roles, obligations, procedures and methods, hierarchical authority, punitive management style, and inhibited lateral communications. In contrast, the learning process corresponds with the type of organisation they call organic – with flexible and changing definitions of roles, obligations, procedures and methods, collegial authority, and free lateral communications. The former is more suited to routine activities in a stable environment; the latter is more suited to adjusting to a changing environment.

SOME PRACTICAL IMPLICATIONS

There are now enough examples of successful professional reversals and implementation of the learning process approach to suggest that these are feasible on a much greater scale. Some of the successes and opportunities (outlined under six headings) can indicate a few of the practical implications.

professional methodologies. Two examples, one from economics and one from agriculture, illustrate the type of challenge offered to normal professional methodologies.

Social cost-benefit analysis is deeply entrenched in the normal professionalism of economics. Whatever the qualifications about weightings for distribution effects, it fits the dominant philosophy which puts growth before people. It is taught worldwide, notably at the core of development cores, the Economic Development Institute of the World Bank, reinforcing the high status it anyway enjoys through its mathematical methods and well defined routines. But social cost-benefit analysis neither puts the poorer people first nor even puts people first. The classic and magisterial guide, *The Economic Analysis*

Table 12.5 The blueprint and learning process approaches

	Blueprint	Learning process
mostly initiated by	governments	voluntary agencies
idea originates in	capital city	village
first steps	data collection and plan	awareness and action
design	static, by experts	evolving, people involved
supporting organisation	existing, or built top-down	built-bottom-up, with lateral spread
main resources	central funds and technicians	local people and their assets
implementation	rapid, widespread, time-bound	gradual, local, at people's pace
content of action	standardised	varied
communication	vertical: orders down, reports up	lateral: mutual learning and sharing experience
leadership	positional, changing	personal, sustained
evaluation	external, intermittent	internal, continuous
error	buried	embraced
associated with	normal professionalism	new professionalism

Source: D. Korten, personal communication, with additions.

of Agricultural Projects (Gittinger, 1982, p. 45), states that 'in most developing countries increased income is probably the single most important objective of individual economic effort, and increased national income is probably the most important objective of national economic policy'. Thinking starts with income and ends with the internal rate of return.

There are, however, alternatives. One is an economic decision matrix (Carruthers and Clayton, 1977) which lays out project alternatives and rates them according to, not just economic internal rate of return, but also other criteria including number of jobs created per $1000 invested; proportion of project income going to the poorest 20 per cent of the population; and location of the project in a priority development area. Another is Charles Elliott's (1982) analysis of who would gain from, and who would lose by, alternative development measures for the Dal Lake in Kashmir. Yet we are so profoundly conditioned by the growth philosophy that the germs of such alternative methods may be ignored until an economic Einstein demolishes and reorders the Newtonian edifice of social cost-benefit analysis. Or will it have to be a Wegener from outside the discipline who dares to articulate the obvious?

Agricultural research methodology is another area of challenge and change. Normal agricultural research is reductionist, measuring a few variables in controlled conditions. It also usually has access to unlimited inputs. The results often suit resource-rich farmers, whose farming and access conditions are similar, and not resource-poor ones, whose conditions vary. Resource-poor farming systems are also often more complex. To meet this problem, farming systems research has evolved. It is an attempt by outsiders to gain enough understanding to identify small farm, and sometimes resource-poor farm, research priorities. But it often involves massive data collection and analysis, while in the meantime resource-poor farmers know what they need and are themselves innovating and experimenting. An alternative last-first paradigm is emerging through the work of Robert Rhoades and his colleagues at the International Potato Centre in Peru and of Jacqueline Ashby in Colombia. The method is to enable farmers to specify their priorities, with scientists as consultants, and to strengthen farmers' experiments with reversals of role (scientists learning from farmers), of location (on-farm instead of on-station) and of evaluation (by farmers instead of by scientists' peers).

rapid appraisal, more usually rapid rural appraisal (RRA), is the term used to describe cost-effective methods of learning about conditions. It involves trade-offs between the amount, relevance, accuracy, timeliness and actual use of information. There is now a large literature, a strong theoretical underpinning, and a growing body of practitioners, with the University of Khon Kaen in Thailand as the most advanced pioneering centre.[4]

The harmony between RRA and the new development paradigm has been pointed out and elaborated by Jamieson (1985). It is flexible, exploratory, interactive and iterative. Increasingly it uses 'triangulation', the checking of the same information in several different ways. The techniques for gaining insights have developed considerably in the past five years, and Conway's (1985) methods for ordering and presenting information have made what seems a quantum leap.

For the new professionalism, RRA has four principal advantages.

1. In conditions of accelerating change it provides for more and faster feedback and learning for professionals from face-to-face contact, in a manner which is relatively sparing of their time and which can lead quickly to a report. A Nigerian investigation of the underutilisation of public sector health facilities using focus groups took two weeks in mid-March 1985 and was presented as a final report in April (Attah, 1985).
2. It provides a quality, depth and range of insight which are impossible with questionnaire surveys. Instead of imposing outsiders' categories on the reality, it allows the reality to generate the categories. Rapid does not mean second best. Information and insight can be much better than with more conventional methods.
3. It is a means of professional reorientation. It has been found effective for professional 'flips' to discover the interest, pleasure and excitement of learning *from* rural people instead of teaching them. It is thus a technique for encouraging and forming new professionals.
4. By its sparing demands on time, it makes space to let in the poorer people. So often they are at the end of the line, the last people to be met or to be learnt from. By consciously offsetting the biases of rural development tourism, and the distancing and overcommitment of large questionnaire surveys, RRA can bring professionals face-to-face to learn from the rural poor.

gaps as centres.[5]   More is known by professionals about the things of the rich than the things of the poor. Mainline disciplinary work in, say, agriculture has in the past fitted the needs of those who are better off and has largely been appropriated by them. The gaps in normal professional knowledge often correspond with the needs and interests of the poor, where the potentials of modern science have been inadequately applied. There are thus opportunities for new technology to develop those gaps and enable poor rural people to command better livelihoods.

Many examples could be given. Three with big potential for the poor are agroforestry, uses of biomass for energy, and common property resources. First, agroforestry falls in the gaps between agriculture, forestry and animal husbandry. Second, the energy crisis has been seen, in normal professional terms, as a problem for the urban and the rich, not as an opportunity for the rural and poor. The increasing value of biomass for energy presents opportunities for new livelihoods, yet there is no international centre for energy or biomass-based livelihoods for the poor, nor, as far as I known, has one ever been seriously considered. Third, almost all rural research, at least in south Asia, has until recently been concentrated on private property resources, especially farming. But common property resources, as Jodha (1983) has shown, can be of much greater proportional importance for the livelihoods of poorer rural people than for those of the less poor.

bureaucratic programmes. The new paradigm appears incompatible with large-scale bureaucratic programmes, tending as they do to be standardised, hierarchical, insensitive to local conditions, and biased towards the less poor. There are, however, ways in which large-scale programmes can serve the new paradigm. Three will be mentioned.

The first is through wide, preferably universal, coverage by a simple standardised programme which transfers power or resources to the poor, or reduces their vulnerability. An early example was the worldwide vaccination which eliminated smallpox from everywhere in the world except Birmingham. It was based on a very simple technique with a hollow needle which held the right amount of vaccine, and was very easy indeed to implement. More recently, UNICEF's GOBI programme, though it has some less simple elements, has similar potential. It puts children and their mothers first. Immunisation reduces vulnerability, and power is transferred to mothers through their understanding of growth charts, and their learning to administer oral rehydration to their children. Above all breastfeeding not only reduces vulnerability to disease but returns self-reliance and control to mothers.

Second, large-scale programmes, like the Employment Guarantee Scheme in Maharashtra in India, can be mounted to provide work at minimum wages when it is needed. The low wages automatically select for the poor – the less poor are not interested; and the system of demand, which gives groups of people the right to demand work or to be paid anyway, ensures that it is precisely when poor people feel the need that they can command income. Much the same can be true of responsive food-for-work programmes.

A third opportunity is bureaucratic reorientation (BRO) (D. Korten and Uphoff 1981; Bagadion and F. Korten, 1985). This can take the form of transforming a hierarchical traditional bureaucracy into a 'learning organisation'. The reorientation of the National Irrigation Administration in the Philippines over almost a decade is a model. Some of the key elements were: continuity of committed leadership; finance and support from an outside catalyst; a working group which included non-government professionals; a built-in research and learning capacity; and adoption of the learning process approach. In this the sequence is learning to be effective, learning to be efficient, and only then, learning to expand (Korten 1984b, p. 183). The approach has been adopted also for community forestry in the Philippines, for four programmes in Indonesia and for two in Thailand.

voluntary agencies are well placed to develop and implement the new paradigm. Many already put the last first. In this, they face problems of scale, staff numbers and replication. Some of the best initiatives are staff-intensive, for instance the formation of small groups at village level as promoted by OXFAM in India. Outstanding voluntary agencies have managed both to empower the poor and to grow without losing their focus. Examples are the Bangladesh Rural Advancement Committee, PROSHIKA, and the Grameen Bank all in Bangladesh, and the Working Women's Forum in south India. The latter has as its members only very poor women for whom it negotiates small loans. It has achieved many simultaneous reversals to create and sustain an enthusiastic and committed counter-culture and to stand on their heads the normal biases of class, caste, gender, learning and hierarchy (the organisation chart has the members on top and the President at the bottom).

The practical challenge for many voluntary agencies is threefold: to maintain a commitment to the poor; to proceed through David Korten's three stages – learning to be effective, efficient and to expand; and developing new approaches which can be transferred to large government bureaucracies, as has occurred with primary health care. To do that, most voluntary agencies need themselves to become more professional.

Finally, changes in *professional training and rewards* are required if there is to be a large shift towards the new professionalism and the last–first paradigm. Some of the points at which leverage can be exercised are: university textbooks; training course materials and syllabi; policies of journal editors; and prizes and other forms of recognition for good last–first work. But change depends on individual professionals and their decisions. Many are trapped in normal professional hierarchies where they have little room for manoeuvre. But most have some scope for some change, and many can find allies who feel likewise and can help. For major shifts do not come suddenly by fiat, though fiats help, but gradually through a multitude of small decisions and actions.

CONCLUSION

The new paradigm which I have sketched is primarily derived from and intended for rural development. But it can be extended to include reversals in international relations and exchanges, and the new professionals are not only those who work in the peripheries, but also those who support them in the cores.

To what extent the new paradigm can solve the problems which have led development to a crisis depends on professional people. They are the key. The problem is not 'them' (the poor), but 'us' (the not poor). The massive reversals needed to eliminate the worst deprivation need professionals to fight within the structures in which they find themselves. The aims are well known and include changes in adverse trends in terms of trade, in the operation of international and bilateral organisations at the macro level, and in policy within both developed and less developed countries. But the basic issue is power. Those with power – 'us' – do not easily give it up. The challenge then is to find ways in which those who are powerful and privileged can be enabled to start and strengthen processes which in turn enable and empower those who are weak and deprived.

As I have argued, this requires new professionals who, in Herbert Butterfield's phrase, 'take hold of the other end of the stick', who stand convention on its head, who put people first and poor people first of all.

Normal professionals face the core
and turn their backs upon the poor
New ones by standing on their head
face the periphery instead

To make reversals requires little of a desk-bound academic. It is harder for those who combine analysis with engagement in practical affairs. But there are role models, people who have combined excellence in their professional work, with a rare and original vision, and a commitment to creating institutions to make the world a better place. Fritz Schumacher is one, stigmatised as eccentric, yet influencing all development professions with the message of his three simple words (1973), his writing, and the organisation he left behind. Hans Singer is another, at one time branded 'revolutionary and even subversive' for his prophetic (1950) views on worsening terms of trade for primary producers. He profoundly influenced development economics with his reversals of view, and policy and practice with his intellectually creative role in the initiation of UN agencies for development. There have always been new professionals, and when they succeed, as Schumacher and Singer have done, in changing the course of thought and action, it is easy later to underestimate their originality and achievement. Without them, much that we take for granted might not have happened. The question is how to multiply such people.

Whether the new professionalism and the new paradigm can spread and transform the development process on anything like the scale needed cannot be foreseen. But there is less and less reason to doubt that they could. Parallel efforts are needed – conversion of the cores and successes in the peripheries. New professionals, wherever they are, have support from much of the rhetoric of development, but the inertia of the normal has been shifted but little. If the new professionalism and the new paradigm do not become a mainstream in reality, the end of the century may see deprivation more awful in depth and scale even than today. But if they gather momentum and become a movement, there will be hope of major changes for the better. To achieve that momentum and movement is now, as we move towards the twenty-first century, the greatest challenge facing the development professions.

Notes

*I am grateful to many people, especially Edward Clay, for comments and constructive suggestions about this paper at various stages; and to Hans Singer for the occasion without which it would not have been written. Responsibility for the views expressed and any errors is mine alone.

1. Since drafting this I have heard that the Makerere University library recently received a large UNESCO grant for purchasing books.
2. Let me thank Hans Singer for at least fifty clippings and papers about bees sent to me over the past five years, ever since he discovered my interest in these 'last' creatures during our work on the second Zambia ILO/JASPA mission.
3. See, for example, the *Rural Development Participation Review* published by Cornell until USAID withdrew its funding support.
4. An annotated bibliography is in preparation under the supervision of Christopher Gibbs of the East–West Center, Hawaii, and should be available by March 1986. The papers of the International Conference on Rapid Rural Appraisal held at the University of Khon Kaen in September 1985 are the most up-to-date theoretical and practical statement, and will be published.
5. These points are presented at greater length in *IDS Annual Report 1984*, pp. 40–2.

References

ASHBY, J. (1984) *Participation of Small Farmers in Technology Assessment* (Florence, Al.: International Fertiliser Development Center).

ATTAH, E. B. (1985) *Underutilization of Public Sector Health Facilities in Imo State, Nigeria: A Study with Focus Groups*, Final Report, unpublished.

BAGADION, B. U. and F. F. KORTEN (1985) 'Developing irrigators' organisations: a learning process approach', in M. Cernea (ed.) *Putting People First* (London: Oxford University Press) pp. 52–90.

BARNES, B. (1982) *T. S. Kuhn and Social Science* (London: Macmillan).

BOWMAN, W. E. (1956) *The Ascent of Rum Doodle* (London: MacDonald).

BROKENSHA, D. *et al.* (eds) (1980) *Indigenous Knowledge Systems and Development* (Lanham, Ma.: University Press of America).

BURNS, T. and G. M. STALKER (1961) *The Management of Innovation* (London: Tavistock).

CARRUTHERS, I. D. and E. S. CLAYTON (1977) 'Ex-post evaluation of agricultural projects', *Journal of Agricultural Economics*, vol. 28, (3) pp. 305–18.

CERNEA, M. (ed.) (1985) *Putting People First: Sociological Variables in Rural Development* (London: Oxford University Press for the World Bank).

CHAMBERS, R. (ed.) (1979) 'Rural development: whose knowledge counts? *IDS Bulletin*, vol. 10(2), Institute of Development Studies, University of Sussex.

CHAMBERS, R. (1983) *Rural Development: Putting the Last First* (London: Longman).

252   *Professionalism, New Paradigms and Development*

CHAMBERS, R. (1985) 'Putting 'last' thinking first: a professional revolution', in A. Gauhar (ed.), *Third World Affairs 1985* (London: Third World Foundation for Social and Economic Studies) pp. 78–94.

CONWAY, G. (1985) *Rapid Appraisal for Agrosystem Analysis*, Aga Khan Rural Support Programme (Gilgit: Northern Pakistan and Centre for Environmental Technology; London: Imperial College of Science and Technology).

DORE, R. (1976) *The Diploma Disease: Education, Qualification and Development* (London: Allen Unwin).

ELLIOTT, C. (1982) 'The political economy of sewage', *Mazingira*, vol. 6. (4), pp. 44–56.

GITTINGER, P. (1982) *Economic Analysis of Agricultural Projects* (Baltimore: Johns Hopkins University Press).

JAMIESON, N. (1985) 'The paradigmatic significance of rapid rural appraisal', Paper for the International Conference on Rapid Rural Appraisal, Faculty of Agriculture, University of Khon Kaen Thailand, 2–5 September.

JODHA, N. S. (1983) 'Market forces and erosion of common property resources', Paper presented at the International Workshop on Agricultural Markets in the Semi-Arid Tropics, ICRISAT Centre, Patancheru, Andhra Pradesh, 24–28 October.

KORTEN, D. C. (1980) 'Community organisation and rural development: a learning process approach', *Public Administration Review*, September–October, pp. 480–510.

KORTEN, D. C. (1984a) 'People-centered development: toward a framework', in D. C. Korten and R. Klauss (eds) *People-Centered Development* (West Hartford, Conn.: Kumarian Press) pp. 299–309.

KORTEN, D. C. (1984b) 'Rural development programming: the learning process approach', in D. C. Korten and R. Klauss (eds) *People-Centered Development*, pp. 176–88 (the fuller original version is 'Community organisation and rural development: a learning process approach', *Public Administration Review*, vol. 40, September–October 1980, pp. 480–510.

KORTEN, D. C. and R. KLAUSS (eds) (1984) *People-Centred Development: Contribution toward Theory and Planning Frameworks* (West Hartford, Conn.: Kumarian Press).

KORTEN, D. C. and N. UPHOFF (1981) *Bureaucratic Reorientation for Participatory Rural Development*, Working Paper, no. 1 (Washington DC: National Association of Schools of Public Affairs and Administration).

KUHN, T. (1962) *The Structure of Scientific Revolutions* (Chicago: University of Chicago Press).

MATLON, P., R. CANTRELL, D. KING and M. BENOIT-CATTIN (eds) (1984) *Coming Full Circle: farmers' participation in the development of technology* (Ottawa: International Development Research Centre, Box 8500).

RHOADES, R. E. (1984a) 'Tecnicista versus campesinista: praxis and theory of farmer involvement in agricultural research', in P. Matlon *et al.* (eds) *Coming Full Circle: Farmers' Participation in the Development of Technology* (Ottawa: International Development Research Centre) pp. 139–50.

RHOADES, R. E. (1984b) *Breaking New Ground: Agricultural Anthropology* (Lima, Peru: International Potato Center).

RHOADES, R. and R. BOOTH (1982) 'Farmer-back-to-farmer: a model for generating acceptable agricultural technology', *Agricultural Administration*, vol. 11, pp. 127–37.
RICHARDS, P. (1985) *Indigenous Agricultural Revolution* (London: Hutchinson).
SCHUMACHER, E. F. (1973) *Small is Beautiful: A Study of Economics As If People Mattered* (London: Blond & Briggs).
SHELDRAKE, R. (1981) *A New Science of Life: The Theory of Formative Causation* (London: Blond & Briggs).
SINGER, H. (1950) 'Distribution of gains between investing and borrowing countries', *American Economic Review*, vol. 40, May, pp. 473–85.

RHODES, R. and BROTH (1984). *Supplementary benefit: a model* ....

RICHARDSON, ... *The social construction of ....* (London, 1982).

ROWNTREE, B.S. (1901) *Poverty: a study of town life* .....
..... (Harmondsworth, Middx: Penguin).

TREBILCOCK, R. (1981) .....*New Society* of ...... and history, from .....
..... (Harmondsworth, Middx: .....

WEBER, ... (1930) .....*The ..... of ..... between poverty and benefits*
..... (London: Academic Press) ..... pp. 1–20, 22, 25–26.

Index